Church and Synagogue Libraries

edited by
John F. Harvey

The Scarecrow Press, Inc.
Metuchen, N.J., & London
1980

Library of Congress Cataloging in Publication Data

Main entry under title:

Church and synagogue libraries.

Includes index.
1. Libraries, Church--United States.
2. Synagogue libraries--United States. 3. Jewish
libraries--United States. 4. Libraries, Catholic--
United States. I. Harvey, John Frederick, 1921-
Z675.C5C52   027.6'7   80-11736
ISBN 0-8108-1304-1

ACKNOWLEDGMENTS

I would like to thank Dorothy J. Rodda of the Church and Synagogue Library Association; Betty Warta and Carolyn Camputaro of Hofstra University; Jane Magill, Deborah Gochie and Linda Ronan of Lyndonville, Vermont; and Herbert Bloom of the American Library Association for extensive and expert assistance in preparing this book. In addition, I would like to thank each and every chapter author for the important contribution which he or she made to the book's success.

CONTENTS

INTRODUCTION
The American Church and Synagogue Library World

John F. Harvey

The object of this book is to describe American church and
synagogue libraries and to identify recent trends in their affairs.
Significant current activity is emphasized, as well as recommended
service policies. The present state of development and the future
direction of one of the library world's newest and least known fields
are described here. This is a pioneer volume in the church and
synagogue library field.

The papers in this volume constitute a comprehensive survey
of the field in its early stages. To a considerable extent, this is
a set of papers for an area which is just beginning to develop and
be recognized and this book should form a relatively comprehensive
description and assessment of it. The book is compromised by the
field's lack of intellectual development, lack of useful and significant
data and research and the lack of information and development in
most of its subfields.

What Is a Church or Synagogue Library?

A church or synagogue library provides reading material and
library service to the members of a specific church or synagogue,
usually in connection with their religious activities. A library is
defined here as one or more rooms containing a collection of print
and/or non-print material organized for use. Of course, houses of
worship of all kinds are included here. Those religious groups
which are neither Christian nor Jewish and which do not call their
worship places churches or synagogues are included in this field,
also. In addition, the phrase "congregational library" refers to a
church or synagogue library. To summarize, church and synagogue
libraries normally encompass Protestant church, Roman Catholic
parish and Jewish synagogue congregational libraries.

Typically, a church or synagogue library is very small and
contains fewer than 1,000 volumes. It is intended primarily for
congregational, rather than the minister's, use. Often it is closely
connected with the program of the church or synagogue school and
has a religious education emphasis, though many a library serves
other church or synagogue groups as well.

Just how small and inadequate a library can be and still fit the definition of a library is not clear.   A room or area with even as few as 100 volumes, one stack section full, if it is organized in some fashion, has a purpose and a client group and receives some use, can be called a library.   Many church and synagogue libraries stretch the definition of a library in several ways.

Though it is a secondary and to some extent a peripheral function, some of these libraries provide a non-religious public library service and circulate books to townspeople who are not members of that church or synagogue.   In many cases, such libraries are open for extra hours each week, perhaps a weekday afternoon and evening, and circulate primarily children's material.   Thus, they are serving a limited function as a small, neighborhood public library. Other libraries restrict circulation to church or synagogue members, but permit or even encourage them to carry out recreational reading.

Usually a church or synagogue library is placed directly under the minister's or rabbi's supervision, but it may be placed under the director of religious education, the assistant pastor or the church or synagogue school head.   Often the minister's own books are excluded from congregational use and are housed in his or her private office.   In other cases, however, his or her library has been merged with the congregational library.

Church and synagogue library staff members are volunteers and usually lack library school training or even college degrees. This is essentially a part-time clerical occupation.   However, in the present book, for the sake of convenience and since it is common practice to refer to the head of any library as the "librarian," that term will be used extensively to refer to the head of the church or synagogue library.   In many cases, of course, the library is operated by a committee of volunteers with a chairperson, and the term "librarian" refers to the entire committee.   Church and synagogue librarians relate to library technicians, also, since graduate library education is lacking in both groups.   However, the technicians are paid and usually are not in charge of their libraries, whereas the church and synagogue librarians are not paid but are in charge of their libraries.

Although only a very small percentage of them have paid professional librarians, and even fewer have full-time paid professional librarians, thousands of these libraries have the advice of professional librarians who are working part-time and voluntarily.   Most of the few paid professional librarians in this field work in synagogue libraries, incidentally.

The church or synagogue library resembles a non-governmental special library in that it serves a private rather than a public institution.   On the other hand, close affinity to a curriculum is one of its similarities to a school library.   Also, its comparatively small size makes it resemble many school and special libraries. As far as can be determined, most professional librarians in churches and synagogues come from the school library field. The church or synagogue library does not relate to a credit-granting school, however. To the extent that its work is focused on the church or synagogue school, it resembles that of a part-time non-credit private school.

The church and synagogue library field relates closely to the public field, also. Many church and synagogue members give their library a recreational reading kind of use. Certain groups develop their collections in cooperation with and in supplement to the local public library. Questions come frequently to public libraries about initiation and development of collections in the church or synagogue. State libraries hear about these libraries occasionally and provide some assistance to them, also. This kind of library should be distinguished from a religious seminary library serving a ministerial education program, from a religious history library, religious publisher's library and religious association library. None of these serves primarily a specific religious congregation. A church, parish or synagogue library does not normally relate in any way to a parochial school and its library, which may be in an adjacent building and which serve parochial school students only. The church and synagogue library relates to a church and synagogue school curriculum, not to a parochial school curriculum.

A church library should also be distinguished from a Christian Science reading room. The latter is a kind of religious non-circulating public library, privately supported, whereas typically the former is open to members of the particular religious congregation exclusively. A Christian Science reading room is usually open long hours and is often located in a business building, whereas the church or synagogue library is open very limited hours and is located directly in the church or synagogue building. In addition, a Christian Science reading room contains primarily Christian Science reading material, whereas a typical church or synagogue library contains a variety of material, much of it religious and from a variety of religious publishers, but some of it merely complementary to the religious material.

Several varieties of church and synagogue libraries exist and these distinctions might be summarized in this paragraph. Normally the term "church library" refers to a library serving a Protestant (specifically Lutheran, Methodist, Presbyterian, Episcopal, Baptist or other) church. It works with the church school, the minister and with other units of the church enterprise. The typical Roman Catholic church library is called a parish or community library and differs from a Protestant church library in not being tied to a church school or curriculum and in being closely oriented toward public library service to adult parishioners. A synagogue, temple or Jewish center library serves a Jewish congregation and is normally closely tied to a synagogue school curriculum. Both the Jewish school and curriculum are more intensively and extensively developed than the corresponding school in the Protestant church.

In conclusion, let me describe a "typical" church or synagogue library. Such a library is open during, before and after
weekly religious services only; has three or four unpaid volunteer
staff members; contains one to five hundred volumes, arranged by
the Dewey Decimal classification, 50 percent or more of them being
classified in religion and one current periodical title; has a typed
card catalog; circulates 10-40 books per week; occupies a room of
100-150 square feet; seats two to three people; has the advisory
services of a former public school library support staff member;
and buys supplies and books at local religious bookstores and through
denominational publishers' approval services. It has an annual budget of about $100 for material and receives numerous gifts.   The
committee works at its library chores every Wednesday and Sunday
morning.   (Incidentally, the average age and gender of church and
synagogue library committee members are interesting imponderables.
In age, they seem to be high, probably over 50 years of age on the
average, and in gender, they are at least 95 percent female.   Volunteers seem most often to be quiet, older ladies, relatively religious.)

Of course, many libraries are smaller and less well organized than this "typical" library, but others are larger--sometimes
5, 000-20, 000 volumes--and may give extensive service.   The folklore of this field says that there are many towns, particularly in
the South, in which the only library is a church library (often Southern Baptist), there being no local public or school library.   In many
of those situations, the church library is said to have grown relatively large and to be providing public library service to the citizenry
as well as church library service to the church members.

The History of This New Field

Much of the background of this field has been covered in two
excellent articles published in Volume IV of the Encyclopedia of Library and Information Science.   These articles, as well as the April
1970 issue of the Drexel Library Quarterly, were prepared by Joyce
L. White[1] and Ruth S. Smith,[2] pioneer leaders in the field.   Rather
than repeat the information which they provide, the reader should
refer to them directly.   The history of the field is described by the
individual denominational chapters in this book, also.   In them can
be seen the elements which led churches and synagogues to establish
libraries.   The field is split by denomination, however, at the present time the amount of cooperation from denomination to denomination still being very small.   Many religious persons consider ecumenism to be a radical and questionable movement, and they are
not interested in cooperating with an ecumenical conference or association.

Church and synagogue library science seems to have gotten
started 30-40 years ago and it has been moving strongly ahead ever
since.   Apparently between 25, 000 and 40, 000 church and synagogue
libraries have developed in the United States, which is as many as

all of the special, academic and public libraries in the country combined.

Historically, the American church and synagogue library movement has been strongly influenced by a) the slow rise in church and synagogue staff professionalism; b) the growth of denominational publishing and religious bookstore promotion; c) the growth and increased professionalism of school and public libraries; and d) the growth and prosperity of suburban churches and synagogues.

Church and synagogue staff professionalism has lagged well behind that of many other social institutions, and this has had a negative influence on their libraries. Beyond the minister and organist, professional qualifications have not been sought. However, a slow improvement has occurred in the staffing area, and the libraries have profited from it.

Probably the strongest force that has pushed the field ahead has been the denominational publishing and bookselling field. Many church libraries were founded with the instigation and assistance of a specific denominational publisher who stood to profit from library market expansion. The influence of the Southern Baptist, Presbyterian, Methodist and Lutheran presses has been especially noteworthy.

The rapid development of school and public libraries in every state has had a strong carry-over to church and synagogue libraries. As the former group has become more professional, the latter group has been guided into professional policies and practice. Another positive factor has been the growth of the large suburban churches and synagogues. Many of the finest libraries in the land are to be found in such places.

Church and Synagogue Library Education

In its short history, library education coverage of this field has been very poor. A few library schools have sponsored workshops for church and synagogue libraries, but only the Drexel University Graduate School of Library Science in the early and middle 1960's made a significant contribution to the field. [3] Perhaps the first library school credit course was offered in the early 1960's on synagogue librarianship at Drexel University and was taught by Sidney Galphan. It was followed by a series of half a dozen annual Drexel-sponsored one-day church library conferences. No regular credit courses have been offered in graduate library schools, and most library schools have ignored the field completely. As a matter of fact, state and national library associations have ignored the field, also. They have not provided programming aimed at this audience. Such neglect is regrettable since it has left the field largely in the hands of untrained volunteers not prepared to move it ahead as fast as professional librarians, library schools and library associations would have.

Persons working in the field have been left to educate themselves through their own conferences, workshops, associations and chapters. Many national, regional, metropolitan area and denominational conference groups exist around the country, and they sponsor annual meetings for member education. One-day conferences and workshops still constitute the primary method of educating church and synagogue librarians.

The Pacific Northwest Association of Church Librarians, the Baltimore Church Librarians Fellowship and the Church Library Council of Greater Washington, D. C. , provide examples of annual conferences. In addition, both the Church and Synagogue Library Association (CSLA) and the Lutheran Church Library Association (LCLA) have developed extensive chapter networks throughout the country to carry on their work locally. The Association of Jewish Libraries (AJL), the Southern Baptist Convention and the Catholic Library Association, Parish and Community Libraries Section (CLA), have several local units for this purpose, also.

For several years, the Southern Baptist group has sponsored week-long summer church library conferences at Ridgecrest, North Carolina, and Glorieta, New Mexico. These conferences provide the most thorough church library instruction now available. They are pleasant study-vacation periods in the mountains of each state and many Southern Baptist librarians take advantage of them. Recent Church and Synagogue Library Association conferences have provided three days of workshops and meetings, and Catholic Library Association conferences, in which the Parish and Community Libraries Section participates, provide several days of programming.

Workshops on specific topics, general programs which are often inspirational and religious book and supply exhibits have constituted the programs of many of these conferences. Cataloging, book selection, reference work, book ordering, circulation techniques, audiovisual materials and publicity are common workshop topics. They introduce the beginner to the most basic elements of his or her new responsibilities. The workshops try to teach these subjects in 90-minute sessions. Often a visit to a good local church or synagogue library is part of the program, as well as a packet of bibliographies, catalogs and instructional material. Most church and synagogue library conferences are geared toward beginning librarians. Apparently their planners assume that the audience will come from libraries still in the establishment phase. Even though the number of libraries may still be expanding rapidly, there must be a trend reducing the new to well-established ratio because of the buildup of five- to ten-year-old libraries.

Obviously, from a professional library education viewpoint, such short conferences are not very satisfactory. Many of the students and instructors would be beyond their depth in doing more than a 90-minute workshop, however. Development has been slowed by the lack of even part-time pay for the librarians' work. Less than normal incentive is offered to learn at conferences or workshops

since attendance cannot be expected to lead to an improved salary
or employment situation or necessarily to an improved library due
to financial limitations.

The ideal qualifications for church and synagogue library
service include Master's degrees in both library science and religious education, followed by several years of experience in a parochial or private school library or experience as a church director
of religious education or of a synagogue school. A religious education and school library background is found in very few church or
synagogue librarians. Library school graduates are needed who
have strong backgrounds in religion and religious education and who
know either adult or children's religious literature well. A thorough
understanding of the church and its potential role in society is needed
also.

The Extensiveness of This Field

The demography of the church and synagogue library field is
covered in Joyce L. White's chapter of this book. A few additional
remarks on aspects of the surprising situation may be in order.
Though it is impossible to locate any accurate statistics on the extensiveness of the field, certain interesting evidence can be summarized here. The first national Directory of Church and Synagogue
Libraries listed 3, 200 libraries in 1967, with a 23-percent return
from the church and synagogue library mailing list. [4] Since that
time, the field has expanded, but more importantly, thousands of
libraries have been located and identified which were not known in
1967.

Estimation of the number of libraries existing nationally can
be carried out in the following manner. We have information on
the number of church and synagogue libraries existing in Maryland
and New Mexico, since careful surveys were made in these two
states in recent years. For New Mexico, Martin and Marilyn Ruoss[5]
identified 302 libraries, and for Maryland, Joyce L. White[6] identified 300 libraries in 1973.

Since the total combined 1970 population of Maryland and New
Mexico equaled 4, 938, 000 people, or 2. 4 percent of the 1970 national
population of 203 million people, it is simple to estimate the total
number of church and synagogue libraries in the U. S. A. If the total
number of these libraries in Maryland and New Mexico, 602 libraries, represented 2. 4 percent of them, then the total for the U. S. A.
was approximately 25, 300 church and synagogue libraries. To what
extent New Mexico and Maryland were typical of the spread of church
and synagogue libraries throughout the country is not known, but this
writer knows of no reason to believe that either state was more or
less plentifully supplied with these libraries per capita than any other
state.

Of course, a much more accurate count than this one is

needed.   Past counts were not representative, however, and an accurate future count is not likely to be available for several years. A recent survey taken by Joyce L. White in cooperation with the Council on Library Resources suffered from a very poor percentage of questionnaire return and by no means approached the size of the universe.   She received replies from only 1, 808 libraries, out of about 10, 000 on her mailing list.   Her survey provided useful information of other kinds, however, as her chapter shows.   Apparently no comprehensive national survey was expected to be taken until 1979 or later, when the U.S. National Center for Education Statistics, Washington, D.C., undertakes a survey of all religious libraries.   Even in a survey under national auspices, however, based on past experiences, the percentage of questionnaire returns from this group can be expected to be extremely low, perhaps 10-25 percent.   The usefulness of such a survey will be limited.

It can be understood that the potential number of American church and synagogue libraries is large.   Certain denominational groups, like the Southern Baptists and the Mormons, have developed extensive church library systems.   Ten thousand or more Southern Baptist church libraries alone are said to exist.   The Lutheran Church Library Association has reached over 3, 500 Lutheran church libraries.   Maryann J. Dotts, in her chapter on United Methodist church libraries, estimates their number to equal at least 14, 000. Other chapters of this book provide additional interesting figures.

Incidentally, certain church and synagogue librarians have developed a debatable theory about the strength and extensiveness of library interest shown by the various religious denominations.   Those groups which emphasize religious education, emphasize a variety of religious sources and texts (rather than just the Bible), and believe Man has responsibility for his own salvation, tend to support libraries relatively strongly and extensively, the theory claims.   Groups which tend to restrict reading to the Bible and believe firmly in predestination tend not to support libraries as extensively.   Undoubtedly, having the funds to support the library and the space in which to put it have much to do with its development as well.

In almost any city, there are more church than school buildings, at least in this writer's experience.   Eventually, if even a fourth of the town's church buildings organize libraries, they will outnumber the school libraries there.   Certainly the potential number of church and synagogue libraries is much larger than the potential number of school libraries.   The grand total number of U.S. libraries is 28, 400, incidentally, excluding school libraries and most church and synagogue libraries. [7]

Based on the estimate of 25, 300 church and synagogue libraries, certain other facts can be extrapolated.   That number multiplied by an average of 300 volumes per library equals 7. 5 million volumes for the entire country.   This is a large collection of material but only a fraction of the number needed for these libraries.

The market of 25, 300 libraries times an average of perhaps
$100 per year equals a $2. 5-million national church and synagogue
library book and supply market per year.   These are neither large
collections nor markets, but both are growing.   It is in the interests
of publishers, jobbers and library suppliers to study, cultivate and
assist in expanding this group.   Probably church and synagogue libraries average about three volunteers apiece.   The 25, 300 libraries
times three volunteers equals 75, 900 volunteers nationally.   Such a
group is almost a third of the number of professional and support
staff persons (235, 000) employed in all of the school, public, academic and special libraries surveyed by the U. S. Bureau of Labor
Statistics in 1970.

Church and Synagogue Libraries and the
Larger Library World

As has been suggested above, there has been relatively little
contact between the church and synagogue library world and the larger public, school, special and academic library world.   Apparently
few church and synagogue librarians have attended a college or library school, so their backgrounds are different from those of other
librarians.   Apparently, few church and synagogue librarians attend
national or state library association conferences since no one would
pay their expenses for such an occasion and very little money would
be available with which to buy copies of the material on display
there.   Recent Church and Synagogue Library Association conferences
have attracted very few people who were neither local librarians nor
national association officers.   The pull on members from other parts
of the country was small.

Of course, the basic principles and procedures of library
science apply in church and synagogue libraries.   They use reference tools from the library world, such as the abridged Dewey Decimal Classification and Relative Index and Sears List of Subject
Headings, and they order the same kinds of supplies as other libraries.   Other sources are hard to find, however, and typical
church and synagogue librarians are hardly conscious that a library
literature exists beyond a few basic titles.   Few ministers, priests,
rabbis or directors of religious education belong to these church and
synagogue library associations.

Contact between church and synagogue library leaders and
other national library leaders has been almost zero, as far as this
writer can tell.   The Church and Synagogue Library Association's
attempts to form an interface with the library world have been relatively feeble and unsuccessful.   The same statement seems to be
true of the Lutheran Church Library Association.   Joint committee
activity to work on common projects and programs which seem so
obvious in the areas of religious literature, cataloging, selection
and reference work, for instance, has been impossible to develop.
Most church and synagogue librarians have no background of library
association activity which would suggest ways of dealing with

professional librarians and library associations. Some of the problems which special librarians faced 50 years ago, when most of
them were clerical, can be seen in the church and synagogue library
field at the present time. Nor is there any strong relationship with
seminary librarians, surprisingly enough.

Isolation from the larger library world is a severe problem.
Because of their need for the education and enrichment it is very
desirable to push church and synagogue libraries closer to the library world. How to enlarge and deepen the meaningful contact between them is hard to know, however.

Current Status and Trends

Clearly, this field is in a very early stage of development.
So little knowledge of it exists that its libraries are largely ignored
when comprehensive directories are compiled. The American Library Directory is discovering an increasing number of them as
new editions are produced, however. Little concern exists for critical book reviews or even for annotations. So few of them are
available in church and synagogue libraries that the point is proven
by that fact alone.

Volunteer committee emphasis is on learning and carrying
out clerical routines, even though more attention is needed for integrating the library and the curriculum. Other professional concerns
are likely to be given minimum attention under those circumstances,
also. Although increasing numbers of these libraries have incomes,
usually regular appropriations from the church or synagogue treasury or from the women's club, probably a majority still do not have
a dependable budget source. Many desirable activities are impossible to carry out under these circumstances.

The library associations of the field--CSLA, LCLA, CLA
Parish and Community Libraries Section and AJL--still charge low
dues rates to their members, usually no more than $5 or $6 per
year. Perhaps it is understandable that volunteers are asked to
pay only a minimum membership fee. The problem is that such
low dues rates bring in so little money that only very limited member services can be provided. Consequently, these associations are
able to push the field forward to only a limited degree.

It is hard to determine trends in a field which is so widely
scattered and on which so little reliable information is available.
Only generalized guesses can be made after having seen a good
sampling of these libraries, perhaps 75 to 100 of them, in this writer's case. A trend seems to be developing slowly in the direction
of increased library professionalism as more professional librarians
become involved with these libraries. As they grow in size and become more fully organized and service oriented, this trend can be
seen more clearly. A trend toward increased religious professionalism in these libraries cannot be discerned by this writer, however.

Closer relationships seem to be developing between the libraries and the church school curricula and study groups. As book and media collections grow, the possibilities of service to study units in the church or synagogue school and in women's and men's group programs become increasingly apparent and are being developed.

Synagogue libraries have led the field for many years, since they were earlier and better developed than parish and church libraries, as were the synagogue schools with thich they have worked. Around 1960, when first visiting Philadelphia libraries, I discovered that the synagogue librarians had been meeting together and discussing their common problems for several years, whereas the church librarians were only beginning to think about such meetings. Now, however, the better libraries in several Protestant denominations equal good synagogue libraries by the scope of their collections and service.

Though no one has reliable data on the subject, the number of church and synagogue libraries is likely still to be growing rapidly. Probably the field is still extending faster than it is improving. Among the larger churches and synagogues, having a library seems to have become fashionable. This writer believes that few church or synagogue libraries are ever abolished. They may move forward more or less rapidly or may even become static, but they are not eliminated completely. Only when the entire church or synagogue is abolished, will the library die. Therefore, the number of these libraries does not decline but must always increase as new churches and synagogues are started or else as libraries are started in existing institutions. In addition, church and synagogue library conferences seem to be attracting larger crowds now than in earlier years, and national association chapters are growing in number. These generalizations are true for both CSLA and LCLA.

The membership growth of both CSLA and LCLA has been impressive. They have grown from 507 to 800 and from 1,250 to 1,450, respectively, in the past three years. Some evidence exists that the larger library world is looking increasingly to the Church and Synagogue Library Association for publications and advice. CSLA publication sales have increased from $755 to $3,541 in 1976.

And finally, a trend can be discerned toward increased use of media material in church and synagogue libraries. This is especially noticeable in Mormon and Southern Baptist church libraries, where much of the collection is available in media form.

The Literature

The field's substantial literature is extremely small. It is at the earliest stage of development with newsletters and manuals predominating. Other publications are booklets and brief bibliographies, relatively superficial and immediate. This literature needs much expansion and improvement. We should have more substantial

books on the theory and policies of the field, such as Lyle's Administration of the College Library and the Introduction to Reference
Work, by Margaret Hutchins.   Such books would enable the church
and synagogue librarian to see his or her role in the larger religious
and library context, to see many development possibilities and to see
the theory behind them.   Explaining "why" policies have been developed would lead the reader to greater understanding and appreciation of his or her work.   We have little more than brief manuals
of good practice now.

        More detailed descriptions and histories of outstanding librar-
ies and their activities are needed.   Three of them are given in this
book.   The inspiration provided by such descriptions is important
but their practical usefulness for imitation should not be overlooked.
Most church and synagogue librarians have never seen an effective
and well-managed library, so it needs to be described in detail and
adapted for them.   More literature connecting church and synagogue
libraries with the greater library world is needed.   Adaptations of
school and special library ideas and of book selection, cataloging,
and reference work titles for this field are needed.   Textbooks
should replace the 90-minute workshops.   Imaginative and experimental projects could develop the field.   Probably some of them
exist already, but little is known about them.   Comprehensive histories of the fine Mormon and Southern Baptist library programs
would provide models for us all to study.   A set of fully rationalized
and appropriate library standards is needed by each one of the three
types of libraries.

        Comprehensive directories of church and synagogue libraries
and librarians are needed.   Such reference tools would be used
daily to facilitate work in the field.   Comprehensive and updated
bibliographies of useful church and synagogue library literature are
needed, so more thorough study will be encouraged.   The literature
is still small enough that a complete bibliography could be produced.
More conferences should publish their proceedings (rarely done now),
so their speeches and workshops can reach larger audiences.

        Books are needed to detail the library's service role in sup-
plementing and firming up the education of the church and synagogue
school, how and why.   A full treatment of this subject has not yet
been done, even once, for any denomination!   Basic and annotated
lists of current and classic books for a synagogue library, each
denomination's Protestant church library and a Roman Catholic parish
and lending library are needed to assist volunteers in evaluation and
selection.   No comprehensive or critical "standard catalog for synagogue libraries," for instance, is available now.

        Books are needed on the reader's advisory problems of church
and synagogue libraries.   Little is known about these problems now.
The same thing may be said about reference work.   Perhaps Ruth
Smith's book on church library public relations will be the forerunner of a more comprehensive and thorough kind of library literature. [8]

Very little research has been carried out in this field. Most of the few library school theses are either surveys, bibliographies or manuals of practice. Hence, the most basic data collection and research have yet to be done. Research is needed on the composition and activities of these libraries. Existing book collections should be compared with comprehensive bibliographies and with "best" book lists to evaluate their quality and bias. What services are offered and how effective are they? How do these services compare with those being offered by other kinds of libraries, in variety and depth, on per capita and per dollar bases?

Before research can be carried out, raw data is needed. Almost no raw data exists on church and synagogue libraries except for partial case studies. We need a national data collection program with well-defined terms and categories, so the present status and future changes in these library programs can be monitored. Information should be collected on staffs, physical quarters and budgets. Such a program would be difficult to develop, however, because strong evidence exists that a majority of these librarians do not respond to questionnaires. Only when comprehensive information is available on these libraries can intelligent recommendations be made on their library education, collection, service and study needs. Only when this information is available can the field be understood and its degree of effectiveness evaluated and improved.

NOTES

1. White, Joyce L., "Church Libraries," Encyclopedia of Library and Information Science. New York: Marcel Dekker, Inc., 1970, Volume IV, pp. 662-73.
2. Smith, Ruth S., "The Church and Synagogue Library Association," Encyclopedia of Library and Information Science. New York: Marcel Dekker, Inc., 1970, Volume IV, pp. 674-81.
3. White, Joyce L., ed., "Church and Synagogue Libraries," Drexel Library Quarterly VI (April 1970), entire issue.
4. Rodda, Dorothy J. and Harvey, John F., Directory of Church Libraries. Philadelphia: Drexel Press, 1967.
5. Ruoss, Martin and Marilyn, New Mexico Church and Synagogue Library Directory. Albuquerque: University of New Mexico Zimmerman Library, 1973.
6. White, Joyce L., comp. Directory of Church and Synagogue Libraries in Maryland. Bryn Mawr, Pa.: Church and Synagogue Library Association, 1973.
7. Bowker Annual of Library and Book Trade Information. 20th edition. New York: R.R. Bowker Company, 1975, pp. 217, 281.
8. Smith, Ruth S., Getting Books off the Shelves. New York: Hawthorn Books, 1975.

PART I:

AN OVERVIEW

HISTORY OF RELIGION, EDUCATION, AND LIBRARIES

Theodore Wiener

In the most elemental fashion, there is a causal relationship between religion, education, and libraries. Every religion, in order to be understood by its committed adherents or by potential converts, requires the help of some kind of education to communicate its beliefs to them. This task of teaching religion may be carried on by the consecrated religious leader, by word of mouth and personal example in the early stages, as Moses and Jesus taught their disciples. When the revelations received by them are written down and become the sacred texts, we have the beginnings of libraries.

In Judaism, learning and study of religious material were indispensable for the true religious life. The Jewish confession of faith recited in every service, "Hear, O Israel, the Lord, our God, the Lord is One" (Deut. 6:4), is followed by the admonition: "And these words which I command you this day shall be on your heart. And you shall impart them to your children when you sit in your house, when you walk on the way, when you lie down and you rise up." Since loyalty to God demanded fulfillment of His commandments, which He had revealed to Moses on Mount Sinai and in the wilderness, they had to be studied carefully. "Assemble the people, the men and the women and the little ones, and your stranger who is within your gates that they may hear and learn and fear the Lord, your God, and do all the words of this law; and that their children, who have not known, may hear and learn to fear the Lord, your God..." (Deut. 31:12-13).

In post-Biblical Judaism the centrality of study as a religious duty was highlighted in the Mishnah, the second century restatement of Jewish law. After enumerating various precepts it concludes that study of the Torah "is equal to them all" (Peah 1:1). Torah in this context is not confined to the Pentateuch, which is transcribed on the Torah scrolls for reading on Sabbaths and festivals in the synagogue, but the whole range of Jewish teachings. Another passage from the Mishnah details the scope of that study: "At five years the age is reached for the study of Scripture, at ten for the study of the Mishnah, at thirteen for the fulfillment of the commandments, at fifteen for the study of the Talmud" (Aboth, or Ethics of the Fathers, 5:21). The Talmud was a further elaboration of the Mishnah that reflected the comments of the Rabbis in their academies in Palestine and Babylonia, and discussed the law and lore of Judaism. It was completed in the fifth century.

3

Other major works making up the basic library of Jewish
legal classics include the digest of the Talmud by Isaac ben Jacob
Alfasi, of Fez, Morocco (1013-1103), and further restatements of
Jewish law in the codes prepared by Moses Maimonides, of Egypt
(1135-1204), Jacob ben Asher, of Toledo, Spain (d. 1340), and
Joseph Caro, of Safed, Palestine (1488-1575).   Alongside these works
there developed collective homiletical commentaries on the Bible, a
genre of literature called Midrash (interpretation), the oldest dated
to the second century.

The purpose of this study was not purely intellectual.   To
know the law was to comprehend the revealed will of God.   Even to
study the tradition for its own sake was considered meritorious.
Whenever people get together and occupy themselves with the Torah,
it is thought that the Shekinah, "the Divine Presence," dwells among
them (Aboth, 3:7).   The traditional Jewish prayerbook includes not
only supplications and prayers, but also selections from the Bible
and the Mishnah and recalls the observances and ceremonies prac-
ticed in the Temple in Jerusalem before its destruction.   The reci-
tation of these passages is to remind the worshipper of the glories
of the past that will be restored in the Messianic Age. [1]   These
daily repetitions are to bridge the gap between past and present.

To bring the personal identification of the Jew with his past
into even more dramatic focus, the Passover Haggadah, the home
ritual for the eve of the Passover festival, which celebrates the
Exodus from Egypt, recounts the many miracles connected with this
pivotal event in Jewish history and admonishes each Jew that he
should feel as if God had delivered him personally from Egyptian
bondage.   The Exodus motif is repeated in every religious service. [2]

When memories of the past played such an important part in
religious faith and practice, it was natural that libraries of one kind
or another would develop.   One of the first to be mentioned in Jewish tradition is a "treasury" of books established by Nehemiah,
which contained "books about the kings and prophets, the books of
David (Psalms) and royal letters about sacred gifts" (II Maccabees
2:13-14).   The discovery of the Dead Sea Scrolls at Qumran leads
us to an actual library that existed at the beginning of the Christian
era.   With the development of the rabbinic literature mentioned
above, they grew in size and significance.   Another reason for their
growth was the practical application of rabbinic law in the internal
affairs of the Jewish communities throughout history up to the time
of the French Revolution.   Thus, in addition to the major classics,
a large literature of Jewish case law, called Responsa, developed,
increasing the volume of books to choose from.

One of the largest private collections of Hebrew books was
accumulated by David Oppenheim, Chief Rabbi of Prague (1664-1736).
It was estimated to contain over 7000 titles, including manuscripts.
In 1829 it was acquired by the Bodleian Library in Oxford as the
nucleus of its Hebrew collection.   Rabbinical seminaries throughout
history had to rely heavily on libraries, however small, for the

training consisted primarily in the teaching and interpreting of traditional texts.   Since study was not confined to the rabbinate, but at
all times was taken up by many laymen, synagogues would also become the repositories of books.   In Verona, Italy, the rules of the
Hebrew school in 1650 required that the library should be housed in
a special room.

This is not the place to trace the history of Jewish libraries,
the great collections in the major rabbinical seminaries, the Jewish
sections in great national and university libraries of today, except
to point out that in the 19th and 20th centuries the secularization
of Jewish thought has brought about a shift of interest away from
the concentration on the Jewish book by the average Jewish layman
to the popular novel or technical work used in his vocation.   Whereas in centuries gone by, the library of his synagogue or of a nearby Yeshivah (the traditional rabbinical seminary) provided the major
access to the world of books, in present-day America, the synagogue library in comparison to the average public library holds
limited interest for him, in spite of the valiant efforts by volunteer
and semi-volunteer workers to attract readers and resources to
make it an important activity of the synagogue.   Thus, while the
original interest in books and libraries certainly derived from the
Jew's devotion to his religion, it must be admitted that the religious
library has been bypassed and occupies now only at best a secondary position in the spectrum of his concerns.   The place of religion in the life of the people is then also reflected in the relative
importance they accord to the religious and secular libraries.

True, in recent years there has been a renewed interest in
the Jewish past, as the traumatic events of the last fifty years, the
annihilation of much of European Jewry during World War II and the
establishment of the State of Israel, have left an indelible impression
on every sensitive Jew.   Study groups and adult classes proliferate,
and libraries benefit in their turn.   But now the synagogue library
ceases to have a monopoly even in the field of Jewish books, as the
public and university libraries include many of the standard works
of Jewish interest, when on occasion even some of these, such as
the recent World of Our Fathers by Irving Howe, become best-
sellers.

Christianity, like Judaism, a religion of the Book, required
at an early stage the establishment of libraries.   The Gospels as
well as the other components of the New Testament comprised the
earliest literary documents in a Christian congregation.   In addition
to the Bible, both Old and New Testament, the former usually in
the Septuagint version for the largely Greek-speaking communities,
church libraries began to accumulate lists of bishops and various
other church officials, lists of charity recipients, festival calendars,
proceedings of the various synods, histories and chronicles of local
congregations, showing the growth of the Christian faith, also stories
of Christian witness, the martyrs, the "Seeds of the Church. "

As a missionary religion, Christianity naturally had to develop

an extensive literature to gain converts as well as works of apolo-
getics against opponents outside and heretics inside the Church.
Thus, the educational task of the Church was implicit in its function.
The message of salvation with which the teachers of the Church were
imbued had to be communicated to the whole world.   Their unshake-
able faith in spite of persecution in their early history by itself had
an educational impact on all those who came into contact with them.
The central teaching of Christianity, Jesus's vicarious atonement
for mankind's sins, had to be repeated over and over again to make
it an integral part of the consciousness of the faithful, and to bring
ever larger numbers into the bosom of the Church.   As the events
described in the New Testament receded into the past, the written
record assumed ever greater importance.

    In the early churches, the manuscripts of the Bible and other
Christian literature were kept in the sacristies along with the church
vessels, possibly cupboards similar to the arks of the law in the
synagogues.   We hear of an early library in Cirta (Constantine, Al-
geria), searched during the persecutions of the Christians under the
rule of the Emperor Diocletian (ca. 300).   In Alexandria, the intellectual capital of antiquity, Christian theologic literature was developed by scholars like Origen (185-254), a man also learned in secular Greek culture.   After being exiled to Caesarea, Palestine, in
231, he established there an important Christian library, which was
used by Eusebius (260-339), who served as archbishop of Caesarea,
in the preparation of his major work: the history of the Church up
to the time of Constantine.   Origen's successor, Pamphilus, who
died as a martyr in 309, had prepared a catalogue of this library,
which also fell victim to the persecution under Diocletian.

    Jerome (ca. 340-420), who produced the Vulgate translation of
the Bible in Bethlehem, also had an important library at his disposal.
Using its resources he prepared in 392 a bio-bibliographical chronology of Christian literature from the beginning up to his own time, a
pioneer work which served as a model for his successors.   With the
establishment of Christianity as the state religion under Constantine,
church libraries received a new impetus.   On the occasion of the
dedication of Constantinople as the capital of the Roman Empire and
the seat of a diocese, he donated fifty illuminated Bible manuscripts
to the Hagia Sophia Church.   These he had ordered from Caesarea,
where they had been produced under the supervision of Eusebius.

    The popes and bishops continued to attach libraries to their
institutions.   A significant one was that of the Church Father Augustine, Bishop of Hippo (d. 430).   The popularity of his writings is
attested by the fact that he had to employ secretaries who would
copy his works on request and thus distribute them to his admirers.
Sometimes they were so busy that they would send out manuscripts
to be copied by others.   A friend of Augustine, the Bishop Paulinus
of Nola (d. 431), had his library in a room left of the apse of his
basilica.   Its entrance bore the inscription: "Anyone filled with the
pious longing to consider the law of God, here he may stay and
study the holy books. "   Yet, libraries could not be protected against

the ravages of invasions and insurrections.   After Paulinus's death his library was incorporated into that of Hippo, where it survived even the invasion of the Vandals.   Not so fortunate was Jerome's library in Bethlehem, which after 386 had become the property of the monastery he had founded there.   It was burned by fanatic Pelagians, members of a fanatical Christian sect, in 416.

Yet, even in the so-called Dark Ages the thirst for knowledge and the endeavor to preserve the literary and cultural heritage of the past were by no means completely lost.   The Church father Flavius Magnus Aurelius Cassiodorus (ca. 490-ca. 583), who had served as chancellor to four kings of the Ostrogoths, established upon his retirement in the year 555 a Benedictine monastery in southern Italy, called Vivarium.   Although he himself remained a layman, he also founded a theological school and wrote an encyclopedic work in two parts--the first devoted to theology, the second to secular knowledge. He actively sought at all times to enlarge the library of his monastery.   On the basis of his magnum opus and from other sources, a catalogue of this library has been reconstructed.   It included both religious and secular works, in conformity with Augustine's saying that the treasurers of worldly knowledge were the gold and silver of the heathens, which had to be taken back by their rightful owners, just as Israel took the spoil of the Egyptians to decorate its sanctuary.

In the later Middle Ages, religious literature began to predominate over that of classic antiquity in the monastery libraries, although the monks were always occupied in copying old works, and indeed, helped to preserve much of the literature of the pre-Christian period.   The regulations of the monks from the fourth century on required the office of librarian.   At the beginning of Lent, the books would be lent out to the monks, as the names of the borrowers and the titles of the books would be read to the whole monastery chapter as part of a solemn service with a sermon and special prayers for the scribes and benefactors of the library who had passed away during the preceding year.   This was also the time for the annual inventory taking.

We see here the organic relationship between religion, the education toward religious faith, and the libraries upon which the education for the faith depended.   The formative periods of Judaism and Christianity point up the early recognition that in addition to the immediacy of religious faith and experience, the faithful require a link to the past and also the guidance of contemporary examples in finding their way to God.

Before the advent of the modern, essentially secular age, religion stood at the center of most men's intellectual experience. This was also reflected in the largely religious collections of books produced during those centuries.   Beginning with the age of discovery around the 15th century, the emphasis in literature began to shift away from the purely religious to the variety of branches of the arts and sciences as well as to secular philosophies.

Revolutionary changes were brought about by the invention of printing, which coincided with the Protestant Reformation. The wide diffusion of the printed word, made possible by the former, and the flood of polemical literature occasioned by the controversies inherent in the latter resulted in fundamental changes in the nature and scope of libraries. This is most clearly indicated in Martin Luther's letter to the authorities of German cities, admonishing them to establish Christian schools dedicated to his religious views. Here, he details the kind of libraries that should be attached to them. In addition to the Bible in the original languages with translations and commentaries, the best of secular knowledge, the liberal arts, law and medicine, chronicles and histories should be well represented.

The closing of monasteries and convents in the Protestant parts of Germany and in England after 1536 placed many of their libraries under more secular auspices, if they were not destroyed. It goes without saying that the explosion of the arts and sciences during the Renaissance was reflected in a much more diverse literature, which sooner or later would result in a parting of the ways between religious and secular book collections.

The religious library which took center stage in the "age of faith" occupies today a much more modest place in the spectrum of the ever more specialized library system, particularly in the United States with its extensive network of public, public school, university, and specialized technical libraries. Just as the Sunday school of today and even the more extended religious education programs of the more active churches cannot compare in development with the many levels of the public school system from kindergarten to graduate school, so the church and synagogue library of today is no match against its secular counterparts. The New Catholic Encyclopedia devotes one paragraph to parish libraries in its detailed article on libraries, indicating the relative unimportance of these institutions in the present context.

The enormous advances in secular knowledge, especially in the sphere of science and technology, have tended to diminish the validity of religious knowledge even in the eyes of the believers. The feeling that religion has lost its central position in the scheme of things for modern man is expressed in a Sabbath meditation in the new prayerbook of Reform Judaism: "For our ancestors, the Sabbath was a sign of God's covenant of peace with the universe. They kept it faithfully.... Our ways are not like theirs. We have many idle days, but few Sabbaths; we speak many words, but few prayers; we make the earth yield to our purpose, but are unsure of the ground beneath us. But here, now, we can begin again. Or, having already begun, we can continue our quest for the wholeness we need."[5] Maybe, as the ending indicates, there is hope for the future. The chapters that follow in this work have much to say about the efforts in churches and synagogues throughout the country to establish and maintain libraries that will serve the needs of the faithful, however estranged they may be from the original wells of salvation.

Even if the laymen do not study the volumes on the shelves in depth, the very fact that they know of these treasures, exemplifying the beliefs and insights of religious leaders of ages gone by, makes for a sense of wonder and may create a quest to fathom the thoughts of these masters. One should not be overawed by the present disparity in size and development between the church and synagogue library on the one hand and the well-equipped and professionally led public library.

This disparity simply reflects the institutional changes that have come about in the last centuries since education and scholarship are now largely under secular authority. The religious library, however, has a special mission to perform. In order to teach religious values to a modern man steeped in the secular thought of the age it cannot counter this by merely offering the traditional interpretations given in the doctrinal works of years gone by. The constant give-and-take between warring secular and religious ideologies, as reflected in the best of current literature, must be made available on its shelves. Beyond this, carefully selected works of fiction, poetry, and biography that testify to the religious spirit, even though they are not strictly religious books, may be featured. The social and political activism of churches and synagogues in recent years has generated an extensive literature, which certainly should be brought to the attention of the layman. This is an element new to our age and may have significant impact on its religious life. In these areas the religious library can render a unique service in support of the work of church and synagogue. Yet, with all of this, we should not be unmindful that education and libraries, while significant in the program of church and synagogue, are only auxiliaries to their main purpose, to transform the lives of their adherents, to give them new direction, and to raise their sights above the ordinary mundane values. Books and education may help, but ultimately we must open ourselves up to the spirit of God. This quest is never ending in our lives. "Seek the Lord while He may be found, call upon Him while He is near" (Isaiah, 55:6).

NOTES

1. Cf. Abrahams, Israel, A Companion to the Authorized Daily Prayer Book. Boston: Herman Publishing Co. , 1966, pp. 24ff.
2. Ibid. , p. 54.
3. Central Conference of American Rabbis, New York. Gates of Prayer. 1975, p. 246.
4. All factual data not otherwise credited have been derived from Encyclopedia Judaica (Jerusalem, 1971), especially the articles "Education" and "Libraries, " and from Herman Erbacher, Schatzkammern des Wissens; ein Beitrag zur Geschichte der Kirchlichen Bibliotheken (1966), pp. 1-30.

COLLECTION DEVELOPMENT IN CHURCH
AND SYNAGOGUE LIBRARIES

Jacqulyn Anderson

> To provide a plentiful supply of good and useful books is
> the college library's raison d'être.   Library materials
> are the core around which sound teaching and other edu-
> cational activities of the college take place. [1]

These words of Paul Bixler begin the chapter on selection
and acquisition in Guy R. Lyle's book on the administration of the
college library.   Substituting "church and synagogue library" for the
college library referred to above, the reader finds an accurate
statement of the purpose of congregational libraries.   No library
stands alone on its own merit apart from the institution or persons
it serves.   Nor can a library be effective unless it provides material significantly related to the needs and wants of its patrons.   Thus,
since the grouping of persons with their peculiar backgrounds and
needs of no two congregations will be identical, no two congregational libraries will be the same in the collection of material provided.   There are, however, some common guidelines which pertain
to all church and synagogue libraries.

General Principles of Collection Development

In viewing the area of collection development in the church
or synagogue library, it should be understood that the collection
discussed here refers to all types of library material, both print
and non-print.   This material includes books, periodicals, pamphlets, motion pictures, filmstrips, slides, sound recordings--disc,
reel-to-reel, and cassette--video tape recordings, flat pictures,
maps, and realia.   Many libraries also house and circulate the electronic equipment required to use the audiovisual material.   Progressive churches are aware of the need to use all forms of media
in their programs, and the library, or media center, is the logical
place from which to make the media holdings available.

All material in a church or synagogue library should be selected carefully with the individual congregation in mind.   The collection should reflect the congregation in respect to age, educational
background, spiritual backgroud, and church or synagogue orientation.   Additions to a collection should be determined by the following factors: 1)   individual needs and requests;   2)   organizational
needs;   3)   financial resources available;   4)   material currently in

in the collection; and 5) accessibility of other library facilities.
Those persons selecting items for purchase should consider each
one in respect to its potential contribution to the collection and to
the congregation.

    In most instances, the library personnel is responsible for
selection, with the librarian often being the one to make the final
decision.   In some libraries, a selection committee may be designated for this work.   It is advisable for selection personnel to have
as guidelines a written selection policy which has been approved by
the congregation.   This policy provides basic direction for evaluating
material.   Such a policy may help to minimize conflicts regarding
items to be added to the collection.   A statement concerning gifts
should be part of the selection policy, and all gifts to the library
should meet the same standards as purchased material.   Persons
should be led to give money to the library so that the staff may secure specifically needed titles.

    Material should be added to the library collection on a regu-
lar basis.   By making a few carefully determined purchases often,
the library staff will be able to develop a better planned collection.
In addition, the staff members responsible for processing will not
be overwhelmed with work at one time, and the congregation will
have the benefit of new items coming in often.

    Just as the collection needs to be developed through additions,
it should also be developed through regular weeding.   Charles Gosnell has said, "A librarian who buys and never weeds will have a
library full of weeds."[2]   Material with out-of-date content and/or
in bad physical condition often should be removed from the collection.
The lack of circulation of an item is not necessarily reason for
weeding it, however, since the problem may lie in the area of promotion rather than content.

Material to Support the Church or
Synagogue School Curriculum

    As in the case of the college library, the material collection
of the congregational library will be selected to support and supplement the curriculum of the educational program of the congregation.
Some denominations suggest that as much as 75 percent of the titles
added should be directly related to the church's teaching and training units.   Not all of this material will be religious, since in most
churches and synagogues there is emphasis on the whole person and
his world rather than just the spiritual aspect of his development.
Material on the family, world conditions, the environment, the community, social concerns, and understanding persons will all be
needed to reinforce curriculum topics.

    Teachers and leaders are often in need of background and
reference material which relates to topics being studied by church
and synagogue groups.   These leaders are dependent upon the

congregational library for supplying this material plus titles which
may be used by group members for assignments, projects, and other
activities which involve participation as a part of the study or discussion.   With activity teaching being used effectively in religious
education, there is an even greater need for related resources than
with the lecture method of presenting facts, interpretation and application.   Especially with the advent of multi-media educational approaches, church leaders find the library an indispensable tool for
their teaching.

        Titles to supplement church school curriculum areas are of-
ten listed in the periodicals for the leaders and group participants.
Curriculum unit topics may be available in advance of the periodical
so that the library personnel may check holdings to see which titles
already cataloged relate to the topics.   The staff may then decide
on other acquisitions in order to secure and process them in time
for the use of the leaders.   Some church related publishing houses
provide lists of specific titles related to the curriculum.   These
lists assist staff members in having the material needed.

        When the church or synagogue library services day schools,
kindergartens, or day care center groups sponsored by the congregation, the library collection will have a greater proportion of secular material than the library serving the regular church program
only.   In some instances, there are separate libraries, with one
for the school and the other for congregation use.

Material in Religion

        The largest single section of the church or synagogue library
will naturally be the one related to religion.   Since a church or
synagogue library is a special library, its collection will be heavily
weighted with titles in this main class.   The titles in each subdivision of the main class will reflect denominational aims.   Works
oriented toward explaining the values and history of the denomination
will be emphasized in admittedly somewhat biased form, since a
single church is served.   However, the broad subject of religion
should be covered as a part of the library's collection.   Reference
works such as dictionaries, encyclopedias, and concordances of religion and the history of religion are needed.   In addition, basic
tools on Christianity are also important in Christian churches.   Libraries will want to have objective works related to the major religions of the world, major denominations of Christianity, and to
comparative religions.   Titles are needed to give information about
sects and smaller religious groups.   The selection personnel may
not want to include the books of doctrine presented by a religion or
denomination with the desire to convert to that belief.   The denominational collection will be biased since it serves a specific church
with denominational material, but it will not be biased because the
works collected are unsound.

        In Christian churches, many titles will be Bibles and books

and other material concerned with Bible study and interpretation.
Many useful translations and paraphrases of the Bible and the New
Testament are now available, and the library should contain as many
of these titles as possible.   Harmonies and parallel translations are
also helpful study aids.

Bible reference books such as handbooks, dictionaries, encyclopedias, commentaries, concordances, and atlases are needed.
Some of these titles are available in abridged or limited content
while others are in exhaustive or complete editions, often appearing
in multi-volume sets.   In some libraries, both types of books will
be needed, with perhaps the smaller volumes being available for circulation and the larger ones being used only in the library.   When
there is great demand for titles in this section, it is wise to purchase multiple copies of the most popular ones.

Bible commentaries are useful in a church library and often
present a selection problem because of the multiplicity of existing
titles.   Commentaries may be one volume on the entire Bible, a
volume on one of the Testaments, or the volume may be about one
book of the Bible.   On the other hand, a set of commentaries may
include as many as twelve or more volumes concerning the Bible or
a portion of the Bible.   Commentaries range in content from the extremely scholarly tomes appropriate for well-trained ministers to
the devotional study guide which may be a companion for personal
Bible study.   Commentaries are available on specific parts of the
Bible such as the many annual titles which treat the International
Bible Lessons.   In some instances, such as with church school lessons, denominations publish their own commentaries, and the library
will purchase those editions.   In addition, some denominational
publishing houses produce Bible commentaries, and these titles will
be especially significant for the libraries of those denominations.
However, many libraries prefer having a variety of commentaries
in order to provide their users with several views and interpretations.

Other Bible-related books deal with the origin of the Bible,
life and customs, geography, and archaeology of Bible lands.   Bible
biographies, collected and individual, provide readers with an insight to Bible persons and are popular study aids.   Children and
adults often come to appreciate the people and events of the Bible
through Bible stories.   Collections of these stories and books containing individual stories are needed on various age levels.   Doctrine books will be an important part of Christian church libraries.
These books will include theological discussions on Christian doctrine as a whole, specific doctrines, and doctrinal concepts of specific denominations.

Titles concerned with the Christian as a person will be needed in a church library.   Here will be books about aspects of the
Christian life such as prayer, Bible study, stewardship, and witness
bearing.   This section will also contain titles related to Christian
ethics.   Devotional books and books of prayers will be included here.

Books about the Christian church, its nature, history, organization, and operation comprise a large portion of the religious section.   Religious education, missions, church administration, the church staff, religious orders and congregations, and worship are covered in a great quantity of titles from which selections should be made.   The complexity and number of materials on these subjects necessitate the local library staff's giving careful attention to those selected.

Each congregation will want to include as many materials as possible related to its own denomination or religious affiliation. Included will be histories, doctrine, educational methods and principles, biographies, local congregational practices and other areas. In addition, the library is often the location for the historical items of the local congregation.   Here would be printed material, pictures, and historical objects.   This material may be on display in cases or protected shelving.   Often valuable church records are placed on microfilm and located in a vault adjacent to the library.

Religious Material Outside the 200's

In addition to the topics covered in the 200, or religion, class of the Dewey Decimal Classification, there are needs in a church or synagogue library for other religious material and subjects treated from a religious perspective.   Psychology and personality development, while not usually thought of as "religious, " are often presented with a religious and/or Christian treatment.   Many books which have a religious approach are available in the field of applied psychology.   The same type of treatment will be found in titles on marriage and the family, sexual values, child care and management, aging, and other subjects in the field of interpersonal relationships.

In addition, church architecture, religious art, religious music, and such literary works as poetry, drama, essays, quotations, and letters are classified outside the 200's but are especially valuable in a church or a synagogue.   The many biographies of religious leaders, past and contemporary, provide an insight into religion in life and should be part of the collection.

Other Non-fiction Material

Since in most congregations there is a wide variety of activities in many fields, usually a complete library collection will cover a broad spectrum of subjects.   However, in some congregational libraries the selection policy restricts the collection to religious material because of the availability of other material in other libraries.

Most congregational libraries will have a reference section, including dictionaries, encyclopedias, atlases, and at least one almanac.   The decision concerning the purchase of an encyclopedia needs to be made after careful evaluation of the work and the potential for its use. Some libraries have found a one-volume encyclopedia to have the type of "ready reference" information usually requested. An unabridged dictionary is often a worthwhile investment in addition to a good standard abridged dictionary. Every effort should be made to keep the reference section current. Reference material should be provided on all age levels.

In the library which does have a wide scope of content, the following subjects, in addition to those mentioned earlier, may be considered:

1. Educational principles and methods;
2. General and applied psychology, personality and group dynamics, social problems, and age group studies;
3. Recreational program aids such as games, parties, banquets, camping, retreats, and sports;
4. Program aids such as puppets, drama, storytelling, group work;
5. Special interests such as hobbies, crafts, cooking, entertaining, antiques, sewing, gardening, mechanics;
6. History and travel including travel guides and atlases; and,
7. Special material for children about nature, community helpers, and vocational stories.

Some libraries provide a "career corner" especially for use with college students containing catalogs, information about college entrance, and vocational guidance. Much of the general and special interest material in a congregational selection may be considered "bait" to get a person to visit and use the library for the first time. He may find items in which he is interested and return later for works which will relate more to his spiritual needs.

Recreational Reading Material

Along with some of the material already mentioned which may be considered as recreational, many congregational libraries contain fiction. In a church library, some of this fiction will be Bible-related or identified as "Christian fiction" which teaches a moral or has a Christian setting. Some general fiction, especially for children and youth, is helpful. Many persons will pick up leisure reading material at the church or synagogue library because of the library's accessibility or the convenience of getting library material since they are already in the building. In addition, some persons are overwhelmed by the volume of fiction available from other sources, and they do not feel knowledgeable about selecting worthwhile reading.

Children and youth often identify with the characters in fiction and may be helped through problem situations. Fiction dealing with such subjects as death, divorce, adoption, racial prejudice, discrimination, handicaps, illnesses, hospitals, and social problems often

communicate valuable concepts and information to readers.   Children
may begin the reading habit and develop an appreciation for good
books through their use of a church or synagogue library.   Their
books should be especially attractive and of good quality both in content and workmanship.

Periodicals and Pamphlets

Along with books, the printed material in a congregational
library should include periodicals, pamphlets, and other ephemeral
items usually placed in the vertical file.   The periodicals will largely be those of a publishing house of the particular denomination or
church group.   In addition, some general religious periodicals may
be included as well as a few secular periodicals such as news magazines and a digest-type monthly.   Usually, limited finances and the
brief time for using periodicals will make an extensive periodical
collection impractical.

The contents of the vertical file will be free or inexpensive
items such as pamphlets from denominational or church headquarters, government publications, and public service material.   Newspaper clippings, flyers, small pictures, maps and other non-perma-
nent items are helpful in updating a general collection.

Non-Print Media

There should be no sight and sound barriers in today's
school library, for an educational program of excellence
demands the multi-media approach to teaching and learning.   Library resources can no longer be limited to
printed material; a school library program designed to
implement a quality educational program must provide all
types and kinds of instructional resources regardless of
media format. [3]

In her book, The School Library, a Force for Educational
Excellence, Ruth Ann Davies makes the statement above in describing the multi-media approach to teaching in the school.   This same
approach should be followed in teaching in churches and synagogues,
and it is only logical that the congregational library should apply
the needed resources.

The last quarter of the 20th century has been referred to as
"The Era of the Media. "   In the current generation, the proliferation of types of media has been mind-boggling.   Though there are
continuous debates about the future of print in education, or actually
the place of the book in the future, most pragmatists agree that
there is both room and need for all types of media today and in the
future.   Therefore, it is necessary that religious leaders, who often have lagged behind other educators in using newer techniques in
teaching and training, must learn and use the many types of media.

The trend appears to be, at least in progressive congregations, toward a strong effort to catch up with more innovative approaches to education.

The use of learning aids in both electronic media and non-projected forms is increasing in religious groups. Often the failure to include these aids is influenced by the limited access to them by local leaders. In many congregations, the principles involving the material are presented to leaders, but no source of the items is provided. It is logical, thus, that the library should become the media center for making the material, or soft-ware, and the electronic equipment needed to use that soft-ware, available.

In addition to housing filmstrips, slides, recordings of all types, pictures, maps, and other items, the media center may provide a media preparation area with supplies and equipment for making learning aids. There may be a drawing board, cameras, a photocopy machine for making overhead cels, posterboard, colored paper, glues, felt-tip markers, overhead transparency material, and film. Having the supplies and a place for making the aids easily accessible, the leader or member will often be motivated to prepare a learning aid when he would not otherwise expend the necessary effort for such an undertaking. Some libraries provide sophisticated equipment such as cassette duplicators, videotape cameras and recorders, and even microfilm readers. While few libraries will have motion pictures as part of the collection, the staff should order rental films for leaders as a service, and money should be provided for this rental.

Flat pictures, maps, globes, objects, curios, teaching games and puzzles, and display cloths add variety and value to the collection. Many libraries contain framed prints of good religious and secular art which are circulated to the congregation for home use. Borrowing these art prints, families may introduce children to good art, and they may "live with" a painting for a period of time before deciding on the purchase of the particular print.

Collections in congregational libraries will vary in size and content in order to meet the demands of the individual congregation with its people and needs. The collection permits the congregation to have an informed faith. While emphasis must be on a single denomination, each library must impart some factual knowledge about other religious and objective works with a denominational orientation.

An adequate, useful, stimulating collection is the goal of every leader in a church or synagogue library. Building such a worthwhile collection is both a challenging and awesome responsibility.

NOTES

1. Lyle, Guy R., The Administration of the College Library, New York: H. W. Wilson Company, 1961, p. 232.

2. Gosnell, Charles F., "Systematic Weeding," College and Re-
    search Libraries XI (April, 1950), p. 138.
3. Davies, Ruth Ann, The School Library, a Force for Educational
    Excellence, New York: R. R. Bowker Company, 1969, p.
    24.

THE DEMOGRAPHY OF AMERICAN CHURCH AND SYNAGOGUE LIBRARIES

Joyce L. White

Summary data for this chapter have been drawn exclusively from a survey of church and synagogue libraries conducted from 1971 to 1975 by the Church and Synagogue Library Association, under the present author's supervision. The denominational groupings used in the data tabulations were taken from those used in the Year-book of American and Canadian Churches (edited by C. H. Jacquet, Jr. and published in 1974 by the Abingdon Press). Data tabulation was done at the Computer Center of the University of Pennsylvania with the aid of a grant from the Council on Library Resources, Inc.

Validity of the Data

The directories and mailing lists used in the survey are listed at the end of the paper. Altogether, the number of libraries listed there equals about 57,000. However, some duplication exists between and in certain cases within the lists. In addition, certain of the libraries listed are no longer active or else do not meet any accepted definition of a library. The author was unable either to study the lists carefully or to undertake the rigorous comparison and purging needed for them, since that would have required a personal visit to each library listed, so the extent of duplication and inactivity is not known. What is known is that a mailing of 10,000 questionnaires was sent out to a sample of these libraries and 1808 usable replies were received.

Informed estimates taken from the mailing and membership lists available to the author placed the number of American church and synagogue libraries at a minimum of 20,000. Certain other students of this subject have suggested that at least 40,000 active libraries must exist. Therefore, the data in the present survey represented 9 percent of the former number, 4.5 percent of the latter number, and 18 percent of the 10,000 questionnaires mailed. Consequently, the survey cannot be regarded as yielding comprehensive or even necessarily typical results for the universe of American church and synagogue libraries. The author does not know the extent to which the present results are typical. It may be guessed that among the respondents, the larger and better supervised libraries were over represented. On the other hand, many small libraries were included, also. In any case, the survey was unique and useful since it obtained the most recent and detailed information available on the world of church and synagogue libraries.

Establishment of the Libraries

One third of the libraries reporting were established between 1960 and 1965, and those two were the most popular founding years, with 1962 being the median library's founding year. Five percent of the libraries were founded before World War II, and four libraries reported founding dates in the nineteenth century. Of course, Table I shows a fourth of the respondents not to have answered the question.

Table I: Church and Synagogue Library Establishment Dates

YEAR	NO. OF LIBRARIES	FREQUENCY (%)
1882-1900	6	0. 4%
1901-1910	4	0. 3
1911-1920	9	0. 6
1921-1930	28	2. 1
1931-1940	26	1. 9
1941-1945	27	2. 0
1946-1950	93	6. 8
1951-1955	130	9. 5
1956-1960	262	19. 1
1961-1965	345	25. 4
1966-1970	243	17. 7
1971-1975	192	14. 1
1976	1	0. 1
Not Reported	457	Missing
TOTAL	1822	100. 0%

In all cases, the tables in this paper are based on 100 percent equaling the total number of usable returns, not the total number of libraries in the sample.

The library for the Brooklyn Friends Meeting of the Religious Society of Friends was founded in 1890, and the Byberry Friends Meeting in Philadelphia, in 1894. The earliest date reported was that for an Episcopal Church library, the Church of the Redeemer in Andalusia, Pennsylvania, which dated its founding from 1882. This is a list of the earliest church or synagogue library for each denomination reporting:

1882   Church of the Redeemer, Andalusia, Pennsylvania
       (Episcopal)
1890   Brooklyn Friends Meeting, Brooklyn
1896   The Temple, Cleveland (Jewish)
1900   First Church of Christ, Congregational (United Church
       of Christ), New Britain, Connecticut; Woodbrook Baptist
       Church, Baltimore
1912   First Presbyterian Church, Charlotte, North Carolina
1915   North and Southampton Reformed Church, Churchville,
       Pennsylvania

1920   Maple Grove Mennonite Church, New Wilmington, Penn-
        sylvania
1930   First Christian Church (Disciples of Christ), Honolulu;
        Old St. Mary's Church, San Francisco (Roman Cath-
        olic)
1934   St. Martin's Lutheran Church, Austin, Texas
1940   North Parish Congregational Church, Sanford, Maine;
        Oneouta Congregational Church, South Pasadena, Cali-
        fornia
1941   Kingshighway United Methodist Church, St. Louis
1945   Church of the Brethren, Elgin, Illinois
1952   First Unitarian Church of Cleveland, Shaker Heights,
        Ohio
1954   Church of the Annunciation (Orthodox), Baltimore
1955   Fourth Memorial Church (Non-Denominational), Spokane
1957   Evangelical Covenant Church, Muskegon, Michigan; Uni-
        versity Religious Center (Inter-Denominational), River-
        side, California
1960   Church of God (Assembly of God), Seattle

Table II: Denomination Breakdown of Church
            and Synagogue Libraries

DENOMINATION	NO. OF LIBRARIES	FREQUENCY (%)
Adventist	2	0.1%
Assembly of God	5	0.3
Baptist	165	9.2
Brethren	16	0.9
Congregational	15	0.8
Disciples of Christ	40	2.2
Episcopal	118	6.6
Evangelical	7	0.4
Society of Friends	29	1.6
Latter Day Saints	1	0.1
Lutheran	560	31.2
Mennonite	22	1.2
Methodist	202	11.3
Moravian	1	0.1
Orthodox	6	0.3
Presbyterian	290	16.2
Reformed	33	1.8
Roman Catholic	66	3.7
Unitarian	10	0.6
United Christian Church	98	5.5
Wesleyan	2	0.1
Non-Denominational	7	0.4
Inter-Denominational	11	0.6
Jewish	87	4.9
Not Reported	29	Missing
TOTAL	1822	100.0%

Denominational Breakdown

Table II shows the absolute number and percentage of valid questionnaires returned from each religious denomination. Certain denominations can be seen to be severely over or under represented in this sample. For example, out of 20, 000 possible Baptist church libraries, according to the aforementioned lists, only 165 reported, or 0. 8 percent. The percent for Latter Day Saints was one out of 4, 000 libraries, or 0. 025 percent. Cokesbury reported 5, 040 Presbyterian churches and the number responding here was 6 percent of that figure, or 290. In an example of another kind, the figure for Lutheran churches, 560 responding, was more than a fourth of the Lutheran Church Library Association mailing list of 2, 000 libraries.

In absolute numbers, Table II shows that the Lutheran, Presbyterian, Methodist and Baptist church libraries dominated the returns with two thirds of the total, and this fact should be remembered in viewing later denomination tables. Almost a third of the returns came from Lutheran churches, incidentally. Other denominations, poorly represented but known to have many libraries--the Latter Day Saints, for instance--made a weak showing in the tables. These figures showed over and under representation by absolute numbers as contrasted with the over and under representation of the "universe" seen above.

States Represented

Table III shows the wide dispersion of church and synagogue libraries throughout the country. The largest number of returns was received from Pennsylvania, Maryland, Minnesota, Washington, and New Mexico. Each one of these states provided 100 or more of the total number of questionnaires returned, and these five states combined provided 40 percent of the total. Study of Table III shows that these five states plus four more, California, Ohio, Wisconsin, and Illinois provided 60 percent of the total number of questionnaire returns.

Table III: Church and Synagogue Libraries
Arranged by State or Territory

STATE	LIBRARIES	FREQUENCY (%)
Alaska	1	0. 1%
Alabama	10	0. 5
Arizona	12	0. 7
Arkansas	4	0. 2
British Columbia	2	0. 1
California	91	5. 0
Colorado	14	0. 8
Connecticut	26	1. 4
Delaware	18	1. 0

(Table III cont'd)

STATE	NO. OF LIBRARIES	FREQUENCY (%)
District of Columbia	20	1.1
Florida	20	1.1
Georgia	12	0.7
Hawaii	4	0.2
Idaho	2	0.1
Illinois	83	4.6
Indiana	30	1.6
Iowa	32	1.8
Kansas	13	0.7
Kentucky	11	0.6
Louisiana	32	1.8
Maine	3	0.2
Maryland	155	8.5
Massachusetts	29	1.6
Michigan	60	3.3
Minnesota	136	7.5
Mississippi	2	0.1
Missouri	21	1.2
Montana	6	0.3
Nebraska	19	1.0
Nevada	2	0.1
New Hampshire	3	0.2
New Jersey	58	3.2
New Mexico	100	5.5
New York	56	3.1
North Carolina	28	1.5
North Dakota	14	0.8
Ohio	89	4.9
Oklahoma	9	0.5
Ontario	6	0.3
Oregon	53	2.9
Pennsylvania	206	11.3
Puerto Rico	1	0.1
Rhode Island	6	0.3
South Carolina	4	0.2
South Dakota	8	0.4
Tennessee	18	1.0
Texas	56	3.1
Utah	1	0.1
Vermont	1	0.1
Virginia	32	1.8
Washington	107	5.9
West Virginia	7	0.4
Wisconsin	86	4.7
Not Reported	3	Missing
TOTAL	1822	100.0%

Although there may be a disproportionate number of church and synagogue libraries in those states, or may not be, it must be noted
that three of them house the headquarters of four of the country's
major church and synagogue library associations: The Church and
Synagogue Library Association (Pennsylvania); the Parish and Community Libraries Section, Catholic Library Association (Pennsylvania); the Lutheran Church Library Association (Minnesota); and the
Pacific Northwest Association of Church Librarians (Washington).
If we can assume that the sample is representative by state, the
Middle Atlantic, Upper Middle Western and West Coast areas are
leading church and synagogue library centers.   Notably missing
from this list of leading library states are those located in the Southeast, Northeast, South Central and Rocky Mountain areas (except for
New Mexico).   Twenty-eight states produced 15 or fewer libraries
or less than 1 percent of the total apiece.   Nevertheless, church and
synagogue libraries returned questionnaires from every state in the
Union except Wyoming.   Returns were received from the District of
Columbia, Puerto Rico and Canada, also.

Access to Library Facilities

The largest number of libraries reporting on access indicated that the library facilities were available whenever the church
or synagogue building was open.   On the other hand, and not in con-
tradiction to the above, 425 libraries reported that they were staffed
one day per week only.   Roughly, the figures seemed to indicate
that most libraries were staffed on Saturday or Sunday, the day of
worship, and whenever a particular meeting was occurring.   Otherwise, the libraries were available on a self-service basis during the
rest of the week whenever the building itself was open.   Table IV
shows this breakdown.

Table IV: Access to Church and Synagogue Library Facilities

Facilities Opened	Staffed	Self-service
One day per week only	425	32
Before and after meetings	226	191
Whenever the building is open	143	890

Number of libraries = 1822

Service

More than 85 percent of the libraries reported that they
were established for use by the entire congregation.   Less than 3
percent reported that they were established solely for the use of
children, and less than 1 percent solely for the use of the clergy.
On the other hand, nearly 9 percent reported a conscious policy of
serving the entire community in which the church was located.   The

latter group of libraries served a public library function in their communities.

Staff Members

One hundred churches and synagogues reported that they had a paid professional person in charge of the library. This could have been either a director of religious education, a synagogue school head, or a professional librarian. In most cases, no distinction was made on the report. In addition, 508 churches and synagogues reported that a professional librarian provided supervision for the library on a volunteer basis. Another 265 returns reported the volunteer services of a professional librarian, but not in a supervisory capacity. These three figures total 873 or almost half of the entire group.

Table V: Church and Synagogue Library Staffing

Persons in Charge	Paid	Not Paid
Professional	100	508
Non-Professional	83	1158
TOTAL	183	1666
Staff Members or Assistants		
Professional	18	265
Non-Professional	28	1459
TOTAL	46	1724
GRAND TOTALS	229	3390

Most libraries reported that they were staffed with non-professional volunteers. The total of 1808 libraries that submitted returns indicated a combined staff of 3619 persons, or an average of about two persons per library. It is not clear whether or not this figure included all volunteers. In addition to the above findings, 229 libraries reported one paid person to be connected with the library in some capacity. Table V shows these figures.

Annual Budgets

Table VI shows the annual budgets of these libraries with almost 99 percent of them reporting. Eighty-five percent of the libraries had annual budgets ranging between nothing and $500. More than 100 libraries reported budgets of over $1,000, however. A typical budget was $250, and this amount of money would buy about 20-30 new adult volumes.

Of the 15 percent with annual budgets above $500, synagogue libraries accounted for a large proportion, Table VII showing

that 70 percent of the synagogue libraries reported annual budgets
in excess of that figure.   Lutheran, Baptist and Presbyterian denominations trailed immediately behind the synagogues in absolute
number of libraries with annual budgets in excess of $500, and Ro-
man Catholic churches trailed the synagogues in percent of libraries
above $500.

Table VI: Annual Budgets for Church and
Synagogue Libraries

ANNUAL BUDGET	NO. OF LIBRARIES	FREQUENCY (%)
Less Than $100	517	28. 8%
$101 to $500	1009	56. 1
$501 to $1000	170	9. 5
More Than $1000	101	5. 6
Not Reported	25	Missing
TOTAL	1822	100. 0%

Table VII: Church and Synagogue Libraries by
Denomination and Annual Budget

DENOMINATION	ANNUAL BUDGET				
	Less Than $100	$101 to $500	$501 to $1,000	More Than $1,000	Total
Baptist	40	90	18	16	164
Disciples of Christ	12	22	4	1	39
Episcopal	44	57	10	6	117
Society of Friends	14	13	1	1	29
Lutheran	185	327	32	10	554
Methodist	59	118	17	4	198
Presbyterian	85	172	27	4	288
Roman Catholic	8	32	16	9	65
United Christian Church	24	63	10	0	97
Jewish	0	25	19	40	84

Number of Missing Observations = 52 libraries

Book Collections

More than one-third of the libraries (703) reported collections
in excess of 1000 books.   Four percent of them reported more than
5, 000 books in their collections, making them substantial collections.
Almost two-thirds of the library collections fell between 500 and
5, 000 books with the typical library having about 800 books.

Table VIII: Church and Synagogue Libraries by
              Number of Books

BOOKS	NO. OF LIBRARIES	FREQUENCY (%)
0 to 100	57	3. 2%
101 to 300	242	13. 6
301 to 500	294	16. 5
501 to 1, 000	486	27. 3
1, 001 to 5, 000	631	35. 4
More Than 5, 000	72	4. 0
Not Reported	40	Missing
TOTAL	1822	100. 0%

Table IX shows the largest number of libraries with collections in excess of 1, 000 books to have been reported from Lutheran
churches.   Jewish and Baptist synagogues and churches led in the
percentage of libraries with more than 1, 000 books, however.   By
this table, Jewish libraries averaged 3, 000 books and Baptist libraries averaged 785 books.

Non-Print and Periodical Collections

This section summarizes questionnaire findings for holdings
of filmstrips, films, phonograph records, and periodicals.   The vast
majority of the libraries responding had small filmstrip collections,
less than a fourth of them having more than 100 filmstrips.   The
Baptists, Lutherans and Methodists reported the largest numbers of
filmstrips in their libraries, but the synagogues, Methodists, Roman
Catholics and Baptists had the highest ratios of large collections.
Tables X and XI show that a third of the libraries failed to respond
to this question.

Few libraries owned more than small film collections.   Among
those few, the Baptists and Methodists led the way.   For the entire
sample, the typical library had about 100 films and filmstrips combined, more of the latter than of the former.   Less than 10 percent
of the libraries had more than 100 phonograph records.   Of those,
the Baptist, Lutheran and Methodist denominations led the way.
Presbyterian and Episcopal churches led in number of periodical
titles received.   Of the 26 libraries reporting 100 or more periodical titles, eight were Presbyterian, five were Episcopal, three were
Lutheran and three were Friends.   Lutherans led all denominations
by having the largest number of libraries with relatively large non-
book collections.   However, non-book material was found in large
numbers in very few of these libraries.

Table IX: Church and Synagogue Libraries for Selected
Denominations by Number of Books Held

			BOOKS HELD				
DENOMINATION	0 to 100	101 to 300	301 to 500	501 to 1,000	1,001 to 5,000	More Than 5,000	Total
Baptist	9	21	21	46	56	11	164
Episcopal	6	23	18	34	31	4	116
Lutheran	15	84	102	162	176	8	547
Methodist	10	22	38	51	73	5	199
Presbyterian	3	44	43	74	116	6	286
United Christian Church	4	14	19	25	30	2	94
Jewish	0	1	5	18	36	24	84

Number of Missing Observations = 68 libraries

Table X: Number of Filmstrips

FILMSTRIPS	NO. OF LIBRARIES	FREQUENCY (%)
0 to 100	940	76. 2%
101 to 300	250	20. 3
301 to 500	33	2. 7
501 to 5, 000	11	0. 8
Not Reported	588	Missing
TOTAL	1822	100. 0%

Table XI: Libraries by Denomination and
Number of Filmstrips

DENOMINATION	0 to 100	101 to 300	301 to 500	501 to 1, 000	1, 001 to 5, 000	Totals
Baptist	85	43	5	2	1	136
Disciples of Christ	20	6	1	0	0	27
Episcopal	61	7	3	0	0	71
Lutheran	290	57	8	1	1	357
Methodist	101	54	4	2	0	161
Presbyterian	159	32	4	0	0	195
Reformed	19	1	1	0	0	21
Roman Catholic	27	7	3	1	0	38
United Christian Church	60	16	0	0	0	76
Jewish	32	20	2	1	0	55

Number of Missing Observations = 607 libraries

Circulation

Circulation statistics were collected on a weekly basis rather than on the traditional annual basis, since church and synagogue library recordkeeping was often poor. It was felt, therefore, that greater accuracy could be obtained by gathering figures at their point of origin. Table XII summarizes library use findings. Most churches and synagogues reported their libraries to circulate between 10 and 25 volumes per week, or between 500 and 1, 250 volumes per year. Between four and five percent of them reported more than 100 charges per week. Table XII shows an average weekly circulation of about 17 volumes and an average yearly circulation of about 900 volumes. Certainly, these are small circulation totals when compared with other kinds of libraries. No figures were collected on browsing use.

Table XIII shows that half of the synagogues reported library circulation figures above 50 volumes per week with a third of the

Roman Catholic churches reporting use above that figure. The Baptists and Lutherans were the other denominations with large numbers of libraries in the higher circulation frequencies. In contrast, most Episcopal churches indicated that their libraries circulated under 10 volumes per week.

Table XII: Weekly Circulation for Church and
Synagogue Libraries

WEEKLY CIRC. CHARGES	NO. OF LIBRARIES	FREQUENCY (%)
Less Than 10	589	33. 3%
11 to 25	643	36. 3
26 to 50	355	20. 1
51 to 100	105	5. 9
More Than 100	78	4. 4
Not Reported	52	Missing
TOTAL	1822	100. 0%

Summary Data

        The typical library was founded in the early or mid-1960's and was open for service whenever the building was open, though it was staffed for only one day a week.   The Middle Atlantic, Upper Middle Western and West Coast areas were the leading centers of church and synagogue libraries.   Lutheran, Presbyterian, Methodist, and Baptist church libraries were found in largest numbers among the respondents.   Data from 1808 questionnaire returns indicated that American church and synagogue library collections averaged about 800 books, something under 100 films and filmstrips, several dozen records and a few periodical subscriptions.   The typical library had available about $250 per year for library operation, mostly spent for print and non-print material purchases.   Circulation averaged 17 charges per week.   For the most part, the collections served the entire congregation but not necessarily the surrounding communities.

        Although most staffs were volunteer and non-professional, many professional librarians were associated with these libraries. Clearly, synagogue libraries outstripped church libraries on many of these tables.   With only an 18 percent return, the generalization about which we can be surest is that the majority of American church and synagogue libraries did not answer questionnaire surveys like this one.

Table XIII: Selected Denominations by Weekly
Church and Synagogue Library Circulation Charges

DENOMINATIONS	Less Than 10	11 to 25	26 to 50	51 to 100	More Than 100	Totals
Baptist	49	56	35	10	7	157
Disciples of Christ	12	18	4	5	1	40
Episcopal	62	39	9	5	2	117
Lutheran	183	193	129	23	17	545
Methodist	70	79	31	11	3	194
Presbyterian	96	119	59	9	4	287
Roman Catholic	7	23	13	8	11	62
United Christian Church	38	41	10	1	3	93
Jewish	6	13	24	19	24	86

Number of Missing Observations = 79 libraries

LISTS OF CHURCH AND SYNAGOGUE LIBRARIES

Printed and Published Lists

List of Religious Libraries Published in the American Library Di-
    rectory. New York: R. R. Bowker Company, 1974. Contains
    400 church and synagogue libraries.

Recipients of Library Citations, 1948-1975. Citations awarded anu-
    ally by the Jewish Book Council of America, 15 East 26th Street,
    New York. Lists 276 synagogue libraries that meet stated re-
    quirements.

Rodda, Dorothy J. and John F. Harvey, Directory of Church and
    Synagogue Libraries. Philadelphia: Drexel Press, 1966. Lists
    3200 libraries with data.

Ruoss, G. Martin and Marilyn M. Ruoss, New Mexico Church and
    Synagogue Library Directory. Albuquerque: University of New
    Mexico, Zimmerman Library, 1973. Lists addresses for 302
    libraries, data information for 83.

Smith, Ruth S., Survey of Church Libraries in the Washington D. C.
    Area. Bethesda, Md.: Church Library Council, 1966. Lists
    132 libraries with summary data.

White, Joyce L., Directory of Church and Synagogue Libraries in
    Maryland. Bryn Mawr, Pa.: Church and Synagogue Library
    Association, 1973. Lists data for 125 libraries from a mailing
    list of 300 libraries.

White, Joyce L., Directory of Church and Synagogue Libraries in
    the United States. In Preparation, 1977. Lists 1808 church
    and synagogue libraries with full data and is summarized in the
    present paper.

Mailing and Membership Lists

Association of Jewish Libraries.
    1975 Synagogue Libraries Membership: 166

Catholic Library Association.
    1975 Parish and Community Libraries Membership: 300

Christian Board of Publication.
    1975 Mailing List to Church Libraries: 2658

Church and Synagogue Library Association.
    1975 Membership Mailing List: 755

Church Librarians Fellowship, Baltimore, Md.
    1974 Membership List: 150

Church Library Council, Washington, D. C.
    1976 Membership List: 125

Cokesbury Church Library Department.
    1976 Mailing List to Presbyterians: 5, 040
    1976 Mailing List to United Methodist Church Libraries: 14, 547
    1976 Mailing List to United Church of Christ Libraries: 3, 615

Congregational Libraries Association of British Columbia.
    1976 Membership Mailing: 200

Evangelical Church Library Association.
    1975 Membership List: 370

Friends Meeting Librarians.
    1973 Mailing List: 102

Church of Jesus Christ of Latter-Day Saints (Mormon)
    1976 List of Meetinghouse Libraries: 4, 000

Lutheran Church Library Association.
    1975 Membership Mailing List: 2, 000

Ontario Church Library Association.
    1976 Membership Mailing List: 225

Pacific Northwest Association of Church Libraries
    1974 Mailing List: 250

Southern Baptist Church Library Department.
    1975 Directors of Church Library Services: approximately
    20, 000

ARCHITECTURE AND FINANCE

G. Martin Ruoss

Architecture and finance for church and synagogue libraries are phenomena of the twentieth century. It is evident that the present library associations of churches and synagogues have created interest in and have set standards for housing, staffing and maintaining the library. Thus, in 1922, the Catholic Library Association arose from the National Catholic Education Association as a result of pastoral leadership in the local parish.[1] In 1927, the Southern Baptist Convention began its epochal development of church media centers. The Presbyterians began their library group in 1944, the Lutherans organized in 1958, and the Evangelicals formed an association in 1972. The Christian Science Reading Rooms and the Catholic Information Centers are usually more specialized types of library service.[2] Today, with more than 300,000 places of worship, it is estimated that there are about 40,000 church and synagogue libraries with an average holding of 500 volumes.[3]

The twentieth century's renewed interest in church and synagogue libraries is in sharp contrast to the nineteenth century's concern for them. Then, they were an integral part, where they existed, of the instructional or worship facilities of the various worship places. This meant, however, that they were poorly located in an obscure building area and were poorly financed. The San Concepcion Mission in San Antonio, Texas, in earlier times, had a library room as a part of the Spanish mission architectural plan.[4] The Sunday School libraries, as such, had their beginnings about 1825 and began as an economical way to reward attendance. For almost a century, Sunday Schools encouraged the establishment of library areas, even if they were but a table and a shelf in a closet or a balcony area.[5]

Today architecture and finance for church and synagogue libraries are current items in most denominational and Jewish groups. Their regular administrative and planning agencies utilize the best architectural advice and service from church finance officers to present information and help to the local congregation.

Architecture

The architectural provision for church and synagogue libraries is normally a low priority item in local administration and planning, but it is included, noted and provided for. One of the major

34

concerns, architecturally, has been to identify a suitable location
for the congregational library.   Historically, the library has been
located in very interesting and unusual areas of the building.   Currently, church and synagogue libraries can be found in all of these
places:

> in a dimly lighted, poorly ventilated and poorly heated
>   basement;
> in an office or corrider corner;
> in the vestibule or narthex of many older buildings;
> in a vacant classroom or other unused area;
> in a glass-walled space on a balcony;
> in a closet;
> in a parish hall (a kind of portable library);
> on a stage;
> in a cafeteria;
> in spare space in a rectory or parsonage, and so on. [6]

Since 1950, space allocated to the church and synagogue library
follows commonly accepted architectural principles, such as the
following:

a.   locating the library near the major traffic area of the
     building--at the hub of activities;
b.   assuring the library of easy accessibility and its con-
     comitant of visibility;
c.   being mindful of the relation of the parking area to
     the library user;
d.   emphasizing functional use of the space rather than
     storehouse concepts--reading areas and wall space
     for shelving;
e.   providing good lighting, adequate ventilation, air con-
     ditioning and heating where required;
f.   using decorative colors and features for bulletin
     boards, book drops, etc.

This situation is a result of the growth of the architectural service
departments found in most denominational groups today.   At the
present time, sufficient information is available in the manuals,
handbooks and serials of the various church and synagogue library
groups to encourage local leaders to assume greater initiative and
responsibility in designating the space to be utilized by the library. [7]

The wide spectrum of church and synagogue climate and
housing styles will be reflected in the spaces available and desirable
for their libraries.   There are such libraries in all of the life zones
from the tropical to the arctic.   This fact helps one to understand
that not all architectural recommendations are acceptable in all geographic areas.   For example, a vestibule library might be practical
in the Southeast or Southwest, but it would not be as desirable in
the North Central or Northeast.   Climate affects the location of
suitable library space.   This is reflected in the requirements for
heating, air conditioning, ventilation, lighting and the like.

A second major factor in architectural services for church and synagogue libraries is a sharpening definition of the library's purpose in local ministries. The purpose for which the local church or synagogue library exists will aid noticeably in determining its location, design, furnishings and financing. To arrive at a purpose for the library, serious consideration must be given to questions such as these:

--How frequently will the library be used? Will it be used only on the main day of worship or whenever there is a meeting in the building?
--Will the library be staffed at some hours?
--Will it be a self-service library?
--Will it primarily serve the administrative and teaching leaders, or will it be concerned with the whole congregation and even the neighborhood?
--Will the library be used by children as well as by adults?
--Will the handicapped be able to use the library?
--Will the library have both a circulating collection and a reference collection, or only one of these?
--Will it house congregational records, archives, rare mementos such as old Bibles, books and artifacts?
--Will the library be a multi-purpose room?

Answers to questions like these will readily indicate to local leaders how to plan wisely and well for library areas. They will be useful to the architect if a new or remodelled building is in process, also.

The location of the library within the main building complex depends upon a judicious response to these concerns:

--Will the parking area abet or hinder the library user?
--Will custodial care be available to the library?
--Will there be sufficient storage areas--especially if the library is a media center?
--Will heating, lighting, ventilation and air conditioning be available for the library at all times? Remember that radical changes in temperature are harmful to books and media as well as to furniture.
--Is the lighting adequate for browsing in all shelving areas or must accent lighting be provided?
--Will the library be staffed by a busy office worker, a volunteer, or a paid staff member?
--Will there be suitable comfortable chairs, a desk and a filing cabinet?
--Will security be a problem?
--Who is responsible for security?
--Are there adequate directional and informational signs to guide the library user?

The work that is customarily done in the library area as well as plans for the future expansion of services, the space requirements and the collection itself affect the architectural space.

For instance, the library staff--whether volunteer or paid--needs a good work area for acquiring, cataloging and circulating library material. This activity requires at least a desk with drawers, a typewriter and stand, a chair, a catalog cabinet and one other filing cabinet. A minimum of 150 square feet seems certain.

The anticipated plans for the future, however distant, require consideration about how permanent the present location will be. One must consider whether or not the library areas can easily be extended, expanded or enlarged. There is today a major concern that the library space be comfortable with enough space to relax and read as well as good shelving space. It must be esthetically pleasing. The trend, as reported in the various issues of church and synagogue library association publications, is toward using the space occupied by the library solely as a library. A full-fledged media center will have additional requirements for storage and shelving; a walk-in closet is desirable.

Today, any church or synagogue can obtain aid in planning, developing, and selecting the best library location inasmuch as architectural services are a viable part of the work of churches and synagogues. Appendix A to this chapter contains a list helpful in designing library quarters. Suggested floor plans appear on pages 38-39.

Equipment and Furnishings

During the previous century, church and synagogue library equipment was chiefly a kind of "locked case or cupboard" because of the exigency of the times, limited building use, and lack of library staff members. This furniture reflected the prevailing nineteenth-century attitude that libraries were storehouses. [8]

The last fifty years of the twentieth century have seen much public and academic library building construction. These buildings should encourage church and synagogue members to envision better library furnishings and equipment. Even public school libraries have had both a direct and an indirect effect upon the desires of church and synagogue libraries to provide better facilities and equipment.

The atmosphere of the library should reflect friendliness. It should be a place where the user can be at home in finding and reading a book. It is better to have a few well chosen pieces of furniture and equipment than to have a random assortment of "hand me downs. "

For the library staff, the minimum requirement for equipment and furnishings would include: A comfortable work chair; a small desk with drawers; a typewriter and stand in the event that the desk does not have an attached typewriter shelf; a card catalog of six or more drawers; a filing cabinet for publishers' catalogs

SUGGESTED FLOOR PLANS

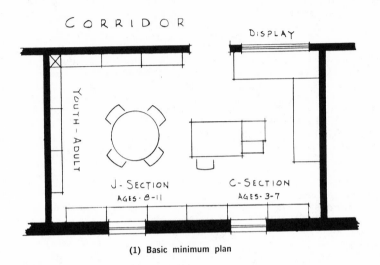

(1) Basic minimum plan

(2) Plan showing use of two classrooms

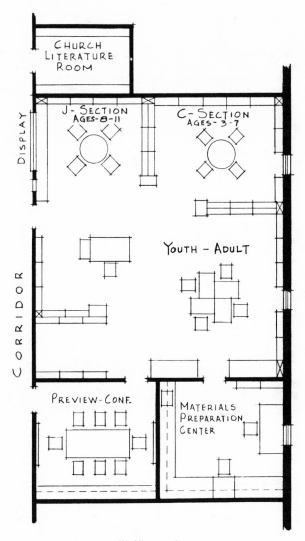

(3) Library suite

and vertical file material; a book truck--particularly if the library
is not near the hub of traffic or if the library staff needs to take
material to other areas; and a good display rack.

For library users, the following are recommended furnishing
and equipment needs: comfortable chairs; small rectangular tables
(even folding tables are useful); a floor lamp for accent reading; a
place to return books when the library is not open.

Other necessary equipment and furnishing needs are shelving--
preferably metal, adjustable, and in sufficient quantity to shelve the
present collection; a display rack for paperbacks and magazines;
and, if media equipment and materials are a part of the collection,
an adequate amount of shelving for phonodiscs, tapes, slides, films,
cassettes, and the equipment they require for effective use.

A few other areas for consideration:

--floor coverings that match the general building floor pattern (chil-
        dren like carpet as a place to sit and read);
--electric outlets for displays and equipment;
--window areas
--types of doors--full glass, half glass or even panel doors; a door
        can usually be used as a place to install a book drop;
--good use of color;
--symbolism that is educative and imaginative;
--display cases, including locked ones if archives and rare items
        are to be on display;
--a telephone line
--directional and informational signs;
--security for money if fines, petty cash and gifts are kept.

Many of these equipment needs and furnishings can be supplied
by regular public library suppliers.   Some religious groups provide
their own recommendations for these items.   Most library staff
members are surprised, on paging through a library supplier's catalog, to discover the wide diversity of help offered.

Income and Expenditures

Libraries in churches and synagogues are expensive to operate.   Income on a regular basis and budgeted expenditures will provide consistent library service.   A wide disparity of practice exists
in financing such libraries.   Some operate on the proverbial shoe-
string while others are so fortunate as to have a regular monthly
allotment, such as First Baptist Church, Greensboro, South Carolina. [9]   Despite the large amounts of volunteer time and donations
of books and supplies, the local church or synagogue library needs
effective regular income for good library service.

The best source of income is an apportioned amount with all
funds handled by the proper congregation fiscal officer.   This method

requires consistent attention to planning book and equipment needs,
including special items, by the library committee. When a budgeted
amount is given by the institution, the library increases in stature
in the eyes of the congregation.

The national Church and Synagogue Library Association suggests appropriately that apportionment of the annual library budget
may be as follows:[10]

Acquisitions	60%
Subscriptions, ephemeral material	5%
Supplies	5%
Promotion and publicity	10%
Equipment, furnishings	10%
Staff needs	10%

Acquisitions should be considered to include purchases of books and
media as well as mending, rebinding, or replacing material on hand
which is worn or outdated.   General proportions may be allocated
as follows:

Reference works	20%
Teaching aids	5%
Adult fiction	5%
Adult non-fiction	30%
Pre-school material	5%
Children and youth fiction	20%
Children and youth non-fiction	15%

Other sources of income exist in addition to the apportioned
yearly amount from the congregation. They include contributions of
money to buy books and material; donations of books (titles should
be accepted only if you would have been willing to buy them); contributions from memorials; collections at specially sponsored library
events; money to honor persons or events; direct mail solicitations;
fund-raising dinners and events; membership dues; fines for over-
dues; book fairs.[11]   Income is the result, in large part, of the enthusiasm and imagination of the library staff, the library committee
and the religious sponsor.

The experience of a wide variety of churches and synagogues
has led to the following suggested norms for local library budget
needs:

A beginning library should strive to build a basic collection
of two items (books, audio visuals, etc.) per church or
synagogue member, not counting duplicate copies.   An
established library may be maintained on a minimum budget not less than 50¢ annually per congregational member.[12]

Expenditure for library material, supplies and equipment is best
done on a regular basis rather than by "spurt and splash. "   The

regular meeting of the library staff to recommend purchases and to replenish supplies is a sure way to keep on top of the funds available for the library.   In some libraries, the staff is paid, and this requires attention to fringe benefits.   Some libraries provide transportation costs for workers and pay the expenses of attending conferences and workshops.   At all levels, the staff ought to know what items cost, when payments are due, and how to verify receipt and payment.

Good stewardship of time and possessions requires the library staff to keep records--simple or complex--but at least a regular tally sheet of what came in from where and what went out to whom and when.   Allied with this is the desire to ask for a yearly audit, small or large as it may be.   Also, some religious groups expect a monthly, quarterly or yearly report.   This is a good opportunity to know where the library has been and where it is going financially. It also provides a medium for promotion and publicity.   Such reports are the stuff out of which history is written on the local level.[13] Page 43 shows a sample financial report form. †

Conclusions

The varieties of architectural provisions for church and synagogue libraries and for their financing reveal that a potential for more and for better religious libraries exists at the congregational level.   It is possible that 100,000 church and synagogue libraries will exist within a decade and thus become the largest single type of library in the country, outdistancing public and school libraries.[14]

It is to be hoped that in the serial publications of the Society for Church Architecture and the Church Architectural Guild a more frequent occasion will be found to discuss church and synagogue libraries; likewise in Church Management.   Above all, it is to be hoped that the current crop of publications by the church and synagogue library associations can be pooled into a means of reporting to all concerned the interests of architecture and finance.

APPENDIX A*

LIBRARY SUPPLY AND EQUIPMENT COMPANIES

American Instructional Materials, Inc., Box 22748, Texas Woman's University Station, Denton, TX 76204.

---

*Reprinted by permission from Gladys E. Scheer, The Church Library: Tips and Tools.   St. Louis, MO: The Bethany Press, 1973, p. 77.
†Opposite: Reprinted by permission from Church Library Record and Plan Book. © Copyright 1973 Convention Press.   All rights reserved.

BUDGET AND FINANCIAL RECORD

Be specific in making budget requests. The following form may be an aid in planning budget needs. For special areas such as redecorating or enlarging the room, make a separate request. Some churches are using the suggestion of 50¢ to $1.00 for library materials for each person enrolled in Sunday School as the annual budget amount.

	Amt. Budget This Year	Amount Spent This Year													Needed Next Year
		Oct.	Nov.	Dec.	Jan.	Feb.	Mar.	Apr.	May	June	July	Aug.	Sept.	
Books:														
Ages 3-7														
Ages 8-11														
Youth and Adult														
Audiovisuals:														
Materials:														
Filmstrips														
Slides														
Motion Picture Rental														
Nonprojected Aids														
Recordings														
Tapes														
Cassette tapes														
*Equipment:														
New Equipment:														
Maintenance														
Supplies														
**Library Meetings														
TOTAL														

*Some churches provide for audiovisual equipment and maintenance in a general church fund. Library furnishings, such as shelving and files, should also be covered in this way.

**Many churches have a general convention and conference fund covering regional, state, and Convention-wide meetings.

Bro-Dart, Inc. Eastern Division: 1609 Memorial Avenue, Williams-
    port, PA 17701 or 56 Earl Street, Newark, NJ 07114;
    Western Division: 15255 E. Don Julian Road, City of Indus-
    try, CA 91746.

Demco Educational Corp. , P. O. Box 1488, Madison, WI 53701.

Fordham Equipment Company, 2377-79 Hoffman Street, Bronx, NY
    10458

Gaylord Bros. , Inc. , P. O. Box 61, Syracuse, NY 13201 or P. O.
    Box 710, Stockton, CA 95201

The Highsmith Co. , Inc. , P. O. Box 25, Fort Atkinson, WI 53538.

Josten's American Library Line (supplies), 4070 Shirley Drive S. W. ,
    Atlanta, GA 30336.

Josten's Library Services Division, 900 East 80th Street, Minneap-
    olis, MN 55420

> The following companies supply furniture and
> metal stacks primarily:

Art Metal Construction Co. , Jamestown, NY 14701.

Estey Corporation, Drawer E, Red Bank, NJ 07701.

Globe-Wernicke, Cincinnati, OH.

Harvard Interiors Manufacturing Co. , Inc. , 4820 Durfee Avenue,
    Pico Rivers, CA 90660.

John E. Sjostrom Co. , Inc. , 1716 North 10th Street, Philadelphia,
    PA 19122.

Remington Rand, Library Bureau, 315 Fourth Ave. , New York, NY

The Worden Company, 199 East 17th Street, Holland, MI 49423

NOTES

1. Sister Marie Angela, "A School-Parish Library, " Catholic Li-
    brary World XXXIX (1968), pp. 334-345.
2. Wilson Library Bulletin XLV (1967), pp. 318-321.
3. White, Joyce, "Church Libraries; Unrecognized Resources, "
    American Libraries II (April, 1971), pp. 297-299. Also,
    Encyclopedia of Library and Information Science, IV (1970),
    pp. 662-681. The bibliographies of these two sources are
    most useful in citing unpublished sources as well as basic
    bibliographical titles.
4. Thrall, Bernard, "Parish Libraries: Vatican II-Lacunae, "
    Catholic Library World XLI (1970), pp. 377-379, 466-471.

5. Briggs, F. Allen, "The Sunday School Library in the Nine-
    teenth Century," Library Quarterly XXXI (1962), pp. 166-
    177.
6. Sister Marie Angela, op. cit., pp. 344-345.
7. See the attractively illustrated leaflet, "Church Library Space,
    Equipment and Furnishings" by the Church Literature Depart-
    ment, Sunday School Board, Southern Baptist Convention,
    Nashville, Tennessee, published in 1970. 24 p.
8. Sister Marie Angela, op. cit., pp. 344-345.
9. Sykes, Marvin, "Greensboro Church Library," Library Journal
    LXXIX (September 1, 1954), pp. 1468-1469.
10. Church and Synagogue Library Association, Standards for Church
    and Synagogue Libraries (CSLA Guide No. 6), Bryn Mawr,
    1977, p. 7.
11. Briggs, op. cit., pp. 166-177. Recall that in 1697, the Angli-
    can Divine, Dr. Thomas Bray, noted his plan to have a library
    in each American Anglican parish: "There is but one objec-
    tion that I can foresee, and that is an excessive scarcity of
    money."
12. Church and Synagogue Library Association, op. cit., p. 7.
13. Parish and Community Library Services of the Catholic Library
    Association. "Standards for Parish and Community Librar-
    ies," Catholic Library World XLIII (1972), pp. 459-460. The
    standards for finance are stated succinctly:
    A. 1. a definite budget
        2. annual needs
        3. notice of yearly allotment
        4. funds readily available to the chairman of the library
            committee
        5. regular accounting and reporting
    B. included in the regular parish budget
    C. additional funds for special needs or equipment from
        gifts and special activities
14. White, op. cit., pp. 397-399. Statistics for 1975 indicated
    that there were 9,190 public libraries in America.

BIBLIOGRAPHY

Association of Jewish Libraries. Standards for Jewish Libraries in
    Synagogues, Schools, and Centers. New York: Jewish Book
    Council of America, 1970. 8 p.

Baptist Heritage History. v. 6, pt. 3, pp. 181-184. (1971).

Catholic Periodical and Literature Index. v. 1- 1888- Haverford,
    Pa.: Catholic Library Association.

CSLA issue in the Drexel Library Quarterly, VI, pp. 112-202. This
    is an excellent series of survey articles.

Hannaford, Claudia. "CSLA," Special Libraries LXI (1970), pp.
    9-14.

Kohl, Rachel. Church and Synagogue Library Resources. Phila-
    delphia: CSLA, 1975. 18 p.

Laugher, C. T. Thomas Bray's Grand Design, 1695-1785. Chicago:
    American Library Association, 1973.

Library Literature. v. 1-   1934-   New York: H. W. Wilson
    Co.

McMichael, Betty, "How to Finance a Church or Synagogue Library,"
    Church and Synogogue Libraries XI (November-December,
    1977), pp. 1&12.

The most complete bibliography on church and synagogue libraries
    is by Murdock, J. Larry, comp. "Church Libraries: A
    Bibliography on Sources of Information from 1876-1969."
    Catholic Library World XLI (1970), pp. 377-379, 466-471.
    When the author completes this work through 1976, it will
    indeed be a valuable reference work for all concerned.

Religious and Theological Abstracts. v. 1-   1958-   Myerstown,
    Pa.

Sunday School Board, Southern Baptist Convention. Church Library
    Space, Equipment and Furnishings. 1970. This is a useful
    planning document for any church or synagogue library.

Trezza, Alphonse F., ed. Library Buildings: Innovation for Chang-
    ing Needs. Chicago: American Library Association, 1972.

Weine, M. Survey of Synagogue Libraries in Philadelphia. MLS
    Thesis, Drexel Library School, 1957. 50 p.

PART II:

JEWISH LIBRARIES

SYNAGOGUE, TEMPLE AND JEWISH CENTER LIBRARIES

Helen B. Greif

Historically, synagogues and temples have always maintained collections of books for the study of Torah. In more recent years, rabbis have added to these collections books to assist them in carrying out their pastoral responsibilities. In addition, many varied collections of Judaica have found their way into the synagogues as bequests or donations from the members. Very few of these collections were organized originally as formal libraries. A typical example is Congregation Rodeph Shalom, Philadelphia, organized in 1802 as the first German synagogue in the United States. It is believed that a library was started at that time with books written in the German language. Through the years, the congregation has had several homes. In 1928, it moved into its present building and the 1,444 library books were catalogued for the first time. This collection has since grown to 6,700 books with an additional 3,000 volumes in a suburban branch in Elkins Park.

Library Survey Results

It is difficult to determine the exact timetable for the current trend in establishing formal synagogue libraries. In a 1947 survey conducted by the National Jewish Welfare Board, 60 percent of the 41 libraries reporting indicated that they had been organized in 1935 or later.[1] In 1967, a similar survey with 131 responding showed that nearly one half of the libraries had been organized since 1960.[2] Based upon the findings of a survey conducted in 1976 by this author for this paper, the largest number of American synagogue libraries was established within the last three decades. In fact, half of the libraries reported establishment since 1960. Four of the libraries date from the World War I period or earlier, however.

In any case, the founding of these libraries was strongly associated with the American middle class trend toward living in the city suburbs. Old congregations moved out from the city and new congregations sprang up to include a mixture of city and country folk. Many of these suburban congregations developed libraries far exceeding the small collections of the older synagogues.

The survey profile of the average synagogue library indicated

that, in its broadest sense, it was an institution for Jewish education. Its aim was to increase the Jewish knowledge of its adult
readers, provide resource material for congregational schools and
create an atmosphere appropriate for stimulating intellectual curiosity, literary appreciation and the enhancement of aesthetic values
in the Jewish community.

The questionnaire for the 1976 survey was mailed to 235
synagogues in 37 states, with the largest number going to the states
having the greatest Jewish population concentration. Seventy-three
librarians in twenty states replied, and this report is based on their
questionnaires. Half of the respondents were in four states: Massachusetts, New York, California and Illinois. Three of these
states, Massachusetts, New York and California, were among the
leading states in percentage of Jewish population. [3]

Three fourths of the libraries had library committees operating as supervisory bodies. These committees determined the library goals, policies and administrative direction. Several other
libraries received direction solely from the librarian or the volunteer in charge. A third of the library committees included members of the synagogue staff, the rabbi, cantor, principal or the executive director, while the rest of the committee were lay synagogue
members. The committee was charged with the responsibility of
determining the library's relationship to the parent organization. In
addition, it often supervised the budget and hired the personnel. It
promulgated the library operating guidelines, shaped the library's
character, defined the community areas to be served and assisted
in book and non-book selection. An important committee function
was to stimulate use by coordinating library activities with those of
other synagogue and community groups.

A third of the synagogue libraries answering the questionnaire
considered themselves to be "school libraries." In addition, three
fourths of the head librarians worked with classes in the library.
The synagogue library's importance as a resource center for the
religious school has grown as the library has become more professional. Where this has occurred, the librarian was often a member of the school staff and attended its meetings. He or she could
then be made aware of future school needs regarding curriculum
changes, special programs, assemblies, class projects and teachers'
needs. The children's librarian of Temple Beth-El, Lowell, Massachusetts, described the function of her library as follows:

> We have become the heart of the school.... Our library
> serves as an extension of the classroom as well as a
> gathering place before school and a place to come when
> the world seems momentarily overwhelming or unfriendly.

The B'nai Jacob Library, Woodbridge, Connecticut, stated in its
descriptive brochure:

> Hopefully we can stimulate an interest in our students for

further study in Judaica beyond the classroom and their
school years at B'nai Jacob.

They reported, as did others, that many of their students returned
later to seek material for high school or college research papers.

In a paper published in the Synagogue School, based on a survey by Judith Segal, "almost all of the libraries had some juvenile
books, ranging from 100 to 1500 volumes. The average number was
491. And, since the average student population was 422, the result
was a little over one book per student. "[4] The Association of Jewish
Libraries suggested that a Jewish school should not consider its juvenile collection adequate with fewer than three books per pupil.

An average of only a fourth of the entire collection of the
libraries in the present survey was classified as children's material.
The average synagogue library fell short of its desired goal of three
books per pupil because of the lack of good Judaic literature for
children. Since publishers have been made aware of this potential
market, the situation has improved.

With a range from 60 to 3,000, the typical synagogue had
500-600 family memberships and an annual library budget of $1300-
$1700, or $2-$3 per family. This typical library had 3200-4200
volumes of which 800-1000 were in the juvenile collection. It is
noteworthy that the top quarter of the libraries in this survey averaged 9000 volumes in size and over $4,000 in the annual budget.
Apparently, certain of the large synagogue libraries in the country
were represented in this group.

In its publication, Standards for a Jewish Library, the Association of Jewish Libraries recommended that each library contain
at least four books per adult borrower. [5] The average number of
books within the range of family membership in the synagogues reporting showed that this standard was being met. In this survey,
the typical synagogue provided between five and six volumes per
family.

Media were often reported with school supplies, not with library holdings. In spite of this error, two thirds of the libraries
did acquire media material in one form or another, though more
than a fourth did not. The emphasis on using media material in
education and its importance in the learning process for young children has been recognized only recently by the religious schools.
This need is most easily fulfilled by library acquisitions. There,
the material can be classified and made available at the appropriate
time to teachers, parents and students, to enrich the educational
environment of the school and the synagogue.

The library media center can provide a language laboratory
for developing fluency in Hebrew language use. Tapes and recordings of guest speakers and programs can be made for future reference. No one communications medium is adequate today to meet

student educational needs.   The multi-media approach is the best
one for maximum motivation and the deepest impact in the learning
process.

Periodicals and newspapers were acquired by the vast majority of the libraries answering the questionnaire.   Librarians recognized that these serials were essential in order to keep the most
current information available for borrowers.

The subject of non-Judaica in the Jewish library has been a
controversial one.   The prevailing philosophy is that the Jewish library should contain only Judaica.   Since public libraries were readily accessible to serve other areas of interest, it was felt that the
synagogue library should serve to broaden the Judaic education of
its congregants.   Most libraries had almost nothing but Judaica.

Most library funds came from outside donations, the synagogue, or the sisterhood.   Usually they were very limited.   No
source of public funding was available.   Outside donations, variable
from year to year, could not be considered a reliable funding source.
Several returns indicated that budgets were privileged information.
Funds were provided by synagogue organizational budgets or combina-
tions of two or more groups.   Large gifts were essential to provide
costly items such as library equipment, encyclopedias or furnishings.
Budgets were often augmented by the proceeds of book fairs and
sales, social functions, library teas and book reviews.   Probably
the lack of funds was one of the main reasons that so many synagogue libraries were still operated entirely by volunteer personnel,
in spite of the recognition of professional staff members' importance.

The amount spent on books, media and supplies can be expressed as a ratio.   In the smallest congregations, the ratios among
the three factors were 81-12-7 and in the largest congregations they
were 69-21-10.   Of course, the amount spent in each category rose
with congregation size.   The ratio spent on media and supplies rose
as the ratio spent on books declined in the larger libraries.

As in all previous surveys of Jewish libraries, the lack of
uniformity of classification systems and subject headings was apparent.   The Library of Congress classification scheme was used by
most of the scholarly Jewish libraries in the United States, but it
was not well known to the general public. [6]   The Dewey Decimal
system presented difficulties for the Jewish librarian because (1)
the specialized Judaica collection required excessive subdivision
within a limited area, and (2) certain subjects dealt within the Jewish library did not fit into the Dewey System well.   However, it was
used in many synagogue and temple libraries.

As a result of these problems, several other systems have
been devised for use in the small Jewish library.   The Golub and
Celnik classification systems are simplified schemes based on letter
classifications.   The Weine and Leikind systems are based on the
Dewey Decimal system, and the Elazar system, used extensively in

the West, is most useful for larger collections. [7] Of the other classifications, the Weine system was the most popular, though a considerable variety of them was in use. With the increase in the use of paid professional librarians, perhaps the use of standardized library classification systems will increase. Though a dozen or more subject heading lists were in use, the Weine subject heading list was most popular with almost 40 percent of the total usage. The Library of Congress and Sears subject heading lists were next in popularity.

The synagogue library movement was built on a base of volunteer help. Without volunteers, most libraries, with the exception of the heavily endowed synagogues, could not have been started. Funds were not available, but of equal importance, few educated Judaica librarians were available. Those people who had some library experience and a basic knowledge of Judaica were in the forefront of the movement. As it grew, they became involved in such organizations as the Association of Jewish Libraries, the Church and Synagogue Library Association and the many regional Jewish library associations. These organizations offered training sessions and workshops devoted to raising the professional standards of synagogue libraries. Most recently, several colleges and universities have developed programs of Jewish studies in conjunction with other institutions offering library science degrees to develop the field of Jewish Librarianship.

A joint Judaica Librarianship program exists under the coordination of Brandeis University and Simmons College in the Boston area. Although not officially a joint program, it does provide the facilities of three institutions: Brandeis, Simmons and Harvard. Applications are submitted separately to Brandeis and Simmons and both sets of graduate degree requirements must be fulfilled. The requirements include eight courses from Simmons and twelve courses from Brandeis. There is a 600-hour supervised internship in the second year of study at the Harvard Judaica Library under the direction of Charles Berlin. In addition, after the first year of study, there is a four-week Brandeis-Israel Seminar. This course of study requires a minimum of two years for completion. It earns an M. A. in Contemporary Jewish Studies from Brandeis University and an M. L. S. in Library Science from Simmons College.

In 1974, the Jewish Theological Seminary in New York received a grant from the National Endowment for the Humanities in Washington, D. C. for a Pilot Program to educate librarians for Judaica collections. Originally, four courses were offered to give students an introduction to the field of Judaica librarianship. The courses were Judaica Bibliography and Reference Works, Special Problems in Cataloging and Classifying Judaica, Hebrew Paleography Workshop and History of the Hebrew Book and of Collections of Judaica and Hebraica. The J. T. S. program began in January 1975 and ended a year later. The students were taking the courses for credit towards their M. L. S. degrees. Each course earned three graduate credits, and a maximum of six credits was transferable to a library school program. The Seminary included an internship in its library for an additional three credits.

In Los Angeles, the Bureau of Jewish Education awarded a "Librarian-Teacher" certificate to each person who completed 50 college credits in Judaic Library Science, Judaica Studies, and Education. Persons earning Certificates were considered to be "Professionals. "

Survey information obtained on the head librarians revealed that they worked in the library an average of about thirteen hours per week and that more than half of them were college graduates. While a seventh of them had graduate degrees outside the library field, 40 percent of them were graduates of schools of library science. More than a fourth of them had had library experience before becoming synagogue librarians, and a fourth of the head librarians possessed some formal Jewish education. Usually, under the direction of the library committee, the head librarian ordered and catalogued the books, dealt directly with the school and implemented congregational programs. Half of the head librarians reported receiving synagogue salaries, and the other half were volunteers. Many of the larger libraries were fortunate enough to have more than one paid librarian.

Their membership in professional library associations revealed that a clear majority of the head librarians belonged to the Association of Jewish Libraries and a third of them to local Jewish library groups. Only a handful of them belonged to either the American Library Association or the Church and Synagogue Library Association. Forty-eight of the head librarians questioned were willing to assist other synagogue libraries as consultants.

The number of hours per week that the libraries reported remaining open during the school year was 10 to 13, a relatively large number. Many libraries remained open on an abbreviated schedule during the summer months. Most of the libraries were open for use by people outside of the synagogue community, though few formal inter-loan arrangements existed between synagogue libraries and others.

The following questions were answered with approximately an equal proportion of affirmative to negative responses: 1) Were the libraries open to other religious denominations? 2) Were they available to other schools in the area? 3) Were they acquiring scholarly books for research? 4) Was the head librarian conducting training workshops for volunteers? and 5) Did the library use volunteers? An area that was not well subscribed to was that of large-print books for senior citizens. The difficulty in securing them may have been the reason for this situation.

It is generally agreed by all sets of standards that the library should be located in a part of the synagogue where it can be seen and reached with ease. It should be aesthetically attractive, physically comfortable and conducive to study and browsing. The survey results indicated that care had been taken to satisfy these basic principles in planning synagogue libraries. The size of the rooms in which the synagogue libraries were housed revealed them to average 600-700 square feet, with a sixth of them occupying more than 1,000 square feet.

Most libraries were located in the central area of the synagogue or the school building. They were air-conditioned and were well-lighted. Almost half were sound-proofed. A majority of them had standard library shelving and adequate seating and work table facilities. They also utilized card catalogues, had bulletin boards and display areas, and maintained special racks for current publications and storage for past issues. Only a fourth of them had a special area for media material, however. Many libraries reported that media material was catalogued in the library but stored elsewhere in the school building.

Every library had a unique character that was influenced by the need which it fulfilled within its own synagogue, its past history and the personnel involved in its operation. Temple Emanu-El of Honolulu, with only three hundred and fifty family members, had the largest Judaica collection in the state of Hawaii and was part of the State Library System. A catalogue card of every book shelved was transmitted to the state system. The library was available for research by all church groups and university students.

The Temple Library of Cleveland, which housed the Abba Hillel Silver Archives, had made a fine contribution to the development of Jewish learning in the United States with its publication of the Index to Jewish Periodicals, edited by Miriam Leikind. This reference tool made it feasible for libraries to collect and store back issues of Jewish periodicals and publications for research purposes. The William G. Braude Library of Temple Beth-El of Providence maintained a card catalogue and an interloan arrangement with Brown University.

Temple Emanu-El Library, also of Providence, had a large collection of volumes on the history of religion, classical religion and Judaism in late antiquity. A recent addition to this area was a collection of original manuscript facsimiles of the Talmud, Midrash Bereshit Rabbah, Early Codes and First Editions of Biblical and Talmudic Commentaries. To quote the head librarian: "This ever developing part of our library collection is a constant impetus to serious Judaic study for our congregation."

There were other areas of specialization. Temple Beth Israel Library, Phoenix, housed an unusual music collection. It included liturgical music, Hassidic and Yiddish songs, Israeli music and a wide assortment of cantorials. They had the equipment necessary to record reel-to-reel tape and cassettes. The reel-to-reel tape was the master file and did not circulate while the cassettes were lent to members.

The Isadore Gruskin Library of Congregation B'nai David of Southfield, Michigan, reported that 90 percent of its users were

under the age of 13.   The suggestions of the young people were taken
seriously.   They were encouraged to decorate the library with posters and signs.   They had their own reading club, a corps of volunteers, a newspaper about the library and a "penspal" corner where
they could correspond with other youngsters in Jewish communities
throughout the United States and Canada.

Sinai Temple Library, Springfield, Massachusetts, had a
monthly Judaica exhibit collected from the community on a subject
relevant to the month or the next holiday.   The exhibits included
crafts, stamps, coins, needlework, art, and sculpture.

The librarian of the Axelrod Memorial Library, B'nai Jacob
Congregation, Jersey City, wrote:

> My committee represented our congregation at the "City
> Spirit Festival" which was held to improve the image of
> the city through its various ethnic, religious and racial
> groups.   Our exhibit on the Judaic heritage included ma-
> terial on Judaic culture, religion, art, music and litera-
> ture.

The synagogue library not only served the members of the congregation and the Religious school but performed an educational service
to the non-Jewish community, also.

Many synagogue libraries received guidance and direction
from the central office of the overall national religious group with
which their institution was affiliated.   The Conservative Movement
of Judaism, for example, under the leadership of the Women's
League for Conservative Judaism, encouraged its sisterhoods to establish and maintain libraries in all of their synagogues.   The central office in New York had a national chairperson in charge of libraries.   She distributed useful information to both the regional office and the library chairperson in each Conservative synagogue.
Regional workshops were held in many areas, and regional office
consultants were available to assist local synagogue librarians.

The synagogue librarian could secure a great deal of information about what Judaica was available from the Jewish publishing
houses, the secular Jewish organizations, such as B'nai Brith, and
from the publications and periodicals issued by various Jewish religious and educational groups.

The Leonard M. Sandhaus Memorial Library, Temple Israel,
Sharon, Massachusetts, represented the typical medium-sized synagogue library in origin, growth pattern, collection and operation.
Perhaps it would be useful to describe such a typical library here.
The Sandhaus Library started as a small collection of 1,000 volumes housed in the Temple's Jewish Community Center building.
When a new school wing was added to the building in 1962, the "library" was moved into a basement room.   The rabbi enlisted the
aid of a sisterhood member who was an experienced synagogue librarian.   A corps of volunteers was recruited from the sisterhood.

Training workshops were conducted. The books were catalogued and the library began lending material. In 1968, a beautiful new library room was built with funds provided by the sisterhood. It was centrally located, comfortably furnished and attractively decorated. By 1976, the collection had grown to 3,500 volumes. It included all classifications of Judaica and a general reference section. There was a separate teachers' reference collection. The children's section included Hebrew books in addition to those in English.

The Sandhaus Library subscribed to thirty periodicals. A small collection of material augmented the school's own media collection. Because of the proximity of Temple Israel to higher schools of learning offering Judaic studies, scholarly texts were acquired. The rabbi was consulted for acquisitions on religion and rabbinics, the cantor for music and the school principal for curriculum books. Suggestions from the congregation were welcomed.

Sandhaus Library operated with a corps of volunteers headed by one professional librarian. The library was open during school hours, before meetings, during adult study classes and on special occasions. Although there was a library committee, the head librarian made the final selection for acquisitions. She was invited to school staff meetings and brought the religious school children into the library periodically for visits and instruction.

The Typical Synagogue Library

A 1976 survey was made by the author of U.S. synagogue libraries, and the following summary reveals the picture of the typical library. Although American Synagogues have had libraries at least since 1802, most of the responding libraries had been founded in the 1950's or 1960's. Half of them were located in Massachusetts, New York, California, or Illinois, leading states in Jewish population. Most of the libraries were supervised by library committees and worked with Hebrew school classes.

The average synagogue library had 500-600 family memberships and an annual budget of $1300-$1700. A fourth of the book collection was devoted to children's literature. Book collections averaged 3200-4200 volumes, or 5-6 volumes per family. Most of the libraries contained media material, periodicals and newspapers. Their collections were dominated by Judaica material. Donations, the synagogue and the sisterhood were the primary sources of funding. The Dewey Decimal and the Weine classification systems were most common as were the Weine, Library of Congress and Sears subject heading lists.

While volunteers were the most numerous library staff members, more than half of the librarians reporting were paid, most of them were college graduates and almost half were library school graduates. Membership in the Association of Jewish Libraries and local Jewish library groups was heavy. The libraries were open

for service for an average of 10-13 hours per week and most of
them served people outside the synagogue community. Most libraries were well located in the synagogue building and square footage
averaged 600-700. Many libraries provided unusual services.

Synagogue Library Challenges

In the past two decades, the synagogue library has made enormous strides in physical plant, personnel qualifications, and the services rendered to the Jewish community. It is apparent, though, that
the library has not yet received full recognition for the importance
of its role in Jewish education. Typically, it is still not fully funded
as part of the synagogue educational facility. It relies too heavily
upon volunteers, professional or otherwise, to operate efficiently.
Under these circumstances, the number of hours which the library
can remain open is often happenstance. The Jewish librarian, along
with the Jewish educator, is bottom person on the totem pole of pri-
orities in the allotment of salary funds. Although the use of standardized classification systems and subject headings has increased,
still, too many libraries rely on homemade systems. Jewish professional library organizations have programmed their efforts toward
correcting these conditions. To accomplish these ends, great changes
must come from within the individual synagogue and from an enlight-
ened Jewish community.

NOTES

1. Summary of Replies to Library Questionnaire. New York: National Jewish Welfare Board, 1947.
2. Survey of Jewish Community Center Libraries. New York: National Jewish Welfare Board, 1967.
3. Fine, Morris and Himmelfarb, Milton, eds. American Jewish
Year Book. New York: The American Jewish Committee;
Philadelphia: The Jewish Publication Society; 1974-75, LXXV,
pp. 305-6.
4. Segal, Judith, "On Jewish Libraries and Standards, " The Synagogue School XXXI (Winter 1973), pp. 15-25.
5. Standards for a Jewish Library. Association of Jewish Libraries, Synagogue, School and Center Division, 1968.
6. Fine and Himmelfarb, op. cit., p. 24.
7. Classification Systems for Jewish Libraries, A Listing of Resources. New York: Jewish Book Council, 1973.

THE RELATIONSHIP OF THE SYNAGOGUE
SCHOOL AND ITS LIBRARY

Maurice S. Tuchman

What is the entity called "the synagogue school library"?
By its very nature it draws, or should draw, its strength and knowledge from two streams--Jewish education and librarianship.   In order for us to assess the functions and services of this type of school
library, we must first look at the context in which it exists.

Jewish Education

In a 1969 analysis of Jewish Education, Walter Acherman
stated, "Jewish education in the United States as we know it today
is rooted in the continued attempts of previous generations of Jews
to develop forms of Jewish schooling compatible with changing con-
ceptions of Judaism, new styles of Jewish life, and the demands of
living in America.   The salient features of this process of accom-
modation, common to most Jewish groups, were acknowledgment of
the primacy of secular studies and a consequent subordination of
Jewish education to a secondary and supplementary role. "[1]

It is a matter of great concern that these Jewish supplementary schools must compete with ever growing forms of entertainment and weakening religious commitment.   Several recent studies
of Jewish education have pointed out its basic weaknesses.   The
schools "make no greater demands of faith, knowledge, or action
commitment than what the mass of people are ready to accept, or
indeed have already accepted.   In other words, Jewish education
can be and often is as shallow as the life it is purporting to enrich. "[2]

Another commentator found that the aim of Jewish education
was to raise a generation of competent and informed Jewish individuals willing to identify themselves with the Jewish people and
committed to personal Jewish living. [3]   Jewish education has tried
to achieve this goal by transmitting the Jewish cultural and spiritual
heritage.   In a study of these schools' curricula, however, it was
precisely this point that was found limiting.   It was felt that Jewish
schools did not give due consideration to the needs of their students
in contemporary surroundings. [4]

59

Despite these findings, a just completed survey of enrollment
in Jewish elementary and secondary schools showed that an estimated
400, 000 students received some form of Jewish education under school
auspices.   Three hundred twenty-five thousand of these students attended the supplementary school programs.   The prominence of the
congregational school in this picture reflected the suburbanization of
the Jewish community and the growth of synagogue membership following the end of World War II.   "If, as most observers agree,
membership in a synagogue is less a matter of religious impulse
and belief and more a means of Jewish identification with American
mores, the congregational school is faced with the extraordinarily
difficult task of attempting to persuade children to adopt a life style
which their parents have rejected."[6]

The Public School Librarian

It is in this complex and difficult socio-cultural context that
the librarian of the supplementary Jewish school is trying to function.
We must not forget that we are discussing a library that is influenced
to a larger or smaller extent by the techniques, practices and, even,
philosophy of the public school library.

The school library's chief contribution to the total school program lies in providing reading guidance, developing study skills and
coordinating and providing materials of instruction.[7]   Despite the
lack of libraries in large numbers of elementary schools, despite
the fact that many educators have omitted the library in their analysis and study of curriculum, school libraries are an essential element of the educational experience.[8]   The school library serves all
school personnel from student, to teacher, to administrator.   It
serves, or should serve, as a coordinating agency aiding improved
pupil achievement, improved teaching and creating experiences for
both.

The librarian works toward this achievement through curriculum enrichment and reading for pleasure.   The librarian must be
aware of subjects for study, the approach of the teacher and the
interests of the children.   In other words, the school librarian sees
the curriculum as a whole.

The scope, the service, the uniqueness of the library's program, rest primarily on the cooperative efforts of teachers and administrators with the librarian.   The understanding shown through
cooperative planning in the use of materials, through stimulating
students to become effective library users, by providing a source
for reading pleasure and individual information needs, and by contributing to curriculum planning, is necessary for the development
of the enriched library program for school students.

Essential Functions of the Library
for the Synagogue School

We shall now see how these two streams, Jewish Education
and Librarianship, are fused in creating the entity called "the synagogue or temple school library." In the introduction to Standards
for a Jewish Library it is stated, "A library is, in its broadest
sense, an educational institution. Hence a Jewish library is an institution for Jewish education. Its aim should be to increase the
Jewish knowledge of its readers, whether by providing books for
formal study or research, or by providing recreational reading on
Jewish themes."[9] It is the responsibility of Jewish educators, rabbis and the lay leadership of the Jewish community to see that Jewish libraries are established and that they meet the highest professional standards.

These school libraries should reflect and support the philosophy of the school and share and implement the school's aims and
objectives. It should be totally involved in the teaching and learning process. Its functions include:

1. A resource center. In it all forms of print and non-
   print material are organized and housed for easy accessibility and use.

2. A learning facility. Provides materials which will both
   enrich and implement the curriculum. It encourages individual exploration and inquiry.

3. A teaching facility. It teaches students how to find information and stimulates new interests. It keeps teachers
   and school administrators informed about new material.

4. A service agency. Procedures are established on the
   basis of assistance and service to students and faculty.
   Schedules and procedures are changed when necessary to
   serve a need. Material is circulated when and where it
   is needed and use of facilities is encouraged at all times.

5. A coordinating operation. It coordinates the use of materials
   between the various classes in the school as well as between individuals and small groups. It coordinates and
   provides the most appropriate type of material, print as
   well as non-print, for the specific learning task.

6. A guidance program. It assists students in studying effectively and makes available materials to help the student
   plan for the future. Teachers should use this material
   in guiding their pupils.

7. A recreational and entertainment service. It provides a
   wide variety of material on Jewish themes, even when
   they are not touched upon or only peripherally discussed

in the school's curriculum.   It fulfills the current needs
of the student body, in general, and the range of interests
and abilities of each individual member of the school.

8.   An introduction to other community resources and to a
     program of life-long learning.   It acquaints the students
     with the resources available within the community that
     pertain to and provide Jewish learning and material and
     makes necessary arrangements for student use.   It en-
     courages their use in adult life and promotes the personal
     ownership of Jewish books and Judaic material. [10]

Identifying the School's Needs

There must be a close correlation between the manner in
which these basic library functions are carried out and the specific
needs of the school.   Several basic questions must be asked and
answered before the library can function as an integral and vibrant
aspect of the school program.   These questions should include:

1.   What is the school's purpose?
     a.   Does it stress the Hebrew language?
     b.   Does it stress Judaism, that is, religion in the form
          of customs and ceremonies?
     c.   Does it stress the cultural heritage of the Jewish peo-
          ple?

2.   What type of school is it?
     a.   Is it an Orthodox, Conservative, Reform or Recon-
          structionist supplementary school?
     b.   Does it offer one, two, three or five day a week
          school programs and/or a combination of these
          programs?
     c.   Does it offer an intensive program for those students
          who wish to pursue their studies further?
     d.   Is it an elementary school, that is, till age 13, or
          does it offer a high school program as well?

3.   What is the school's philosophy?
     a.   Is it child-centered with an activity program?
     b.   Is it structured both in scope and sequence?

4.   What is the philosophy of learning inherent in the school's
     program?
     a.   Is it cognitive or emotive?
     b.   Is it textbook oriented or does it take into account
          different media as well? [11]

Curriculum Planning and the Library

While most books and articles on Jewish education omit the

library, some do give casual mention to it. One such survey
states: "One of the most important teaching aids is the school library. Indeed, in modern education, the library is conceived as
'the heart of the school'...it is essential both for children's self-
study assignments and for supplementary recreational reading. "[12]
This survey, which examined 80 schools in 18 sample communities,
reported that only 56 schools (70 percent) had some sort of library.
In these libraries, 62. 5 percent of the school librarians never participated in staff meetings and only 26. 8 percent participated regularly. [13] The relationship between curriculum planning and the library has not changed to any great extent since this survey was
made.

        Despite the lack of input by librarians in curriculum planning,
several articles and brochures have pointed out the obvious need
for librarians to participate fully in such planning. Dorothy Schroeder, Librarian, Wilshire Boulevard Temple, Los Angeles, states,
"Every librarian should be a member of the faculty because the
closer relationship of the teacher to the librarian will give both a
better sense of how to implement teaching programs as well as a
knowledge of each other's strengths and needs. "[14] By being involved in curriculum planning, the librarian will be able to stay
one step ahead of the students, teachers and supervisors. In knowing important, exciting and new resources, the librarian can assist
in formulating a curriculum that does not include boring and inac-
curate texts and dated programs. It is the duty of the librarian to
know the curriculum because only then can there be genuine knowledge of classroom requirements and the different methodologies of
individual teachers. The Jewish supplementary school has an obligation to students and the Jewish community to implement these new
directions in the religious school curricula so the school can fulfill
its potential in making its pupils knowledgeable, informed and identified Jews.

        The Standards for a Jewish Library states that the basic re-
lation between curriculum planning and the library should be as follows: "If the institution has a school, the librarian should be considered part of the faculty. He should be familiar with the curriculum and the planned activities of the school, and should coordinate
the library with the classroom. "[15] Another recent commentator,
Judith Segal, writes, "Of course, the library must coordinate itself
with the educational program: its staff must be involved in curriculum development, in training of research methodology and the organization and maintenance of educational material for teachers. "[16]

        There is, however, a wide discrepancy between what should
be and what is. Though, in a few schools, librarians participate
in curriculum planning, in an overwhelming majority of cases they
do not. The Jewish education--be it principal, rabbi, or director
of Bureau of Jewish Education--is basically responsible for this
critical neglect.

Relationship of the Synagogue School Library to the
Public Library and the Public School Library

"The Jewish supplementary school library should not be regarded as a substitute for a public library or public school library
but rather as a supplement to it, by providing Jewish material which
these more general libraries cannot, or by their very nature should
not, be expected to provide."[17] The various manuals on the organization of the Jewish library mention this relationship.   A guide written in 1948 notes that Jewish libraries are needed because, as a
rule, the local public library does not provide Jewish books.[18] The
public librarian is seldom in a position to direct and guide an individual in Jewish reading.   A manual written in 1962, while changing
the emphasis, still basically repeats that "even though the public library can provide many of the materials, it will not usually have
the quantity, quality and variety of specifically Jewish materials that
are needed."[19] A manual published in 1968 discusses the exchange
of ideas between the public librarian and the congregational librarian
and the fact that means of mutual assistance may be found.[20]

The Temple Library, Cleveland, has been a pioneer in developing a sound and beneficial relationship with the public library
specifically and the entire community in general.   This congrega-
tion/school library has made Jewish Book Month each year an event
of major community importance.   The public librarians, from the
county, city and suburban libraries are invited to a meeting that
plans Jewish Book Month for the entire system.

It is important for the synagogue librarian to become active
in the community and known in the public library and public school
system.   Information is two-way communication.   The Jewish school
librarian assists these librarians with problems in the field of Judaica and they, in turn, help in the general field of librarianship
and education.

The relationship between the Jewish school librarian and the
public librarian and public school librarian is one based on cooperation.   The Jewish school librarian can and should offer:

1. Guidance in answering questions relating to the various
    aspects of Judaica.
2. Assistance in selecting material for acquisition.
3. Information regarding Jewish topics and resources.
4. Planning regarding exhibits on Jewish themes or topics
    for study, both formally in the school system and infor-
    mally for small group projects.
5. Bibliographies that can be used as acquisition tools and
    reading lists.

The public librarian and public school librarian can, likewise, provide guidance, assistance, information, planning and bibliographies on general subjects or on general educational topics,
e.g., curriculum, methodology, equipment, that would be of interest
to the Jewish supplementary school and its library.

Working with Individual School Teachers

The functions of the library and the specific needs of the school create a close working relationship between the librarian and the individual school teachers. Teachers and librarians should work closely together in specific areas of the library program, such as book selection, classroom visits, curriculum development, faculty committees, bibliographies for units of study and presentation of new material. The teacher with a specific knowledge of classroom interests and actual use of material can suggest definite areas of need and titles of books. There must be careful planning by teacher and librarian before library visits are made, so that they are made meaningful to the students. It is particularly important for the teacher and librarian to check about information available on a new topic so there will not be a frustrating library experience for the class.

In a sense, librarian and teacher are participating in a team teaching program during class visits. Teacher participation in the library during the class visit is very important. The librarian is acting in the capacity of teacher, introducing material he or she knows in depth. It is only through interchange of information between teacher and librarian that both can become fully aware of the range of comprehension and the breadth of interest of the students so that significant material is made available.

The attitude of the teacher toward the library has a direct bearing on the student's attitude and the use made of the library facilities. If the teacher dumps the class at the library there should be little wonder that the class has little enthusiasm for reading, reference work or the exploration of new interests in specific class projects. Basic to this is the real acceptance of the librarian by by school administrator and not the mere mouthing of platitudes.

It is a two-fold program in cooperation. There should be participation from the teacher, but the librarian must develop skills in human relationships. There must be respect of the standards and professionalism of the teacher but the librarian must retain professional values. The librarian must make an effort to implement, to broaden and to interpret services and the teacher must express interest in the overall program of the library and expand the use of library facilities.

Basically, the library provides teachers with two kinds of service: that related to the curriculum and that related to their own professional needs. Specifically, these needs include:

1. A need for structuring innovative educational experiences for students.
2. A need for instructional planning assistance.
3. A need to create and modify media as it correlates with changing modes of instruction.
4. A need to learn of the potential of library material and facilities.

5. A need for assistance in selection of material.
6. A need for interaction between material, students, teachers and librarians on a continuing basis to foster general improvement of the teaching staff.
7. A need for assurance that their expectations for students are being met.
8. A need for the opportunity to be creative and effective in their work. [21]

The Standards for a Jewish Library include several statements bearing directly on the librarian-teacher relationship. "The members of the professional staff of the institution should also be aware of their obligation to cooperate with the librarian in seeing that the necessary books are purchased and made available. Because they are experts in their fields, they may be aware of gaps in the collection which should be called to the librarian's attention."[22] A synagogue which has a congregational school should provide pedagogical works for the use of the teachers.

> A regular schedule of library visits by each class is most desirable, but other devices may be used, such as a book truck with suitable books brought into the classroom, a library shelf in each classroom, or storytelling for younger children. Bibliographies should be provided to assist teachers and students in carrying out class assignments. [23]

The literature on Jewish school libraries provides articles describing the use of one or another of these techniques. Many of them have been extremely beneficial in creating a good working relationship between librarian and teacher. In one school, an orientation talk for teachers was presented at the first faculty meeting of the school year. Each class was scheduled for twenty-minute library sessions on the alternate weeks of weekend religious school. [24] At another school, book reports were a normal part of the class routine and the teacher kept a record on the bulletin board of the child's name and title of the book. This library, which was "a rolling library," had, at the request of the class teacher, included specific reference volumes or a group of them on a cart from which members of a class could choose to seek information to meet a class assignment. [25]

Still another school brought the younger students to the library to teach them its use and how to take care of books. It was the responsibility of the teacher to be familiar with the material available in the library. The teacher was urged to view the collection as a continuous teaching aid and direct students to it. Library visits were regularly scheduled and carefully planned to develop reading as a habit. [26]

Book talks were an exceedingly good way to interest students in the library but demanded close planning between teacher and librarian. One librarian stated, "I think the only way a librarian can be effective is to go into the classroom and offer her services to the classroom teacher, or the rabbi or to the education director. Get in the classroom.... Tell them that there are stories that are just darn good reading. "27 There must be close coordination between the librarian and the teacher, whether in preparation of bibliographies, class visits or storytelling. Only through this cooperation can students receive the full benefit of the school program.

Working with Individual School Pupils

The library can fulfill the needs of the student from two distinct areas--those related to the curriculum of the school and those related to individual personal Judaic needs.

Student use and needs are dictated by three different types of situations, as individuals, in small groups or in class-size groups. Each one raises different concerns and relationships and must be dealt with differently by the librarian.

The supplementary Jewish school library can assist the student to interpret himself or herself in relation to others and develop a better understanding of the world in which he lives, arouse true intellectual curiosity, introduce him to the rich Jewish cultural heritage and instill an understanding of the intrinsic importance of reading and libraries in an informed nation and as an identified Jew. The library program attempts to develop attitudes of good citizenship, such as an understanding of the care and sharing of public property, the assumption of personal responsibility and the importance of an orderly arrangement of material.

The librarian must have a knowledge of the individual pupil's interests and capabilities and should be able to present material that will awaken an interest to pursue the study of Judaism deeper and to a higher level.

The pupil should be brought to the library upon entrance into the Jewish school and introduced to its treasures. The student should learn that the library can be fun and that books are there to be shared.

Library material should appeal on three levels:

1. Information. Specific knowledge required for classroom study.
2. Enlightenment. General knowledge required to answer specific individual questions about Judaism and the Jewish people.
3. Recreation. An understanding that the Jewish experience is not a chore nor a category but an intrinsic part of the child's total environment.

The school library should create a social-emotional climate which is warm and friendly, devoid of unhealthy pressure and competition. Each student in this situation feels self-confident and secure,

free to speak his mind, to question and criticize constructively.
There should be an on-going concern with the well-being of each individual pupil, making the student feel wanted and respecting his
ideas and views.   The librarian can, and should, assist the pupil
in resolving conflicts and providing experiences conducive to self-
fulfillment--intellectually, emotionally and socially.

The librarian can be instrumental in encouraging the pupil to
develop personal interests and creative abilities; putting a premium
on originality, on creative interaction, on thinking rather than mem-
orizing.   The librarian can expose the student to challenging ideas,
novel experiences, controversial projects and different points of
view.   The librarian can help the child become an independent learner and a thinking and creative individual.

It is through techniques such as story-telling and book talks
that individual children may be introduced to the cultural heritage
of Judaism.   It is through individual guidance from librarians that
the pupil learns to use different material and can be awakened to a
better understanding of Judaism.   It is through the total library experience that students can begin to reach their potential as knowledgeable individuals and informed Jews.

Reference Work in the Synagogue Library

Reference work is the one area in the library where true
two-way communication between the librarian and the user can occur.
Through reference work, the librarian not only can foster and encourage intellectual curiosity and a better understanding of Judaism,
but can make the library a "happy place" where people--students,
teachers and congregants--want to go.

Reference work is a satisfying experience and furnishes the
librarian with a chance to keep in close touch with the procedures
in the classroom as well as an opportunity to be innovative and use
every bit of information previously acquired.   The purpose of reference work is two-fold: 1) to provide the answer to a specific
question; 2) to guide each student or questioner to materials that
will allow him to work effectively and efficiently toward completion
of specific work.

Guidance for students should be personalized and continuing.
The student should know what service is available, whom to seek
out for assistance and should feel confident that help will be forthcoming when needed.

Reference service is, or course, not only limited to the student.   Teachers need assistance in using bibliographic tools and in
locating and selecting material for use with a class, group or individual pupil.   Good reference work is possible only where there
is an adequate collection of reference material.   The Standards for
a Jewish Library specifically declares that "all libraries should have

the basic reference works, such as Jewish encyclopedias, dictionaries, atlases, basic Jewish texts, etc. "[28]

The duties of the librarian in a temple or synagogue school
library include providing material and guidance for reference and
research.   The librarian must be able to instruct the reader--stu-
dent, teacher, and congregant--in the proper use of this material.
The catalog, of course, is an important tool in both reference and
research work, and it should be the responsibility of the librarian
to see that the user understands how to use it.   Librarians in
schools should provide regular instruction in the use of the library
for students and faculty so significant reference and research work
can be done on all levels of ability.

Conclusions

The Jewish supplementary school library has, indeed, been
the forgotten aspect of the school.   Jewish educational journals and
books rarely mention the concept of "library."   Only three or four
substantive articles, four or five theses and two surveys of the condition, potential or philosophical bases of these libraries have been
written during the last thirty years.   These, in general, have pointed
out shortcomings, noting such factors as unsympathetic administrators and lay leaders, penny-pinching boards, short-sighted princi-
pals, poor personnel, lack of funds and budget and low Jewish educational standards.

Nevertheless, this library has the potential to be a potent
and vital force in the total school program.   It has the capacity to
reach student and teacher creatively and dynamically.   The two way
communication between library and school and library and user must
be used immediately.

REFERENCES

Bennett, Alan D.   A Manual for the Congregational Library.   Cleve-
     land: Cleveland Bureau of Jewish Education, 1975.

Chaikind, H. K.   Religious School Libraries in Temples of Reform
     Judaism: Factors for Success.   M. S. Thesis.   New Haven:
     Southern Connecticut State College, 1963.

Galfand, Sidney, "Organized Jewish Libraries," Library Journal
     LXXXVII (January 1, 1962), pp. 31-34.

Goldberg, Isaac, "American Jewish Libraries at Mid-Century,"
     The Jewish Horizon XII (January, 1951), pp. 3-5.

Halporn, Roberta, "The Temple Library," Pedagogic Reporter XXII
     (September, 1970), pp. 20-22.

Hamburger, Lewis Davidson. A Study of the Failures and Dilemmas
    of Part-time American Jewish Education and Implications of
    Elements from Talmudic Schools and Educational Camping.
    Ph. D. Dissertation. College Park, Md.: University of
    Maryland, 1971; Ann Arbor, Mich. , 1972.

Leikind, Miriam, "Cleveland's Jewish Libraries, " Ohio Library
    Association Bulletin XXXII (April, 1962), pp. 21-25.

_____. "Reader's Services in the Special Library, " Association
    of Jewish Libraries, Proceedings of the Seventh Annual Con-
    vention, Toronto, June 18-21, 1972, pp. 28-33.

"Library Programs, Promotion and Public Relations, " Association
    of Jewish Libraries, Proceedings of the Ninth Annual Con-
    vention, Chicago, June 23-26, 1974, pp. 26-29.

Lowrie, Jean Elizabeth, Elementary School Libraries, 2nd ed.
    Metuchen, N. J.: Scarecrow Press, 1970.

Pilch, Judah. A History of Jewish Education in America. New
    York: The National Curriculum Research Institute, American
    Association for Jewish Education, 1969.

_____. and Meir Ben-Horin. Judaism and the Jewish School: Se-
    lected Essays on the Direction and Purpose of Jewish Educa-
    tion. New York: Bloch, 1966.

Schwartz, M. G. Conservative Synagogue Library: An Analysis
    and Evaluation. M. A. Thesis. Bloomington, Ind. , Indiana
    U. , 1962.

Singer, Mrs. M. M. , "The Jewish Library in its Setting, " Associ-
    ation of Jewish Libraries, Proceedings of the Third Annual
    Convention, Cincinnati, June 23-26, 1968, pp. 25-27.

Slesinger, Zalmen, "Guidelines for Judging the Quality of a School, "
    Pedagogic Reporter XIV (March, 1963), pp. 11-12, 26-27.

Weine, Mae, "Libraries for the Jewish Layman, " Jewish Book An-
    nual XXIV (1966), pp. 50-54.

_____. Report on the Library Questionnaire of the Synagogue,
    School and Center Division, Association of Jewish Libraries.
    1971? Unpublished report.

_____. Survey of Synagogue Libraries in Philadelphia: The
    Synagogue Library as a Factor in Jewish Education. M. S.
    L. S. Thesis, Philadelphia: Drexel University, 1957.

NOTES

1. Ackerman, Walter I. , "Jewish Education -- for What?" American Jewish Year Book, New York: American Jewish Committee; Philadelphia: The Jewish Publication Society of America; LXX, 1969, p. 3.
2. Donin, Hayim, An Inquiry into the Value Presuppositions Un-
   derlying Jewish Education in Metropolitan Detroit, Ph.D.
   Dissertation. Detroit: Wayne State University, 1965; Ann
   Arbor: University Microfilms, 1972; p. 171.
3. Gelbert, Gershon I. , Jewish Education in America, a Manual
   for Parents and School Board Members. New York: Jewish
   Education Committee Press, 1968, p. 2.
4. Skolnick, Irving H. , A Guide to Curriculum Construction for
   the Religious School. Chicago: College of Jewish Studies,
   1969, p. 4.
5. "Special to the JTA, Dire Consequence Seen for Communal
   Life in Jewish Schools Enrollment Drop, Birthrate Decline, "
   Daily News Bulletin, Jewish Telegraphic Agency, XLIII (November 9, 1976), p. 4, and (November 10, 1976), p. 4.
6. Ackerman, op. cit. , p. 5.
7. Freund, Roberta Bishop, Open the Book. 2nd ed. New York:
   Scarecrow Press, 1966, Foreword.
8. Prostano, Emanuel T. , The School Library Media Center.
   Littleton, Colo. : Libraries Unlimited, 1971, p. 13.
9. Association of Jewish Libraries. Synagogue, School and Center
   Division. Standards for a Jewish Library. n. p. , 1968,
   p. 2. For later edition see Association of Jewish Libraries,
   Synagogues, School and Center Division, Standards for Jewish
   Libraries in Synagogues, Schools and Centers. rev. ed.
   New York: Jewish Book Council of America, 1970.
10. Nickel, Mildred L. , Steps to Service, a Handbook of Procedures
    for the School Library Media Center. Chicago: American
    Library Association, 1975, pp. 1-2.
11. Kanner, Ruth, "Non-book Materials: Sources and Selections, "
    Association of Jewish Libraries, Proceedings of the Fourth
    Annual Convention, Atlantic City, New Jersey, June 17-20,
    1969, p. 36.
12. Dushkin, Alexander M. , Jewish Education in the United States.
    New York: American Association for Jewish Education,
    1959, p. 195.
13. Ibid. , p. 197.
14. See remarks of Dorothy Schroeder in Dan Berger, "The Role
    of the Library in Implementing the Educational Program, "
    Library Light, Association of Jewish Libraries of Southern
    California, I (October, 1971), p. 1.
15. Association of Jewish Libraries. Synagogue, School and Center
    Division. Standards.... op. cit. , p. 12.
16. Segal, Judith, "On Jewish Libraries and Standards, " The Syna-
    gogue School XXXI (Winter 1973), p. 16.
17. Association of Jewish Libraries. Synagogue, School and Center
    Division. Standards.... op. cit. , p. 2.

18.   Golub, Jacob S. , The Jewish Library in School, Center and
      Synagogue: New York: Jewish Education Committee, 1948,
      p. 1.
19.   Cedarbaum, Sophia N. , A Manual for Jewish Community Center,
      School and Congregation Libraries. New York: Jewish Book
      Council of America, 1962.
20.   Celnik, Max, The Synagogue Library, Organization--Administra-
      tion. New York: United Synagogue of America, Library
      Service Bureau, 1968, p. 18.
21.   Prostano, op. cit. , p. 36-37.
22.   Association of Jewish Libraries. Synagogue, School and Center
      Division. Standards. . . . op. cit. , p. 6-7.
23.   Ibid. , p. 12.
24.   Cohen, Frances L.   "The Birth of a Synagogue Library, " Peda-
      gogic Reporter XXIII (September, 1971), p. 26.
25.   Kahn, Ruby, "A Rolling Library, " The Jewish Teacher XXX
      (December, 1961), p. 17.
26.   Leviton, Elsie, "The Temple Library ... Fact or Fiction, "
      The Jewish Teacher XXXII (December, 1963), p. 14.
27.   Daniels, Mrs. Richard, "Children's Literature, " Association
      of Jewish Libraries, Proceedings of the Fifth Annual Con-
      vention, New York, June 21-24, 1970, p. 42.
28.   Association of Jewish Libraries. Synagogue, School and Center
      Division. Standards. . . . op. cit. , p. 5.

THE TEMPLE LIBRARY, CLEVELAND

Miriam Leikind

The stronghold of Judaism has always been its books. Not until recent years, however, has the Jewish library expanded its functions beyond the Synagogue and Sunday school. Now, art collections, book fairs, archives, and story hours offer a variety of innovative ways to introduce Jewish culture through the library to families starving for closer links with their heritage.

By tradition, books were treated by Jews as special, treasured objects. When they grew old or frayed, it was thought sacrilegious to throw them out. Old books were placed in a synagogue's attic. When space ran out, books were solemnly buried, in a ceremony fit for the burial of a saint.

Even books the Jews hated were never burned but were called "apocryphal" or "outside" and were locked away or hidden. Rabbinical liberature is full of admonition about the solemn duty of a Jew to lend books to others (so that learning will be increased); of the obligation of every community of Jews to build a library; of meticulous advice about the binding, airing, care and preservation of books and manuscripts.

Along with the mitzvah (blessing) attached to the ransom of enslaved Jews was one for Jews who bought back books which had been captured by brigands, pirates or robbers of synagogues. Thousands of prized Talmuds and rabbinical writing, stolen from Jews, were bought back by them or other Jews.[1]

In the Beginning

The Temple in Cleveland pioneered in developing a library to serve its community.[2,3,4] Within its doors, a room for books and magazines was provided as early as 1898. A librarian was hired and general literature as well as books of Jewish content could be found on the library shelves. The library soon became a favorite neighborhood social and educational center. The doors were open to all in the community as well as the Temple membership and school. So much activity was engendered by the book shelves that

a librarian was engaged in 1903 who also had to double as a gym
teacher.   He soon realized that justice could not be done to either
function, and he resigned.   The Temple sought the guidance of William Brett, Librarian, Cleveland Public Library.   With his help, a
unique cooperative program was developed.   The Temple would furnish the room and the public library could operate a branch there.
The only stipulation was that the Temple would have use of the library for its students on Sunday.

        Children of the congregation attended either morning or after-
noon sessions on Sundays, for religious instruction.   The Temple
Library books were kept in locked cases and opened when classes
were in session.   There was a Jewish librarian and the books, of
course, were of Jewish content.

The Temple Judaica Library, 1924

        The present Temple edifice was completed in 1924 and the
public library connection was severed.   The Temple reestablished
and expanded its Judaica library and filled its shelves with books,
pamphlets and periodicals.   The library was housed in an attractive
small room near the entrance to the Temple corridor.   We gradually
outgrew the room and had to find other areas for books.   Notwith-
standing, the library was a most popular place for both adults and
students.   The rabbi, the late Abba Hillel Silver, was very much
interested in its function, as a library and stronghold of Judaica
information.   Our library has developed along those lines and is
used by the greater Jewish community.

        When I arrived on the scene (in 1933), the library was a
busy place.   The school, the teachers and the congregation used it
continually.   Then and now, a close contact was maintained between
the Education Department and the library.   I soon realized that the
school should use the library to a greater extent as a research center.   This was a divided school.   Children from the kindergarten
through fifth grade attended classes on Sunday, and young people
from the sixth through ninth grades came on Saturday.   Therefore
we worked with both groups as independent units.

        The little ones were invited to the library to borrow and re-
turn books each Sunday.   When a class had time, a new book was
introduced and sometimes a story was told.   Jewish Book Week was
an important event in the life of the school.   It is even today.   Book
marks were a treat.   At assemblies, a play about Jewish books was
written and dramatized by a class.   Authors writing juvenile books
were often invited to speak.   This was of special interest to junior
high school students.   Gradually, the school began to place increasing emphasis on the role of the library as a teaching resource.   We
worked together on projects as well as providing help on routine
subjects.   The library was introduced to the elementary department
by inviting the classes one at a time for a library experience.   The
library was explained to the children.   The privilege of borrowing

books or records was discussed. The junior high school student
was taught to use the catalogue and books of reference, as well as
periodicals. Early in my career in a special library I realized the
importance of magazine material. My homework was taking home
the periodicals and indexing the important articles by author and
subject on cards and filing them for use. I was amazed at their
usefulness. Jewish magazines were not indexed anywhere. This
indexing was in the back of my mind for years until finally three of
us started to publish the Index to Jewish Periodicals.

A Stamp Club started meeting on Saturdays once a month.
Students in the Junior High School Department would come in to ask
for foreign stamps. Since the library received foreign mail, the
stamps were saved. The rabbi added to the collection, also. I
watched to see what happened to these stamps and did not like what
I saw, so the Stamp Club was born. We brought our lunch and remained after school. After lunch and a cold drink we met in the
library. At first we brought our albums. I asked a friend who is
a philatelist and a member of the Temple to assist. We taught the
collectors how to take stamps off envelopes. We suggested where
and how to purchase new stamps. And also how to develop collections. Even I started collecting Israeli stamps. Many of the students did likewise and over the years developed beautiful collections.
Once a year the group went to an exhibit and short course. Some
of the students entered exhibits and won prizes. What excitement
among the group when that happened!

Another activity was the Reading Club. Students who read
10 books or more received a prize. Today the students in the lower
grades also come in every two weeks to return books and take others. New books are brought to their attention. Many write a short
review that is placed in a scrap book and students look at it for
suggestions of reading matter. The Children's Book Fair was an
annual event in the life of the Cleveland Public Library Children's
Department. Again the students in the Reading Club were invited
to attend. If we arrived early, we would be taken on a guided tour
through the Main Library. That was also a highlight of the day.
The programs were always interesting and to see the many books
on display was inspiring. What a thrill to see on exhibit some of
the books that we had on our own shelves!

When UNESCO met in Cleveland, one of the students could
not attend through his school. He appealed to me for a ticket since
the schools were invited to attend. Since I knew the Superintendent
of Schools, I was able to secure tickets for six of us. What a time
we had attending sessions. I had stipulated that we would have to
make reports since we would be excused from Sunday School to attend. During that week we asked one boy to speak for us. With
help he was able to write a speech to present to the assembly. The
rabbis and faculty were amazed at the material the student absorbed.
The audience was most attentive to this report.

The library handles all of the visual material for the school.

Many film strips are previewed. A catalogue has been made so that
each teacher has her own copy. They are then requested by the
teacher to be shown in her class. When scheduled, the library
takes the film strip, narrative, machine and screen to the room.
The machine is run by the page and the teacher reads or tells the
narrative. The pages often come back and say how much they have
learned themselves. They also have their favorite ones. The library has pictures, maps and pamphlets that students use for Temple work as well as public school homework. Many of them are
working on such topics as the Holocaust and Israel and cannot find
enough information in their schools, so they find their way to this library for pertinent information.

For many years the Bible contest was the highlight of the
winter. After the interest in the Chanukkah play died down, this
contest came into its own. Questions by the hundreds were made
during the summer months. I even dreamt Bible. The contest ran
for six weeks. Each week fifty questions were handed out. Twenty-
five would be asked on the test the following week. They were then
graded and the grades posted in the library. There were two sets
of questions each week as the 6th and 7th grades had their own
tests and the 8th and 9th grades had theirs.

Books such as the Concordance, the Bible, and histories
and commentaries of the Bible were set aside on a reference shelf.
Encyclopedias were also nearby for consultation. Before the tests
were handed out I told the students how to use the books. The library was swarming with boys, girls and many parents. Then
started the phone calls to teachers and to me. I also had to alert
the libraries in the areas where the students lived since those libraries were overrun by our students, also.

What excitement reigned in the Temple in those weeks!
During the week when the results were posted, even that was exciting. Then came the spelldown. Students had to know all the
questions, even the ones not asked in the weekly test. In the event
of a tie, other questions were ready. The audience was made up
of rabbis, parents, students and teachers.

Debates in the high school were also important. Suggestions
of subjects were taken care of in the library. Subjects came from
National when the debate was inter-temple. Material and even the
writing of the presentations were part of the library life. Listening
to the speeches at which I became a specialist was also library
work. Students learned their way around the library and many said
when in college that this know-how was important to them.

Jewish Book Month was celebrated in the Temple. Book
lists were made and handed out to the congregation and borrowers
of the library. Today the book lists are prepared by members of
the Jewish Library Association. Many of us belong to the Jewish
Book Council and are active in the various programs that are sponsored by the community. For many years the city public libraries
would come to me for help in making displays for Book Month.

Facing New Challenges

     As the Temple Library grew in scope, the demands for its services broadened. Not only did the congregation, the Education Department and the community call upon us for help, but scholars from all parts of the nation, and some from distant lands, sought information. An artist was interested in material and information on Jacob and the Twelve Tribes. He was making windows for a Temple. A card company wanted to change its Jewish holiday cards and came for ideas. A collection which I started was New Year's cards from all parts of the world. Many were from early days. "What a find!" the artist said.

     Moreover, the number of Jewish magazines and periodicals had increased dramatically. Current history is now recorded in excellent articles on the pages of many publications of special interest to the Jewish community. How could this material be made available? To take home the periodicals and index the important articles became quite a chore. Three librarians, myself included, indexed about 50 magazines. For the past 13 years we have published Index to Jewish Periodicals. Subscribers include libraries, universities, and scholars here and abroad. So far as I know, this is the only author/subject index available to selected American and Anglo-Jewish journals of general and scholarly interest.

     In Cleveland, as in many other cities, synagogues have followed their congregations to the suburbs. They developed new libraries, often staffed with volunteers or non-professionals. Inevitably, they came to me for assistance. I realized that it was necessary to train and develop Jewish librarians. My first step in this direction was to invite the librarians to a Teacher's Luncheon, held annually in Cleveland at the various temples. Out of our discussion was born the Jewish Library Association, the first of the Jewish Library organizations interested in developing Judaica centers in communities. At a later date, I was able to organize a national body. [5] Through this organization we gradually developed better libraries. We became known in the community and before long we won recognition as the book people in circles outside our congregations.

     When local chapters of the national Jewish organizations needed book reviewers, help with discussion groups and program assistance in activities, they consulted the Jewish Library Association. We even helped some of the agencies to staff and stock their professional libraries, serving only themselves.

     In the meantime, The Temple Library developed as an important Judaica collection, used by a number of universities in the area, the congregation and the community at large. Since we are a part of the Cleveland area Union Catalog, many institutions need our books and they are loaned freely, even to England. In Cleveland, through the Jewish Community Center, there is a Book Council activity which arranges Jewish Book Week programs during Book

Month and the other times.   Not only do we loan books for the exhibits, but the Temple Library is also active in programming.   This
year, an extremely interesting exhibit and lecture were arranged at
the Cleveland Public Library as part of a Bicentennial Ethnic Series.
I believe it is important for the librarian to be active in community
affairs.   When Sunday School teachers hold workshops and lectures,
the librarian has an opportunity to introduce books through displays
and group discussions.   Our national organization has chapters in
many cities and is growing, despite many early frustrations.   We
get together to solve mutual problems in book selection, methods of
classification, and means of reaching out to the public.

Much can be gained through cooperation.   The national group
even held a convention in Israel.   What a thrill it was for the Israeli and American librarians to discuss our common goals on sacred ground!   When the American Library Association met in Cleveland, I wrote to the National Jewish Book Council and suggested
that whenever ALA meets we should also have a Judaica exhibit.
The idea was accepted and was introduced for the first time here.
Among the many spectators were a large number who had never
seen Jewish books before.

When Rabbi Abba Hillel Silver passed away, his papers, the
tapes of his sermons and other memorabilia were given to the Temple.   These are classified and preserved in the Rabbi Abba Hillel
Silver Archives, a room separate from the library itself.   Scholars
and students from all parts of the world come to use the Archives
or write to me for information.   The entire library contains 2500
volumes, subscribes to 25 periodical titles regularly and has 32
vertical file drawers of material.

In retrospect, this has been a most interesting library in a
field which has received too little attention.   My personal growth
as a librarian has been immeasurable--and no wonder.   At the helm
of the Temple have been great and inspiring leaders.   Among those
who use the services of the library are individuals whose scholarship has won wide recognition.   The field I cover is limitless and
constantly growing and changing.   The people with whom I work
range from tots whose toes barely touch the floor, to teachers and
rabbis, and even to octogenarians absorbed in the ancient lore of a
civilization which has enriched every major religion.

NOTES

1.   Rosten, Leo, Treasury of Jewish Quotations.   New York: Mc-
     Graw-Hill, 1972.
2.   The Temple Yearbooks, 1898-1950.
3.   The Temple Minutes, 1950- .
4.   The Temple Bulletins, 1917- .
5.   Papers of the Jewish Library Association, both local and nation-
     al.

PART III:

CATHOLIC LIBRARIES

ROMAN CATHOLIC CHURCH LIBRARIES

Jane F. Hindman

The clergy, both Catholic and Protestant, who came to America as missionaries to the immigrants pouring into the country in the early 1800's, realized that books were a necessary adjunct to their efforts. Volumes were tucked into their luggage to provide solace for themselves and their people. Bishop Simon Bruté carried with him as he trudged through the woods on his missionary journeys in Kentucky and Indiana. So good was his collection that after his death a special building was erected in old Vincennes to house his books. [1]

In the 1820's, a young Bohemian felt a strong call to travel to America to help the German-speaking Catholics who were emigrating to the new country. This young man, John Nepomucene Neumann, will soon be acclaimed America's first male saint. Sympathetic clergy and laity whom he met on his travels, instead of providing him with money for his journey, gave him books which he either carried or shipped at his own expense. He deprived himself of many meals so that he could save enough to bring these books to the new world. [2]

As Father Neumann and other priests settled in their parishes, they sent home for more reading matter. Considering the scarcity of books and the difficulty of transportation, the libraries of priests in the early days of America were truly remarkable.

The interests of the priests were varied. All were deeply concerned about the spiritual welfare of their flocks. They imported books on prayer, dogma, lives of the saints. In addition, to provide for their own mental stimulus, they begged for secular books. Saint John Neumann always carried a book on botany. As he saw the great need, he added books on the medicinal value of herbs so that he could help his people by practicing simple medicine. These were not his only interests. He owned books on astronomy, mathematics and history. The pioneer priests were truly catholic in their interests.

In 1801, St. Augustine's Church was established at Fourth and Arch Streets, Philadelphia. Its pastors not only established a library, but made it a community center, including on its board of

managers, representatives from three older parishes.   Between
1836 and 1839 it circulated 2, 000 volumes and was a powerful force
in educating Catholic adults.   This community effort was called a
Library Association.   To supplement the library, St. Augustine's
Youth Literary Institute was formed in the 1840's.   It was organized
for the purpose of furthering the education of the parishioners, who
as a rule had four to six years of schooling.

      In 1844, the Nativist rioters descended on St. Augustine's
Church and it was burned.   Not content with this holocaust, the mob
broke into the rectory and threw out of the windows a theological
collection of from three to five thousand volumes, all of which went
to feed the bonfires.   The lending library suffered the same fate. [3]

      Although St. Augustine's Parish Library no longer existed,
others of far less value endured for a time.   The size and scope
of each library depended on the interest of the priest and his parishioners.   Sunday schools and literary societies were the vehicles used
for helping the immigrant to attain literacy.   The parish library
supplemented the teaching effort by making books available to all.
These libraries contained secular as well as religious titles.   As
books became more plentiful and less expensive, parishioners became better educated and more affluent.   Personal libraries became
the vogue, hence less and less demands were made on parish libraries and they fell into disuse.   If a parish library did exist, it
consisted of a few books on a shelf in the Sunday School room or in
the rectory.   Seldom used, rarely was a book added to the collection.   A new pastor, seeing the books unused, and needing the space,
was apt to sweep them off the shelves and sell them at the next
rummage sale.

      Much more effective were the books lent by the priest from
his own library to fill the specific need of a parishioner.   They
were more relevant to the reader's problem.   From these personal
libraries, the missions in the Midwest developed storehouses of literature and archival material priceless today.   The Franciscan
mission outside San Antonio, Texas, for example, houses a collection of books and manuscripts that is a joy to scholars.

      In the latter part of the 19th century, when high school and
adult education became more available, interest in self-education
took a terrific up-swing.   "Literary Circles" became popular.
Chautauquas were springing up throughout the country.   The Columbia
League, a Catholic organization of young men's clubs, was formed.
Another group, the Xavier Alumni Sodality of New York (1863) invited alumni of Catholic colleges in the area to "form reading circles to promote the study of good books. "   This group pre-dates
Chautauqua by a decade.

      Brother Ryan, in writing of Reading Circles, says: "The
Reading Circle movement sponsored by churches, church libraries
and schools was an important learning effort with national impact
between 1885 and 1900, culminating in the formation of the Reading

Circle Union, 1899. [4]   The Reading Circles provided book reviews,
book discussion meetings, lectures and cultural events.   They were
a forum for the discussion of Catholic concerns about social re-
forms, political pressures, cultural interests and moral issues.

Members of these clubs found that libraries were an effective
means of obtaining the books which they wished to study.   Not enough
books of Catholic interest were included in the now-popular Carnegie
public libraries.   These small libraries, generally housed in the
meeting room in the church or in the rectory, were designed to fill
this deficit.   The purpose of these libraries was to explain the faith
of the Catholic Church, to urge through books the performance of
humanitarian works, and to counteract some of the secular books of
the day.

Financial problems caused these libraries to be uneven in
scope.   They varied from the "elegant to the grubby."   Much depended then as now on the money available and the ability of the
librarian.   If interest waned, the library fell into disuse and was
closed.   Parish libraries are closely linked to other church organizations, especially for funds.

The credit for building up a parish library must be given to
parish priests and/or interested laity.   The Catholic Church neither
sets down guidelines for libraries, nor does it mandate them.   However, in the Documents of Vatican II, in the section on priestly life,
the Vatican Council advocates the "setting up of libraries and appropriate programs of study conducted by suitable persons."[5]   In the
section on the laity, the document does say, "There arises for each
believer the right and duty to use his gifts in the Church and in the
world for the good of mankind."[6] Librarians can apply this admonition and the following quotes to themselves and to their libraries.
In the same section, the document reads, "the laity must make
available the moral and spiritual aids by which the temporal order
can be restored in Christ."[7]

There is no hierarchical control over libraries.   The diocesan
offices neither ask for reports on libraries, nor do they set down
guidelines for conducting such enterprises.   In the past there have
been diocesan libraries in Buffalo, St. Louis, New York, Wilmington,
and other dioceses. [8] Some of them were extremely active.   Mother
M. Agatha, O. S. U. , in an article in the Catholic Library World
gives a good description of the activities of the Wilmington Diocesan
Library in the 1940's. [9] It conducted study clubs, book talks, weekly
radio programs, and public forums at which prominent people spoke
on various subjects.   This library made a great contribution to the
culture of the city.

None of these diocesan libraries has survived, but there is
a resurgence of interest at the diocesan level as religious educators
begin to see the need for resource centers.   Any effort on the parish
level to form a library is left to the desires of the pastor and the
parishioners.   Since so much depends on their enthusiasm and their

ability to finance the project, the parish library will continue to be unstable.

Another cause for the demise of many libraries was their attempt to cover all angles. Such diversification resulted in not enough books to satisfy the readers in each special group. Those libraries which survived longest were those which aimed their ac- tivities at one segment of the church population. In a college town, a parish library put all of its efforts into supplying the special needs of the college students and was successful. Several others directed their efforts towards children. These, too, were successful and flourished until state laws began to demand libraries in the schools. In these cases, the children's parish library was quickly absorbed into the school library and then was administered through the school structure.

An example of this is the parish of St. Vincent de Paul, Al- bany, New York. The pastor was extremely book-minded. In 1918, he and a group of volunteers established a library. It flourished for a while as a general library, but with a religious tone. In due course, a public library was built across the street. At that time it was decided rather than to make a feeble effort to compete, books bought henceforth would be only in the field of religion. A third change came about when the New York State Regents demanded a reference library for high school students. The library was then absorbed into the school, and the parish library as such ceased to exist. [10]

Parish library personnel consists for the most part of enthu- siastic volunteers who may not be professional librarians. Lucky is the committee that can boast of a retired librarian among its members. Sometimes the work of the library is carried on by one person, but unless the librarian is paid and has some library ex- perience, the effort is rarely successful. It has been found that while a library committee is harder to manage, it makes for more continuity.

Some library committees have extended their efforts to in- clude sponsoring book review programs and cultural meetings. Oth- ers have conducted trips to shrines and other points of interest. Still others have sponsored book fairs. Advice to parish library personnel is offered by the Catholic Library Association in its Par- ish and Catholic Lending Library Manual which is currently being revised to meet the present needs of parish librarians. [11]

More than half of the Catholic parishes conduct elementary schools, and, in addition, many either provide a high school educa- tion or support the diocesan high schools, all of which maintain ad- equate libraries for their pupils. Since adult reading has fallen to such a new low, the pastor who struggles to meet the mounting bills resulting from these monumental efforts to educate the children of- ten feels that he cannot divert funds to a project which at best will be used by only a small percentage of the community. Therefore, many parish librarians raise the needed funds for their projects by the usual church means of bake sales, tag days, or by soliciting donations. No matter what method is chosen, the result is an uncertain income and frustration for those who give their time to this effort.

There are two schools of thought as to the scope of parish libraries. One is that of a highly specialized collection of books of good general reading, including books on religion and secular books that have a good moral and ethical theme. No one can claim that one type of library is better than the other. Much depends on the location of the church and its proximity to other libraries in which their collection may be duplicated. No matter which type of library is established, the librarians must make a determined effort not to be a dumping ground for discards from attics and to tactfully explain that books are accepted on the proviso that if they do not fit into the collection, they will not be put into the library.

Where to house the parish library is an ever-present problem. In old churches there is no place in the mainstream of traffic that is available for use. Vestibules are small and drafty. The basement of the church is dark and dingy and the stairs steep. A library is truly buried there. Parishioners are reluctant to go to the adjoining school even if there is a room that can be spared. Newly built churches may have more room, but these churches are often in rural and suburban areas. Everyone drives. The parking problem is monumental. A giant problem is caused by those who stop to browse. Because of vandalism, most churches are locked after the daily morning mass. Books are not available except when the church is being used. Thus, the hours when library service may be offered are severely limited.

Until recent years, not much thought has been given in the Catholic Church to a concerted effort at adult religious education. In America, in the 1970's, each diocese is establishing a Religious Education Office staffed by professionals to further the religious education of those children not attending Catholic schools, and also to update the religious education of adults. This latter phase of religious education has not heretofore had the attention of the hierarchy. Slowly, religious educators are realizing that the generic book, both audio-visual and printed, is a powerful aid in their work. In this visual generation, the film and the filmstrip have had priority in their thinking, but now, they are coming to realize that the book is of great importance in their work. Now is the opportunity for the parish library to become a powerful adjunct to this teaching arm of the church, just as early parish libraries provided help for the schools.

Kelly Fitzpatrick, librarian at St. Mary's College, Emmitsburg, Maryland, made a 1975 survey of Parish and Community Resource Centers. He found that little long-range planning had gone into the development or even the organization of these centers. The personnel usually did not include an educated librarian to aid in

selection and organization of material.   Those in charge failed to
secure the advice and cooperation of librarians on a volunteer basis.
Budgets were low.   From the replies received, he concluded that,
as in any new effort, there is waste motion and a great deal of help
needed.   However, he also says: "Apparent in the replies is an
inherent enthusiasm for the work being carried on by the Parish and
Community Centers. "[12]

     Catholic publishing houses, which are few, have not given
much thought to the parish library except to express the vague hope
that it would purchase their books.   There is no official Catholic
publishing house in America.   From time to time, religious journals
have carried articles expressing the author's views, pro or con, on
the parish library.   The Catholic Library World, the official organ
of the Catholic Library Association, has been the champion of the
cause.   It regularly carries information of interest to parish librarians.   Further, the Catholic Library Association has evidenced
its concern by giving parish libraries status as an interest section
of the Association.

     While certainly not a typical parish library as they stand at
this point in history, the library of Corpus Christi Parish, Chatham
Township, New Jersey, is an ideal for which all parish librarians
can aim.   The library is blessed with a generous budget and an
imaginative librarian.   This is a combination hard to beat.   In an
article in the Catholic Library World one of the columnists explains
why she feels the library to be outstanding.[13]   It is extremely progressive in its views.   Corpus Christi parish library uses modern
techniques to interest parishioners, for example, poetry readings,
art exhibits, crafts and hobbies loaned by community members.   It
has a liberal lending policy, including books that some consider too
precious to be on loan.

     The parish library concept in the Catholic Church seems to
have taken an upswing.   Librarians can take new heart when they
read Patrick Casey's evaluation of their future.   He says: "My
hope would be that with collaboration between religious educators
and skilled librarians, new and effective ways will be created to
make the parish resource center a dynamic force for total religious
education of the entire community.   I believe that the librarian who
is genuinely serving the learning needs of the average parishioner
is exercising one of the most important ministries of the church. "[14]

NOTES

1.   Thomas, Aurelain, "Catholic Lending Libraries," Catholic Edu-
      cator XXV (February 1955), pp. 356-60.
2.   Curley, Michael J., C. SS. R., Venerable John Neuman, C. SS. R.,
      Fourth Bishop of Philadelphia.   New York: Crusader, 1952,
      p. 46.
3.   Ennis, Arthur J., O. S. A., Old St. Augustine's Catholic Church
      in Philadelphia.   n. p., 1965, pp. 27, 39.

4. Ryan, Leo V., C.S.V., "Reading Circles and Parish Librarians: The Earliest American Catholic Effort in Adult Education?" Catholic Library World XLVII (February 1976), pp. 313-14.

5. Abbott, Walter M., The Documents of Vatican II. New York, American Press, 1966, p. 571.

6. Ibid., p. 492.

7. Ibid., p. 498.

8. Murphy, Lucy, "Parish and Diocesan Libraries: A National Survey," Catholic Library World XII (April 1941), pp. 208-17.

9. Agatha, Mother M., O.S.U., "A Diocesan Library in Action," Catholic Library World XIII (April 1943), pp. 203-7.

10. Charles, W.R., "Parish Library at Albany Offers Distinct Service to People," Catholic Library World III (May 1932), p. 64.

11. Schneider, Vincent P., ed., The Parish and Catholic Lending Library Manual. Haverford, Pa., Catholic Library Association, 1965.

12. Fitzpatrick, Kelly, "Parish and Community Resources Centers: What and Where?" Catholic Library World XLVII (November 1975), p. 178.

13. Bennett, Janet M., "Needed: Parish Libraries with Vision and Common Sense," Catholic Library World XLVI (May-June 1975), p. 444.

14. Casey, Patrick, "The Parish Library of the Future," Catholic Library World XLV (March 1974), p. 386.

THE CATHEDRAL LIBRARY, BALTIMORE

Adele-Ethel Reidy

The Cathedral Library, located in the Cathedral of Mary Our Queen, 5200 North Charles Street, Baltimore, Maryland, is a free lending library open to any person in the metropolitan area regardless of church affiliation. The library is a project of the Catholic Evidence League, and its maintenance is not the responsibility of the Cathedral parishioners.

History and Development

The Catholic Evidence League was founded in 1923 under the patronage of Archbishop Michael J. Curley. The League objective, as stated in its Constitution and By-laws, "is to increase in its members a knowledge of the history, teachings, and laws of the Catholic Church, and to make more effective the application of these teachings to our own lives and to the general life of the community." The program presented to Archbishop Curley specified monthly meetings, a twice monthly Bible Study Group, Days of Recollection and Retreat, and the establishment of a library.

In the very early years of the League, the members purchased books, suggested them to friends, and exchanged books. Two of the young ladies went into the countryside recommending and lending books. At this time the books were stored in the homes of members who had extra shelf space. Soon a small store on Cold Spring Lane was rented to house the books and make them more accessible to the public. It was a very modest beginning, no central heating, and little more than four bare walls. In 1939, the library could boast of having one hundred eleven books. After World War II, the Catholic Evidence League was offered the use of a room, with bookcases, for meetings at St. Mary's Orphanage. When the Orphanage was closed in 1959, the League was able to hold its meetings in the Conference Room of the new Cathedral of Mary Our Queen.

In the Cathedral plans, a room beneath the vestibule was designated as a museum. A member of the League suggested that the room be used instead for a library which the Catholic Evidence League would sponsor and maintain. This suggestion was graciously accepted by the Rector of the Cathedral, Monsignor Thomas A. Whelan. The group of women who planned the library visited church libraries in Washington, D. C., conferred with librarians, and sought the advice of Fr. James Kortendick, Chairman, Department of Library Science, Catholic University. Fr. Paul Cook, an associate pastor of the Cathedral, aided in selecting and cataloging print material according to a modified 200 classification of the Dewey Decimal System and the two figure Cutter System. Msgr. Whelan approved the purchase of furniture, cart, typewriter, file cabinet, card catalog, additional shelving, and the installation of a telephone. The League paid for other basic supplies and provided an annual sum for operating expenses.

On October 9, 1960, after months of moving and processing nearly one thousand donated and purchased books, the library was dedicated by Fr. Kortendick and opened to the public. The opening of the library in its new location and the success of its initial years of operation owe much to the unceasing work and devotion of its first chairwoman, Mrs. W. Richard Ferguson.

The library was re-dedicated on November 12, 1973 by the then Rector of the Cathedral, Monsignor E. Melville Taylor, to the memory of the foundress of the Catholic Evidence League, Anne Warfield Martin. Miss Martin, member of a prominent Baltimore family, was a successful business woman who owned and managed a public stenographic service and was one of the two young women who went out into the country in the early days of the League with a supply of books.

Scope and Characteristics

The Cathedral Library endeavors to offer its borrowers the best books available on the many aspects of religion. Although the inventory is composed mostly of books dealing with Roman Catholic teaching, the selection of books is not restricted to this point of view. The Book Selection Committee wishes to meet the needs of the readers; acceptance, growth, mental stimulation, and openness are the key words in its philosophy.

Personnel

The library is staffed entirely by part-time, non-professional volunteers, most of whom are League members. Several of the staff members have served the library for over fifty years; since the library moved to the Cathedral many volunteers have worked for hundreds of hours. The administrative staff, also volunteers, meets in the library each Monday to attend to the many tasks involved in maintaining the library.

The chairwoman and the co-chairwomen are responsible for selecting and purchasing the new books and selecting the books to be kept from among the donated books. The staff encourages its patrons to make recommendations for purchases, and all efforts are made to honor these requests, within the overall goal of the library.

Books purchased are listed in an Order Book with information on author, title, source, price, date ordered, and date received. Each new book is noted in an Accession Book with similar information together with the catalog number. One chairwoman writes commentaries on new books and on books which are of current interest to the members of the Cathedral parish, and these commentaries are printed in the weekly parish bulletin. Another person arranges the monthly art exhibits which are part of the library's program.

Still another co-chairwoman schedules the duty hours of the volunteers; at least one volunteer, preferably two, are on duty daily. Each volunteer serves at least one day per month. The chairwoman of the staff (there have been four since 1960) orders books and materials, handles finances, tabulates the weekly records of circulation and income, attends to the correspondence, acts as a liaison between the library, the parish, and the League. Together with the other members of the administrative staff, she formulates library policy. There is a great flexibility among the administrative staff and duties are shared. Staff members type, mend, and process books, update indexes, shelve returned volumes, mail overdue and reserve notices, place orders for and stock the pamphlet and magazine racks in the narthex as well as replenish supplies of postcards, holy cards, and greeting cards. There are a few retired men who are active in the library's work.

At the annual volunteers' luncheon given by the administrative staff, library policy and procedures are reviewed. At all times a notebook of procedures is on the desk for instant reference.

Finances
_____

The library receives from the Catholic Evidence League a sum to cover annual operating expenses, and this sum has been periodically adjusted to meet the increased costs of service. The Cathedral parish pays the utilities and provides janitorial service. Memorial funds have made it possible for the staff to add shelves for one thousand more books, to expand the collection of writings by and about Fr. Pierre Teilhard de Chardin, S. J., and the collection of writings on Biblical scholarship. Gifts of book ends, a clock, a moveable cart to hold two sets of encyclopedias (also gifts) and very fine specialized books have been gratefully received.

A successful venture which we recommend to any small library is the used book sale. About eleven years ago the library held its first sale of used books, books withdrawn from the shelves and donated books which were not suitable for library use. In time, this semi-annual sale became an on-going library activity. The prices are nominal and lists of requests for books by certain authors or on certain subjects are posted in the library work room. Books which are valuable because of their contents or age are donated to appropriate institutions, for example, the Maryland Historical Society, the Maritime Museum, St. Mary's Seminary and University.

Not all of the used books are sold.   Some are donated to
schools, recreation centers, prisons, rehabilitation centers, hospitals, church missions, and beginning church libraries.   Many car-
tons of books have been donated to the annual book sales sponsored
by Smith College and by Brandeis University.   The library, however, does not sell or dispose of used textbooks.   The library also
carries a small selection of greeting cards, note paper, Christmas
cards, and Advent calendars as a convenience for its patrons and
as another source of income.

Collection

The one hundred-plus books of 1939 have grown into a collection of four thousand volumes.   The subject matter is wide and varied: scripture, theology, hagiology, philosophy, psychology, ecumenism, the charismatic movement, catechesis, liturgy, sociology,
world and church history, travel, fine arts, biography, spiritual
readings, world topics, fiction, and books for juveniles.   The twelve
volume Catholic Encyclopedia for School and Home Use and the thirteen volume New Catholic Encyclopedia are available.   Also available
for reference is a group of books about Maryland, a rapidly growing
collection.   Because the Baltimore Diocese was the first American
diocese, information on this region is of great importance in the
history of the Catholic Church in the United States.   Directories,
almanacs, and dictionaries are available, also.   The number of
books in each classification varies depending upon the need and the
interest of the readers as well as the publishers' offerings of suitable material.   The greater percentage of books are hardbacks, although some paperbacks are now on the shelves.   The advice of experts in areas of specialty such as Biblical scholarship, liturgy and
theology is sought.

At first, church-related periodicals and newspapers were
stocked but when shelf space became at a premium the limited read-
ership for these materials did not justify its continuation and the
staff decided to concentrate the library resources on bound books.
Moreover, these materials can be purchased in the vestibule of the
Cathedral.   The Confraternity of Christian Doctrine maintains its
own well-stocked office in the parish school, so there is no need
to supply audio-visual equipment and teaching materials for the Sunday School classes.   There have been a few requests for tapes, but
the demand for them does not justify their purchase.

Physical Quarters

Two oak-panelled, terazzo-floored rooms under the narthex
of the Cathedral are designated as the library area.   A third, un-
finished, room is used for storage.   The main room, which houses
the collection and the circulation desk, is forty-three feet by seven-
teen feet with two alcoves seven feet square.   In addition to the
desk, shelves, and card catalogs the room is furnished with two

tables each large enough to seat eight persons.   Comfortable chairs, upholstered in orange, add brightness to the windowless area.   Several dozen folding chairs are available to accommodate large groups. A cork bulletin board is hung on the wall between the alcoves.

In the eight by fourteen foot work room are four large tables, two typewriters, a typing stand, bulletin board, vertical file for Catholic Evidence League storage and library records, and table-top metal file cabinet for shelf list cards.   As the name implies, the storage area contains the necessary library supplies, an overflow of books, as well as bundles of guide books to the Cathedral of Mary Our Queen.

Service

The Cathedral Library is open every day throughout the year, except for holidays.   The hours are: Monday to Friday, 1:30 p.m. to 4:00 p.m., Saturday, 3:30 p.m. to 5:00 p.m., Sunday, 10:00 a.m. to 2:00 p.m.

All Library patrons are asked to fill out an application card with name, address, telephone number, and (if applicable) school and grade.   This information is kept in a Rolodex card file.   When a book is borrowed, the volunteer on duty writes the borrower's full name on the circulation card and the due date of the books borrowed.   The date the books are due is also noted in the back of the book.   The circulation card is then filed alphabetically according to author.   Books are loaned for a two-week period and may be renewed unless there is a reserve on the book; books may be renewed by telephone.   Reserves are filled in the order in which the book is requested.   A few books, because of their length, are loaned for one month; they are not renewable.   The encyclopedias are for reference only, as are the old books on Maryland.   The fine for overdue books is five cents per day with a maximum of one dollar per book.   If the library is closed, books may be returned to the Cathedral rectory.   Overdue notices are mailed one week after the book is overdue; often a telephone call has proven more effective than a mailed notice.   If a reader loses a book he or she is asked to reimburse the library for the book.   Unfortunately, the library has suffered a number of thefts of its books.

Books are listed in the card catalog under author and title; the subject catalog is contained in two loose leaf notebooks.   A daily record is kept of the books circulated and the monies received; these are totaled weekly.   The annual report of the library to the Catholic Evidence League contains the number of books circulated and money received for the year.

Periodically, the library has a coffee and cookies "open house" to acquaint new patrons with its facilities and to renew old friendships.   Notices of the meetings are sent to academic institutions, the daily press, neighborhood newspapers, and the Cathedral parish bulletin.

Every effort is made to coordinate print materials with the Confraternity of Christian Doctrine office.   Lists of suitable books are prepared for the teachers and leaders of the Adult Discussion Groups.   The parish priests are kept informed when books which are useful in their work are received.

Relationship to the Parish Priest, the Congregation, and Catholic Publishing Houses

The rapport between the library staff and the clergy of the Cathedral parish is excellent.   Each Rector has offered his support; the library is used frequently by the priests and the nuns of the Cathedral School.   Retired priests have donated their personal collections of books to the library.   Many members of the parish use the library, and, in particular, the children's books are in great demand.

Books are purchased through the Catholic Book Club, The Thomas More Association, and The Thomas More Book Club.   Occasionally, books are purchased from the Abbey Press, The Liturgical Press, or The Paulist Press.   The greatest percentage of the books are bought from the Baker and Taylor Company.   Local bookstores are seldom used.

The Unified Magazine Program of New Jersey supplies most of the magazines available in the narthex, but Bible Today, America, and Commonweal are sent to the library directly from their publishers.   The Paulist Press Pamphlet Service and local religious bookstores are the sources for the carefully chosen pamphlets in the popular paperback rack in the narthex.   The Fortress Press has some excellent offerings.   Literature for children as well as for adults is stocked.

Other Activities

During the past sixteen years the library has been the scene of many activities: Board meetings, Parish Council sessions, lectures, poetry readings, Bible discussions, summer reading and movie programs for juveniles, tutoring, book talks, quilting classes, reading to the blind.   It is also a collection center for clothing which is sent to Inner City distribution centers.   The staff has shared its experience with others who wished to start libraries in their parishes. The Cathedral Library is a member of the Church and Synagogue Librarians Fellowship and has hosted one of its workshops.   Members of the Church and Synagogue Library Association visited the Cathedral during the 1972 national meeting.

An organization working with indigent persons requested permission to have a table in the library on which they would display small articles they sell to help support their work.   Care of this table is a responsibility of the volunteers.

In 1971, Mrs. Robert H. Dyer, then the Chairwoman of the
library, inaugurated a series of art exhibits, featuring the work of
Maryland artists.   Mrs. Dyer continues to coordinate these exhibits
of graphic arts, needlework, and photography.   There is a new exhibit each month, they are well publicized, and the staff of the library and the artisans have been pleased at the enthusiastic response
of the public.   Socially, ecumenically, as well as artistically, they
have been rewarding endeavors; many have been reached who might
not otherwise have ventured into the Cathedral.

The staff constantly strives to expand the library membership,
to serve our members, and to encourage reading of the many excellent works in our special subject areas.   The staff would like the
congregation of the Cathedral parish and the community at large to
make more use of its facilities.

PART IV:

PROTESTANT AND OTHER
CHRISTIAN LIBRARIES

LUTHERAN CHURCH LIBRARIES

Wilma W. Jensen

The Lutheran Church has been known as a teaching church. As such, libraries (or collections of books) have been important aspects of the teaching ministry. During the latter part of the nineteenth century, some American Lutheran churches had book collections for use by the laity. Many of these books were written in the German or Scandinavian languages. Recently, a small book written in Swedish came to our attention. Inscribed on the inside cover were words indicating that the book had been placed in the "Swedish Evangelical Lutheran Church Library" in the early 1900's. [1] Few of these libraries are still in existence.

During the 1930's a new interest in church libraries became apparent in the Lutheran community. At that time, a few churches in the Minneapolis and Chicago suburbs, for instance, began to assemble books into libraries for use by congregation members. An example was the library begun by Mrs. Frank Dominick, a member of the county public library staff, at Gethsemane Lutheran Church, Hopkins, Minnesota.

Very little about these libraries appeared in the church press. It was not until 1958 that an association was founded to help these churches and their libraries. Since then, it has been difficult for this author to separate the history of Lutheran church libraries from that of the Lutheran Church Library Association (LCLA). Post-1958 surveys revealed that a number of Lutheran Church libraries had existed for many years.

The Library's Mission

A resource center which is the heart of the educational program and which undergirds the entire congregation ministry is a description of an effective Lutheran church library. It provides a place where laymen "may study the teachings of their church, learn about its history, and find inspiration and aid in their development as thinking, growing Christians." [2] Literature of the Lutheran Church Library Association indicates that an effective church library will enrich individual lives, enlarge the Christian ministry, extend the Church's witness and enlist men for Kingdom service. [3]

Not only the scope of the library collection but also the service offered by the librarian and library staff become important aspects of the mission to be accomplished. To find the right book (or media) for the right person at the right time becomes a necessity in order to fulfill the mission. Resources for the educational program (Sunday School, adult Bible study classes, confirmation classes and educational work in general) are of primary importance to this mission.

Scope and Characteristics

Libraries are located in the U.S.A., in Canada and in several other parts of the world. More than one-half of all Lutheran churches have some type of library. A survey of Lutheran churches in the United States and Canada is planned for 1977 in preparation for the twentieth anniversary of the Lutheran Church Library Association. Up to this date only LCLA members have been included in its surveys. LCLA, in an effort to learn more about these libraries and stimulate them to upgrade their services, have covered such areas as the scope of the collection, finance, and the services offered. More than 3500 church libraries have used LCLA services through workshop attendance, publications, or membership.

Most church libraries were established to serve the congregation's educational program. Certain churches had school libraries which served the day schools Monday through Friday. Recently, many of these school libraries have been available to the congregation on Sundays. In many instances, too, the church and school libraries have been combined. A fine example of this combination can be found at Gethsemane Lutheran Church, St. Paul, Minnesota. When a new building was erected, the library was placed adjacent to the classroom wing so during the week it was an integral part of the educational building. One door of the library, however, opened into the lounge where many church activities were held. Individuals could read library books while enjoying the comfortable lounge. The lounge, in turn, was near the narthex and main sanctuary so the library was not far from the general traffic pattern. Congregation members found this to be a very workable version of the combined church and school library.

All Lutheran church libraries are open on Sunday mornings during, before and/or after the worship hours. Some are set up for self service, but better service can be offered when the libraries are staffed. Certain libraries have been recognized for their accomplishments. The Trinity Parish Library, St. Peter, Minnesota, was the first church library to receive the John Cotton Dana American Library Association Public Relations Award. In 1968, Marian Johnson, Librarian of Trinity, was presented with this award.[4]

Library Personnel

The library staff varies with the size of the library. Size

ranges from one to as many as forty volunteers.   Suggested duties
are listed in material sent to new Lutheran Church Library Association members.   They include

> Formulate a library purpose;
> Determine the scope of the collection;
> Prepare a summation of the philosophy underlying material
>   selection;
> Provide for financial support;
> Prepare an annual budget;
> Select the library's location;
> Present an annual report to the congregation;
> Promote library growth.

Many church libraries have a librarian with a number of volunteers.
Some libraries have a regular group of aides serving when the library
is open each Sunday morning.   These libraries offer experienced help
to persons who request it.   Some churches have women's circles which
help to prepare the books and media for the shelves and mend books. A
Nebraska library had a young people's corps serving as "Librari-
Anns" and helping shelve books and type cards.   These high school
women worked on alternate Saturday mornings.   On other Saturdays
young high school men joined them to make puppets and prepare the
story hour to be presented to the next day's Sunday School classes.

Very few libraries have salaried personnel.   Our Savior's
Lutheran Church Library in Milwaukee is an exception.   This church
employs a lay assistant who is half-time church librarian, Ken Nord-
by.   Central Lutheran Church in Minneapolis has two part-time librarians and offers some remuneration to cover their expenses.
Occasionally, the Director of Christian Education supervises the
church library.   Rose Mary Ulland, First Lutheran Church, Eau
Claire, Wisconsin, a past president of LCLA, is a Director of
Christian Education.

Some of the professional library volunteers serve as library
directors while others serve as consultants or else catalog and clas-
sify.   Association workshops help them to serve their congregations.
All Lutheran professional librarians are urged to assist their libraries.   A future goal is for each church library to have a salaried
professional librarian.   Just as the choir director and the organist
receive some remuneration, so should the professional librarian who
works in the church library ministry.

Library Finance

Funds are provided primarily by budgets and gifts.   A few
libraries receive a considerable portion of their income from gifts.
The budgets involved are the general church budget and certain
church organization budgets.   The church budget is more important
to the library, not only because of the funds received but because
this implies interest in the library by the church leaders.   Many libraries were started with gifts from one or more church organizations

and were not added to the general church budget until they had prov-
en their value to the congregation.

Ideally, the library should be founded with the financial support of the church governing board.   This support should then be
augmented by budgeted gifts from various church organizations.   The
Grace Lutheran Church Library of Deephaven, Minnesota received a
quarterly gift of $15. 00 from the Sunday School to purchase refer-
ence material for its staff and students.

A 1969 survey of LCLA membership revealed that 70 percent
of the libraries were on the general church budget.   Others relied
only on gifts from individuals and church organizations, with 78 percent getting financial help through gifts.   Most libraries received
financial support through both gifts and budgets.   Budgeted funds
varied from $25. 00 to $2, 800.   The latter budget follows:

Adult books	$1, 000
Youth books	600
Framed pictures	400
Recordings	200
Periodicals	100
Special items (including cassettes)	400
Supplies	100
TOTAL	$2, 800

Memorial gifts continue to be the main revenue source for many libraries.   They vary greatly in size, and some libraries have been
furnished entirely with them.   Not only memorials but birthday and
anniversary presents, or gifts given at Christmas, Easter, confirmation and other occasions become important.

Some libraries regularly hold book fairs where carefully selected material from the local bookstore or church supply house are
placed on display.   A program including a guest speaker or book
reviews at a church organization meeting is often involved.   Church
members are free to browse and to buy books or media to present
to the church library.   They sign a form indicating their choice of
material.   It may read "Please use my gift to purchase the following
books or media for the church library. "   Spaces for signatures are
provided beside each title. [5]

Library Collections

All libraries start with books forming the major portion of
their holdings, and most of them continue to contain more books
than other kinds of material.   More than half of the libraries sending
in reports indicate that periodicals form part of their collections.
Almost one-half of these libraries have film in the forms of slides,
filmstrips, movies or cassettes.   Many of them have as many as
100 films.   Others start taping sermons and special music.   These

tapes are used to share the message with shut-ins and are then
placed in the permanent collection.   One library tapes a special
study series for the church women.   Several copies of each tape
are needed to meet the demand.

Clippings and pamphlet files are important in the reference
collection.   Mounted and circulating pictures are found in one-third
of the libraries.   Art masterpieces (framed pictures) form a growing
portion of library holdings.   Each issue of Lutheran Libraries features some art work to remind librarians of the value of having art
in their collections.   Many church libraries have extensive phonograph record collections for circulation, so reviews of recordings
are likewise featured in Lutheran Libraries issues.   Many church
libraries augment their media resources by cooperating with other
area libraries.   In the fall, 1971, six churches in the Moorhead,
Minnesota area formed the Audio-Visual Resource Center where each
church was invited to pool media material. [6]   The center was financed by the churches participating.   They sponsored media workshops and scheduled television programs.   One of the finest cataloged and mounted picture collections can be found in the Second
English Lutheran Church Library, Baltimore, begun by Margaret
Ballard many years ago.

Not only do libraries have books, but art objects, maps,
globes, teaching toys, and illustrative materials, also.   They can
be used in the classrooms or the private homes of congregation
members.   Some libraries have puppets which are used by library
personnel in telling stories to church school classes.   Media equipment, likewise, is part of the library circulating collection.   Projectors, portable phonographs, cassette players, and tape recorders
can be used in church classrooms or private homes.

Physical Quarters

Quarters vary from one book cart to two rooms for service
and two rooms for work and storage.   A new Lutheran mission may
include a library even before a permanent house of worship is built.
The departments of architecture in the larger churches are aware
of the need for specific library space.

A recent survey indicated that one half of the libraries had
separate rooms, the most desirable situation.   Some libraries share
the space with church school classes.   Other libraries are located
in a lounge where they are very visible.   One library committee
worked hard to promote a separate library room.   After persuading
the church council to budget carpeting, shelving, furniture, card
catalogs, comfortable chairs, wall paper and drapes, the library
was ready to use.   Then the library committee discovered that almost every church group, including those which had opposed funds
for the library facilities, wanted to hold their meetings in the beautiful room.

The ideal library was housed in its own room and located near heavy Sunday morning traffic, near church school classes and the worship center.   Many well used libraries did not have choice church space.   Promotion and the contagious spirit of the librarians counteracted poor locations.   A library in Eau Claire, Wisconsin opened a room on the lower floor.   Parishioners had no trouble finding it, however, because an attractive brochure, complete with floor plan, was given to all members at worship services.

Service

Service is the keynote of any effective library.   The church library which can offer the best service is the one which has carefully selected material and a library staff fully aware of the congregation's needs.

Service to the congregation educational program tops the list for most Lutheran libraries.

The library may contribute to congregational life in many ways: It

a.   supplies historical and background information for the teacher;

b.   provides a better understanding of teaching in terms of the philosophy of Christian education, theories of learning, methodology, and application of techniques;

c.   offers insight into the nature of the student, the teacher-pupil relationship, personality development, and levels of learning and achievement;

d.   focuses attention upon the basic objectives and goals of Christian education and the relationship of those objectives to the process of teaching and learning, and

e.   stimulates the leader to see his task in a total perspective as he attempts to employ and coordinate the varied resources at his disposal. [7]

In addition to strengthening the parish educational program, Lutheran libraries seek to serve the various congregational organizations. Help in program planning, sources for devotional messages, background information on speakers, topics and avenues of service are provided and bibliographies compiled.   A reserve collection can be set aside for a particular group.   Book, art, phonograph records, or reviews may be given by library staff members.   Topical guides can be provided for the auxiliaries.   Certain libraries tape sermons, guest speakers, study topics, seminars and worship services.   They are catalogued and shelved for future use.   Many librarians take books, records and other media to shut-ins.   Some offer this service through a "sunshine committee" and others offer it through a program

where one individual adopts a shut-in and always takes material to
that particular person.

Many libraries sponsor book discussion groups. Once a week
the book discussion group meets in the library to discuss a particular book or its author. Membership in these groups may extend beyond the congregations, thus providing a community service. Other
libraries sponsor camera clubs. Often church librarians present
talks at organization meetings or community programs. [8] On Sunday
mornings books and media may be checked out, reference questions
answered, and new books and media found on display.

Relationship to the Minister, the Director of Religious Education and the Church School

In most libraries, the pastor or a member of the pastor's
staff is a library committee member. A number of libraries get
the pastor's approval before any item is purchased. Others are
well organized and function without such supervision. A pastor who
has confidence in the library staff can work most effectively by al-
lowing them to make most of the decisions. Many Lutheran churches
are blessed with pastors who mention the library in their sermons
and quote from the books found therein.

Just as the pastor can influence the policies and promotion
of the library, so, too, can the Director of Christian Education.
Rose Mary Ulland, Director of Christian Education, First Lutheran
Church, Eau Claire, Wisconsin, works closely with the library committee. The library was begun under her direction, and her talents
are used in its promotion and policy-making. She designed an attractive brochure to introduce the library to church members. She
produced an interesting "Resource Go-Round" to introduce church
school teachers to library resources. She wrote many interesting
articles about the library for the church press. [9]

It is customary for the Director of Christian Education to
have responsibility for some phase of the library program. Many
directors work indirectly through the church school. Others are
church library committee members. Some committees are part of
the congregation board of parish education and are under the Director of Christian Education's supervision. In Our Savior's Lutheran
Church, Milwaukee, the lay assistant divides his time between general educational programs and the library.

Every Lutheran church library is closely associated with the
church school, whether this means the Sunday School, weekday
school classes, confirmation classes or the adult education program.
For most Lutheran libraries the first accessions were those resource
materials which could best serve the church schools. From the
early libraries in the nineteenth century to those being organized
today, the purpose of serving the church schools and the congregation's educational program has been of primary importance. An

interesting bit of cooperation between church schools and libraries
is found in those libraries which are eager to "employ" former
church school teachers during the Sunday hours.   They are most
conversant with the resource materials and know how to use them
in answering reference questions.   One church librarian with the
help of church school staff members compiled an extensive bibliography of library material which would augment the curriculum for
each class in the church school.   It was divided by units for each
class and contained only that material with was appropriate for that
age group in the particular subject.

Relationship to Lutheran Publishing Houses and Religious Journals

The three major publishing houses of the Lutheran churches
in the United States are the Augsburg Publishing House, Minneapolis;
Concordia Publishing House, St. Louis; and Fortress Press, Philadelphia.   These houses are owned, respectively, by The American
Lutheran Church (headquarters in Minneapolis), the Lutheran Church-
Missouri Synod (St. Louis) and the Lutheran Church in America
(New York and Philadelphia).   Each one of these church groups and
publishing houses has shown interest in the church library ministry.
This interest is visible in many ways.   The publishing houses offer
discounts to all church libraries.   The Departments of Publication
take part in library workshops and meetings throughout the nation.
Some of them serve on the Lutheran Church Library Association
Board of Directors.   Helpful displays of the newest and most important books for church libraries are provided for workshops.   The
publishers cooperate through an organization known as "The Lutheran
Editors and Managers Association" which has a church library committee.   This committee serves as a liaison between the boards of
publication and the church libraries.   Often Lutheran journal editors
publish articles about church libraries.   Some of them serve as
LCLA officers.   Still others are active in their own church library
programs or lead book discussion groups in their own congregations.

A Typical Library

Libraries vary as much as individual persons do.   The library described here reflects the type of service and the size of
the library collection which is common in Lutheran churches.   Grace
Lutheran Church, Deephaven, located in the outer Minneapolis suburbs, organized a library in 1958 with only $37.50 to spend for
material.   At a congregation dinner meeting, carefully selected
books from a Lutheran book store were on display.   After hearing
a speaker (an author who had written a number of excellent books),
members were given an opportunity to pledge the price of the books
which they would like to see in the new library.   At the close of
this meeting the librarian was able to keep all of the books taken
on consignment and still had the original $37.50 to spend for library
supplies.   Thus, the Grace Library was begun.

The library was first located on book shelves placed in the entry way to the church offices. Later it was located in the classroom area of the church building and was one of the most attractive rooms. Blue carpeting and wallpaper, walnut shelving, attractive drapes on the two North windows, comfortable chairs and a folding table, walnut card catalog to match the shelving and a librarian's matching desk made this room functional as well as attractive. Four shelving sections were used for the children's corner. Slanting shelves were used for the picture books. Permanent dividers were added to some of the shelves to keep the books from sliding so the children were not afraid to remove books from the shelves. When the new room was dedicated every shelf was not needed for books, so display areas were available on the shelves. A member of the library committee kept this display area filled with appropriate arrangements to match the church year. This display area was in one of the six shelving sections used for the adult collection. Books for junior and senior high school students were shelved among the adult books. The library included 2533 volumes, a number of periodicals, a file of mounted teaching pictures, cassettes, a vertical file and a small art collection.

Many books were purchased with memorial funds. While the library was on the general church budget for a nominal sum which varied from year to year ($50, $100, $200), most accessions were purchased with gifts in the form of memorials, birthday presents, gifts from Sunday school classes and gifts given to "feed the kitty" when one had books overdue. The library received funds through the budgets of the Altar Guild, the Church School and the Church Women. The church council, in addition to providing a small amount in each year's budget, provided funds for furnishing the library.

Mrs. Lloyd (Betty) LeDell, Grace Librarian since 1966, is now assisted by an active library board of eight members. This board is in charge of purchasing, processing and circulating library material. Work days are scheduled throughout the year. The library is staffed every Sunday morning during the school year from 8:45 until 12:15. During the week and during the summer, all books can be checked out on a self-help basis.

A few years ago Mrs. LeDell opened a Narthex Branch Library. On Sunday mornings when parishioners are coming and going from the worship services, they find the branch library very convenient to use. Recent books pertaining to the topic of the day or the season of the church year are displayed on the four shelves in this narthex branch. A member of the library board is always on duty when the branch library is open.

Grace Library's reference collection includes many concordances, commentaries, Bible atlases, Bible dictionaries and encyclopedias. Bible versions include the King James, the Revised Standard, the Jerusalem Bible, Phillips translation, Oxford annotated Bible, The Living Bible, The Duay Bible and many other translations,

including a unique interpretation of the Old Testament published in
newspaper format and printed in Israel entitled "Chronicles." Grace
finds the multiple copies of great use in work with the church school.
All of the reference material circulates. Church school teachers
can check out books for more than two weeks and keep them for the
time needed or until the books are needed in the library. One hundred and fifty new accessions were added to the library in 1975 when
the average per week circulation was 60 items.

The Lutheran Church Library Association

A small group of church librarians met in Minneapolis in
October 1958 to consider the possibility of forming a church library
association. After initial planning by a steering committee, the
first meeting was called. More than sixty church librarians attended
and adopted the by-laws. Provisions were made for a Board of
Publications and a Library Services Board.

The purpose of the Association, according to the by-laws,
was "to further the growth of church libraries in Lutheran churches
by 1) publishing a quarterly journal to be known as Lutheran Libraries; 2) furnishing lists of books recommended for Lutheran
church libraries; 3) assisting member libraries with the technical
problems of setting up and operating a church library; and 4) providing meetings for mutual encouragement, assistance and exchange
of ideas among members."

Since the initial meeting, the by-laws were changed to include
personal memberships and open the membership to all church libraries. Today the membership includes fourteen denominations
and faiths other than Lutheran. Membership grew from the fifty-
nine charter members to 164 churches by the end of the first year.
Today that membership includes 1440, covering every state, six
provinces in Canada, four countries in Europe (Great Britain,
France, Germany, Switzerland), three in Asia (India, Japan, Hong
Kong), Africa and Australia.

Members of the Association receive annotated bibliographies
which have been compiled by the Library Services Board and specialists in specific fields. They include books for children, young
adults, and adults. Short lists such as "Books for the Church Library and for Christmas Giving," "Books Too Good to Miss," or
"Books in Large Print" are sent to members from time to time.
Service Bulletins compiled by the Library Services Board are published as the need arises. At one time they appeared regularly
twice a year in the pages of the quarterly, Lutheran Libraries. To
date, nineteen service bulletins have been published.

Perhaps the most important Association publication is the
journal, Lutheran Libraries, edited by Erwin E. John. Having
served as the Association's first president, John edited the first
issued of Lutheran Libraries and has continued to edit it since that

time.   While the first issue was published at a cost of $120, the
current annual budget for publishing four issues is $7100.   This
figure does not include remuneration for the editor nor the volunteer
staff which meets quarterly to prepare the publication for mailing.
Lutheran Libraries covers such topics as success stories about
church libraries, media and services.   A special feature of each
issue is the book review section where one finds books from more
than twenty publishers.   Each book reviewed is complete with suggested subject headings and Dewey Decimal classification number.
Books are reviewed by church librarians and by specialists in the
field.   New Association members receive a six-page outline entitled
"The Church Library: Organization and Administration" written by
Wilma W. Jensen and revised periodically.   This outline covers the
philosophy or purpose, personnel, policies, procedures and promotion
of a church library.

The first workshop for Lutheran church librarians was sponsored by Gustavus Adolphus College in St. Peter, Minnesota in the
summer of 1959.   Since that time, many workshops have been held
at Lutheran colleges or churches throughout the nation.   Since 1963,
most of these workshops have been sponsored by the Association.
It is not uncommon to find the LCLA executive secretary taking part
in such workshops each weekend during the spring and fall seasons.
Workshops have been held in such cities as Chicago, Dallas, Eau
Claire, Fargo, Harrisburg, Los Angeles, Milwaukee, San Diego,
San Francisco, St. Paul and Minneapolis.   A large volunteer staff
of professional librarians and dedicated church librarians participate.

The first Association three-day conference was held to observe the LCLA fifth anniversary.   Since that time, a tenth conference and a fifteenth conference have been held.   Because of requests an "interim" conference was held on the campus of Gustavus
Adolphus College in 1975.   With the theme, "Take Wings to Serve"
librarians were inspired to find new avenues of service in their own
congregations.   At this conference they learned of new material
available, new techniques and new ways in which to promote their
libraries.

The Duluth, Minnesota - Superior, Wisconsin area requested
the first chapter.   In LCLA's tenth year, the tenth chapter was
formed.   Today 27 chapters meet for "mutual encouragement, assistance and exchange of ideas among members" (as provided in the
Association's by-laws).   The states of California and Minnesota have
five chapters each.   Wisconsin has six.   Chapter activities are recorded in the pages of Lutheran Libraries.   They include church
library bus tours, author's luncheons, technical demonstrations,
book and art fairs, poster and book exchanges, guest speakers and
all-day workshops.   An Advisory Board of twelve church leaders
chosen from the three major Lutheran bodies and representing widespread geographical areas is an important part of the Association.
These key people, working through the regional chapters as well as
the national office, offer their services in promoting the church library ministry.

Association income comes from three major sources: active memberships of churches and individuals ($6 and $12 annually); contributing, donor and patron memberships ($25, $100 and $500 annually) and grants from the Lutheran churches through their respective publishing houses.   LCLA's official seal is a red flame rising from an open book taken from the motto: ex libris spiritus sanctus. This motto can best be expressed in the words of Erwin E. John, "That the spirit of God may emerge from a book to take wings in the lives of its readers. "

Relationship to the National Church Leadership

LCLA is an autonomous association.   It has its own by-laws, budget, and board of directors.   Yet, it is a definite part of the "Lutheran family" and was officially recognized by the Lutheran Council USA in 1969.

A former president of the Lutheran Council, Malvin H. Lundeen, is a current member of the LCLA Advisory Board.   Dr. Lundeen has served as national secretary of the Lutheran Church in America and has been an LCLA president.   The president of the American Lutheran Church, David Preus, has been a keynote speaker at LCLA conferences.   Alida Storaasli, Director of Education for the American Lutheran Church Women, is a past president of LCLA. Members of the Board of Christian Education and of the Board of Publication of the Lutheran Church-Missouri Synod have spoken at LCLA national conferences.

These examples indicate the close relationship between the national Lutheran church leaders and the church libraries.   The Association is most grateful for this full cooperation which has been expressed in a most tangible form through the annual grants received from the boards of publication of the three major Lutheran churches in America.   Without these grants, LCLA could not continue to serve church libraries throughout the world.

Lutheran Church Library Association Chapters

The Alamo (San Antonia area)--organized in 1970
Chicagoland (Greater Chicago)--organized in 1967
Colorado Mile Hi (Denver area)--organized in 1975
Elkhorn Valley (Nebraska)--organized in 1974
Granite City (Central Minnesota)--organized in 1972
Hawaii (Honolulu)--organized in 1972
La Crosse (S. W. Wisconsin)--organized in 1974
Lake Superior (Duluth-Superior area)--organized in 1962
The Lone Star (Dallas-Fort Worth)--organized in 1969
Los Angeles Area (California)--organized in 1966
Madison (Wisconsin)--organized in 1968
Milwaukee (Wisconsin)--organized in 1966
Minnesota Riverbend (S. Central Minnesota)--organized in 1975

Orange County (California)--organized in 1975
Red River Valley (North Dakota)--organized in 1968
Rib Mountain (N. Central Wisconsin)--organized in 1975
Rockford (Illinois)--organized in 1969
San Diego County (California)--organized in 1975
Sheboygan (Wisconsin)--organized in 1976
Shetek (S. W. Minnesota)--organized in 1964
Sioux Valley (South Dakota)--organized in 1971
Southern California Inland--organized in 1971
Tres Condados (California)--organized in 1974
Twin Cities (Minnesota)--organized in 1966
Valley of the Sun (Arizona)--organized in 1971
West Central Minnesota--organized in 1966
West Central Wisconsin--organized in 1967

Lutheran Church Library Association Presidents

1959 Erwin E. John, Librarian, Mt. Olivet Lutheran Church, Min-
      neapolis
1960 Harold J. Belgum, Director, Adult Education, American
      Lutheran Church, Minneapolis
1961 Mrs. Chester (Marian) Johnson, Librarian, Trinity Lutheran
      Church, St. Peter, Minnesota
1962 Clarence Lund, Asst. to President, Synod of Northwest,
      ULCA, Minneapolis
1963 Mrs. E. T. (Wilma) Jensen, Librarian, Grace Lutheran Church
      of Deephaven, Wayzata, Minnesota
1964 Rev. Paul Krause, Pastor, Gethsemane Lutheran Church,
      St. Paul
1965 Sister Gwen Ellsworth, Director of Christian Education, St.
      Paul's Lutheran Church, Minneapolis
1966 Rev. Rolf Aaseng, Assoc. Editor, Lutheran Standard, Min-
      neapolis
1967 Mrs. Charles (Elaine) Graham, Librarian, Westwood Lutheran
      Church, St. Louis Park, Minnesota
1968 Rev. A. Curtis Paul, Librarian, Northwestern Lutheran Theo-
      logical Seminary, St. Paul
1969 Mrs. Roger (Barbara) Livdahl, Librarian, Olivet Lutheran
      Church, Fargo, North Dakota
1970 Gary Klammer, Concordia Publishing House, St. Louis
1971 Carl Manfred, Assistant to the President, LCA Minnesota
      Synod, Minneapolis
1972 Rose Mary Ulland, Director of Christian Education, First
      Lutheran Church, Eau Claire, Wisconsin
1973 Mary Huebner, Librarian, St. Andrew's Lutheran School,
      Park Ridge, Illinois
1974 Malvin H. Lundeen, former President, Lutheran Council in
      the U. S. A., Sun City, Arizona
1975 Alida Storaasli, Secretary of Education, ALCW, American
      Lutheran Church, Minneapolis
1976 Mrs. H. O. (Thilda) Egertson, former Los Angeles School
      Librarian, Seal Beach, California

Lutheran Church Library Association Publications

LUTHERAN LIBRARIES, a quarterly, edited by Erwin E. John.
v. 1, 1958--. 122 West Franklin Avenue, Minneapolis, Minnesota 55404. Reviews of books and media including art masterpieces, phonograph records, tapes, cassettes; articles about
church libraries, authors, publishers, techniques and library
skills, ideas for promotion and service of libraries.

BASIC BOOKLETS, edited and revised by the Library Services Board
of the Lutheran Church Library Association. 1959--. Annotated
lists of books recommended for church libraries with a Dewey
Decimal classification number and suggested subject headings
for each entry. Booklists include:
A Suggested List of Books for Children
A Reference Book List for Church Libraries
Books in Christian Education
Books on Theology
Devotional and Inspirational Books for the Church Library
Books on Church History
Marriage and Family Living
A Booklist for Young Adults
Inspirational Biography
Worship and the Church
Fiction for a Church Library

SERVICE BULLETINS, edited and revised by the Library Services
Board of the Lutheran Church Library Association. (no. 1,
1963--.) Service bulletins in print include:
No. 1 Bibliography of Aids for Church Librarians
No. 3 Suggested List of Recordings for Beginning Collections
No. 6 Periodicals for the Church Library
No. 7 Art in the Church Library
No. 9 A Reformation Bibliography
No. 10 Library-Sponsored Book Discussions
No. 11 A Human Relations Bibliography
No. 12 A Glossary of Library Terms
No. 13 Visual Aids in the Church Library
No. 14 The Church Library Picture File
No. 15 Environmental Concerns--A Bibliography
No. 16 Contemporary Music in Worship
No. 17 Book Fairs
No. 18 Library Service for Men
No. 19 Cassettes in the Church Library

OUTLINES and Mimeographed materials used in Church Library
Workshops:
The Church Library: Organization and Administration
Library Activities for Children
The Library Serves the Education Program of the Congregation
Locating and Furnishing the Church Library
Organizing the Book Collection
Poster Making
Promotion of the Church Library

BIBLIOGRAPHY

Periodical Articles

Burckhard, A. L.   "A Church with an Art Gallery; Lutheran Church
    of the Good Shepherd, Minneapolis, " International Journal of
    Religious Education (July 1967), pp. 4-6.

Ericson, K. M.   "Lutheran Libraries: The Man Who Got Them Go-
    ing, " The Lutheran Journal, pp. 20-22.

Groff, Betty.   "Use Church Library for Isaiah Study, " Scope (Janu-
    ary 1977), p. 23.

Hollabaugh, Elaine and Mark.   "Layman's Love for Books Helps
    Lutheran Libraries' Growth, " The Lutheran Layman (March
    1974), p. 24.

Huebner, Mary.   "The Resource Center for the School and Total
    Parish, " Lutheran Education (Sept-Oct. 1975), pp. 3-13.

Jensen, Wilma W.   "The Lutheran Church Library Association, "
    Drexel Library Quarterly V (April 1970), pp. 148-149.

John, Erwin E.   "A Church Library Needs Good Administration, "
    International Journal of Religious Education (July 1967), pp. 6-7.

John, Erwin E.   "Mt. Olivet Lutheran Church Library, Minneapolis,
    Minnesota, " Drexel Library Quarterly V (April 1970), pp. 132-
    133.

Johnson, Marian.   "After Fifteen Years, LCLA Sticks to Goals, "
    Lutheran Libraries XV (Fall 1973), pp. 86-88.

Johnson, Marian.   "Church Libraries Benefit from Ten Years of
    LCLA Growth, " Lutheran Libraries X (Fall 1968), pp. 4-5.

Johnson, Marian.   "A Church Library That Won a Prize, " Drexel
    Library Quarterly V (April 1970), pp. 139-142.

Johnson, Marian.   "The Church Needs the Parish Library, " The
    Advance (Minneapolis, Lutheran Minnesota Conference of Augus-
    tus Lutheran Church) (March-April 1960), p. 9.

Johnson, Marian.   "Placement, Space, Equipment, " International
    Journal of Religious Education (October 1966), pp. 8-9.

Johnson, Marian.   "Trinity Parish Library; Trinity Lutheran Church,
    St. Peter, Minnesota, " Church and Synagogue Libraries IV
    (March 1970), pp. 5-6.

Klammer, Gary.   "One Library Best for Parish, School, " Lutheran
    Education Association News (St. Louis, Lutheran Church-Mis-
    souri Synod) (November 1976), p. 3.

Lundeen, Lorriane. "The Church Library and You," Lutheran Wom-
en (November 1960), pp. 27-28.

Storaasli, Alida. "The Role of the Church Library," Scope (Minneapolis, American Lutheran Church Women) (April 1975), pp.
38-39.

Stupp, Irene M. "The Church Library Can Use Other Library Resources," International Journal of Religious Education (October
1966), p. 18.

Newspaper Articles

"Church Libraries More than Pius Tomes," by Joan Bastel. Man-
kato (Minn.) Free Press. (April 5, 1976), (Accent page), p. 7.

"In Ten Years Church Library Grows to National Recognition."
Minneapolis Star. (Friday, January 10, 1969), (Women's News
Section), p. 88.

Encyclopedias

Encyclopedia of Library and Information Science. New York: Marcel Dekker, 1975. "Lutheran Church Library Association" by
Marian Johnson XVI, pp. 363-366.

Encyclopedia of the Lutheran Church. Philadelphia: Fortress Press
(and Minneapolis: Augsburg), 1965. "Christian Education: Libraries for Church Schools" by Donald W. Prigge, I, pp. 441-
442.

Encyclopedia of the Lutheran Church. Philadelphia: Fortress Press
(and Minneapolis: Augsburg), 1965. "Libraries in Lutheran
Churches" by Marian Johnson, II, pp. 1289-1290.

Yearbook

Bowker Annual of Library and Book Trade Information. New York:
R. R. Bowker Company. 1973- . "Lutheran Church Library
Association."

Books and Pamphlets

Huebner, Mary. "The Parish Resource Center," St. Louis: LC-MS,
Board of Parish Education. March 1976. (Performing our
Patterns, #19).

Jensen, Wilma A. "The Church Library: Organization and Administration," Minneapolis: Lutheran Church Library Association,
rev. 1976. 6 p. (mimeo).

John, Erwin E. "The Key to a Successful Church Library," Minneapolis: Augsburg, 1967. 47 p.

Johnson, Marian. "Promoting Your Church Library," Minneapolis:
  Augsburg, 1968. 48 p.

Paul, A. Curtis. "Church Library Workshops and Their Effect on
  Church Libraries," Master's Thesis, University of Minnesota,
  1968.

NOTES

1. First Lutheran Church Library, Ottumwa, Iowa.
2. Johnson, Marian, "Libraries in Lutheran Churches," In: Encyclopedia of the Lutheran Church, J. Bodensieck, ed., Minneapolis: Augsburg, 1965. II, p. 1289.
3. Jensen, Wilma W., The Church Library: Organization and Administration, Minneapolis: Lutheran Church Library Association, 1963, rev. 1976, p. 1.
4. Johnson, Marian, Planning and Furnishing the Church Library,
   Minneapolis: Augsburg, 1966.
   Johnson, Marian, Promoting Your Church Library, Minneapolis:
   Augsburg, 1968.
5. "Book Fairs," Service Bulletin of the Lutheran Church Library
   Association, no. 17.
6. Bartz, Mrs. Albert E., "Six Churches Cooperate to Form Audio-
   visual Resource Center", Lutheran Libraries XIV (Fall 1972),
   pp. 98-99.
7. Prigge, Donald W., "Christian Education: Libraries for Church
   Schools", In: Encyclopedia of the Lutheran Church, J. Bodensieck, ed., Minneapolis: Augsburg, 1965, I, p. 441.
8. "Small Church Library Becomes Resource Center for Community," Lutheran Libraries XVIII (Summer, 1976), pp. 52-55.
9. Ulland, Rose Mary, "First Lutheran, Eau Claire, Wisconsin,
   Demonstrates Library Use in Education," Lutheran Libraries
   XIV (Fall 1972), pp. 92-95.

SOUTHERN BAPTIST CHURCH LIBRARIES

Wayne E. Todd

History and Mission

In giving the chronology of Southern Baptist church libraries, we see that the Southern Baptist Convention, established in 1845, moved early to support church libraries.

1866   Records show that the Southern Baptist Convention wanted some "library books" published.

1892   The Sunday School Board came into being with clearly defined responsibilities. One instruction was to make a list of books that could be recommended to the Sunday Schools.

1927   The Sunday School Department of the Sunday School Board saw that the churches needed guidance in organizing their libraries. One person was assigned on a part-time basis to develop church library concepts and material. Marie Estes Stopher and Leona Lavender Althoff, respectively, filled the Sunday School Department post for several years.

1937   Convention Press published The Church Library Manual by Leona Lavender Althoff.

1941   The Church Library Bulletin, a mailout to churches, published its first issue in July, 1941.

1943   The Church Library Service was organized with Miss Florida Waite as the first secretary. Its work grew and soon the pattern was established of one new church library begun, on the average, for each day of the year.

1947   The first Associational Library Council was established in the St. Louis (Missouri) Association. An Associational Council consists of several persons in a given geographical area banded together to foster library service development.

1959   After Miss Waite's retirement, a Mississippi pastor, Wayne E. Todd, became the second secretary of church library work. He brought men into the denominational promotion of the church library ministry.

114

1960   The Church Library Magazine began publication.

1962   The Sunday School Board changed the name from Church Li-
        brary Service to Church Library Department.   The name Li-
        brary Council was changed to the Associational Church Library
        Organization.

1963   The number of church libraries recorded totaled 10,000

1966   Responsibility for the program and promotion of audiovisual
        education was assigned to the Department.   Audiovisuals have
        long been an important part of the educational ministry.

1968   The Church Library Development Plan, Stages 1-3, were re-
        leased to train library workers in planning, organizing, pro-
        moting, and processing library media.

1969   Library Service in the Church, Convention Press, compiled
        by Wayne E. Todd, was released as a church library concept
        book.

1970   A new name with a new concept, Media: Library Services
        Journal replaced The Church Library Magazine.   Media seeks
        to convey the concept of the library as a unit designed for
        service to the entire church.   Library workers are aided
        with suggestions on how to provide a comprehensive collection
        of resource material and to develop skill among library users
        in proper media selection and utilization.   Expanding concepts
        of library services now include the addition of ordering, stor-
        ing, and distributing literature and of cataloging and housing
        the church's music.

1972   The number of church libraries registered with the Depart-
        ment totaled 20,000.

1973   The Department established and began operating model media
        centers at the Glorieta, N.M. and Ridgecrest, N.C. Con-
        ference Centers.

        How to Make Audiovisuals, Convention Press, by John Hack,
        was released.

1974   Media on the Move: Reaching Out with Resources, Convention
        Press, compiled by Wayne E. Todd, was released to encour-
        age church libraries to move beyond the four walls with re-
        sources.

1975   The Media Center Serving a Church, Convention Press, by
        Wayne E. Todd, was released to convey the need and know-
        how to update library service.

1976   The Learning Team: The Learner, the Leader, and the Li-
        brary, Convention Press, by Keith Mee, was released. This

work was designed to aid members in developing skill in
using media in leading, learning, teaching, and witnessing.
The Baptist Sunday School Board gave the assignment of
Tract Development and Distribution to the Department to be
administered as a suggested expansion of library service in
the churches.

The First National Library Week/Church Library Emphasis
promotion kit was released with the theme, "Reading Rings
the Bell. "

1977   The second annual National Library Week/Church Library
        Emphasis promotion kit was released under the theme, "See
        America ... the Media Way. " A 54 frame Broadman film-
        strip, The Church Media Center, became available. This
        filmstrip with cassette and manual presents an overview of
        all areas of church media center work.

1978   Three new books, How To Administer and Promote a Church
        Media Center; How to Process Media; and How to Classify,
        Catalog and Maintain Media were released. These books,
        published by Broadman, make up The Church Media Center
        Development Plan and replace The Church Library Develop-
        ment Plan. A set of four cassette tapes with worksheets
        were also released. These tapes, known as the "Media Cen-
        ter Techniques Series, " relate to classification, cataloging,
        subject cataloging, and cross references.

The National Library Week/Church Library Emphasis promotion kit for 1978 featured the theme "Enrich Family Living...the Media Way. "

The history of church library work among Southern Baptists
is a long and lustrous one.   Search efforts by the Baptist Sunday
School Board's Church Library Department have brought responses
such as the one from Olivet Baptist Church, Beaverdam, Virginia,
which indicated that they had a circulating library as early as 1850.
Another church reported an April, 1854, resolution to form a library of books of the Baptist order.   Word came from the First
Baptist Church in Richmond, which indicated that their library was
started in 1820.

The function of a library is to be the church's arm in encouraging the use of that material of instruction, information, and
inspiration which should lead toward Christian maturity.   Whatever
this statement may lack, it is of such solid construction as to apply
to the first Southern Baptist Sunday School library of the early 1800's
and to Southern Baptist church media center/libraries of the last
quarter of the 20th century.

Scope and Characteristics

Smallness in numbers describes 22, 479 out of 34, 902 Southern

Baptist churches. Two thirds of them contain fewer than 300 members. Obviously, however, smallness is not a deterrent to growing a dynamic church. Many of these small churches are indeed great. Smallness is not a barrier to churches with vision. Twenty-five percent of the small churches in open country and villages report having a library. Many of them have fine libraries. Obviously, they have overcome the handicap of a small congregation and small church budget by convincing church authorities of the importance of library service.

Some which started small have become large. Among the "small beginners" are Two Rivers and Woodmont Baptist Churches in Nashville. The Two Rivers Library was started in simple boxes on the first Sunday of full church activities in 1962. Fifteen years later, Two River's membership totaled 3,000, its Sunday School attendance averaged 1,400, and the church maintained two libraries in two locations in the building complex.

Woodmont Baptist Church began its library work in 1947, soon after the church was organized, in an out-of-the-way room under the stairs. The services performed were so significant that the church agreed to give it prime space in a new building. Today, the library has grown into a model media center consisting of a comprehensive collection of print and non-print items, operating by a committed and capable staff, open and active on a maximum service schedule.

From the smallest to the largest church, there is both a need and a possibility for having a functioning library. First Baptist Church, Dallas, with 19,000 members, represents the position taken by larger churches concerning library support. Occupying a suite of rooms and staffed by several paid librarians, this media center is at work relating resource material to persons and programs every day with special night hours scheduled for Bible Institute students.

Library Personnel

The nominating committee working with the pastor should seek the best qualified person--man or woman--to serve as Media Center Director. This person should encourage the church to see the potential of a complete media center and to enlist additional staff members. The organization responsible for operating the media center/library is called the "media center/library staff." The staff should consist of dedicated, patient, tactful persons who are loyal church members and willing learners.

The size of the media center staff should be determined by the vision of church leaders, the number of services offered, the variety of material to be handled, the amount of financial support, and the time, devotion, and ability of the workers. Most important of all, staff size should be determined by the congregation size and their demand for service. It will be advantageous, after careful

study and analysis, for each library staff to have an organization
chart of its own operation so that each staff member can see how he
or she fits into the overall picture

        Each position on the chart represents groupings of similar
functions.   In practice, any individual in a given position will probably help in other areas but the primary concern will be the assignment represented by the position on the organization chart shown
opposite.

        The Media Center Director serves on the church council and
in other capacities where church programs are coordinated.   This
person plans for and coordinates staff training and meetings, leads
in planning and evaluating media center services, supervises all
directors of specialized activities, and reports to the church on library services.   Even when a full-time paid Media Center Director
is employed, a volunteer staff is still needed.

        The Circulation Director has responsibility for all activities
required to keep material or equipment in circulation.

        Since the Processing Director performs or leads in completing
all processing operations, he or she should learn library techniques,
be careful with details and develop a systematic approach to processing and cataloging media.   He or she should think logically and
follow printed directions.   The Church Media Center Development
Plan has been created to meet the needs of staff persons whose library training and experience are limited, and, like the other publications mentioned in this paper, was published by the Southern
Baptist Convention Church Library Department.

        Media must be kept in usable condition.   The Media Mainten-
ance Director is in charge of care and repair tasks on all media,
including books, audiovisual material, and equipment.   The Media
Education Director supervises the process of educating members
and leaders in the use of the various media.

        Media center promotion involves activities which inform
church leaders and members of available media and services and
encourages theis use.   Information may be found in Promotional
Ideas for Church Libraries.   The Special Services Director works
with projects which relate to collections of circulating media designated for a specific use.   For example, the media center may handle
church literature, work with the pastor's library, keep study course
records, or maintain the music library.   The persons designated as
"directors" on the media center staff make up the media center
council.   This group meets regularly to plan media center activities.
The council is presided over by the Media Center Director to whom
other council members are responsible.

Library Finance

        A budget, representing money available for media and services,

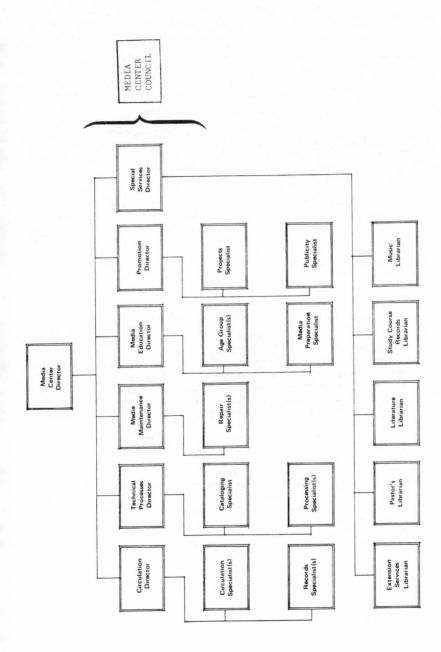

is necessary for the effective operation of a church media center.
Though some money may come from gifts and other sources, the
regular church budget should be the major source for media center
funds.   The following areas should be considered in a budget being
planned.   Types of media center material should be evaluated, quantities of new items (print and non-print) projected, and costs determined.   A media center staff needs continued training for effective
service.   Training opportunities should be planned in the annual
budget.

        A budget and financial page is included in each annual issue
of the Church Media Center Record and Plan Book.   A similar one
is reproduced here (see page 121) as an example of the way a budget may be itemized, records kept for the current year and projected
for the coming year.

        Some media center staffs request funds on a per capita basis,
usually fifty cents to one dollar for each church member.   Other
churches have followed the formula of one-half of one percent of the
total annual church budget as a fair amount for the media center.
Whatever the system followed by the church in budget building,
making purchases, and paying for items received, the library staff
members should work within the guidelines.

Library Collection

        Guidelines are followed in every area of life.   The church
library must keep in mind the tastes, needs, and wishes of its
users.   The church library is to provide tools for all church workers.   The library staff selects material to help all workers prepare
themselves in their areas of responsibility.   The church library
provides resources for extending all teaching-learning processes.
The staff should select material to assist workers and class members to prepare for and go beyond group study periods.   With the
new teaching methods, rapid advances in teaching-learning media,
and the enlarging stores of knowledge, churches must provide material to keep Christian education current.

        The church library supplies help for everyday living.   Li-
brary staff members should seek material which church members
can use as personal and particular needs arise.   Staff members
may be involved in visitations, also.   A key step in visitation involves "finding a point-of-contact. "   Possible point-of-contact situations may be divided into three sections: events, interests, and
circumstances.   Regardless of the situation, certainly there are
some library items related to it.   Church visitors should become
skillful in matching material with people's concerns.

Physical Quarters

        A library that is attractive, easy to find, simple to use and

BUDGET AND FINANCIAL RECORD

Be specific in making budget requests. The following form may be an aid in planning budget needs. For special areas such as redecorating or enlarging the room, make a separate request. Some churches are using the suggestion of 50¢ to $1.00 for materials for each person enrolled in Sunday School as the annual budget amount.

	Amt. Budget This Year	Amount Spent This Year												Needed Next Year
		Oct.	Nov.	Dec.	Jan.	Feb.	Mar.	Apr.	May	June	July	Aug.	Sept.	
Books:														
Ages 3-7														
Ages 8-11														
Youth and Adult														
Audiovisuals:														
Materials:														
Filmstrips														
Slides														
Motion Picture Rental														
Nonprojected Aids														
Recordings														
Tapes														
Cassette tapes														
*Equipment:														
New Equipment:														
Maintenance														
Supplies														
**Media Center Meetings														
TOTAL														

*Some churches provide for audiovisual equipment and maintenance in a general church fund. Furnishings, such as shelving and files, should also be covered in this way.

**Many churches have a general convention and conference fund covering regional, state, and Convention-wide meetings.

efficiently laid out encourages effective utilization of its resources.
A church provides media center service in order to meet the needs
of its people for printed and audiovisual material. The space needs
should be measured by the total number of persons to be served
rather than the number of books and audiovisuals presently owned.
The media center room should be rectangular in shape, in the proportion of 3 by 5, and with sufficient wall space to allow for shelving. In churches with more than 250 members, it is wise to provide at least one square foot of floor space for each church member.
If the media center handles church literature and operates a media
preparation area, as much as $1\frac{1}{2}$ square feet per church member
should be considered. The space for public use is the area most
often identified as the "media center." In this area, the book
shelves, vertical file, audiovisual material, card catalogs, and circulation desk are located.

Consideration should be given to providing space--either in
the library or in an adjacent room--for media preparation, study,
and previewing audiovisuals. A media preparation area is a place
where teaching aids and other items may be made. A section of
the main media center room may be partitioned for this service, a
separate room may be provided, or workroom space can be used.
Many materials are being produced which employ programmed instruction techniques. Multimedia kits including pictures, workbooks,
cassette tapes, slides, filmstrips and other types of media should
be provided by the media center. Individual study activities are
enhanced when study carrels or booths equipped for using tapes, recordings, slides, and filmstrips are provided.

Every media center should have a growing collection of large,
bulky items to be stored. Examples are puppets, audiovisual equipment, floral arrangements, framed pictures, and mounted maps.
These items are kept for circulation, but ordinarily they are not
used for public display. Space for their safe storage and easy location is needed. Because of heavy storage needs, dated church
literature and music material require adequate space. Since neither
one of these considerations involves open circulation in the same
sense as books or audiovisuals, space needs are somewhat different.
In most cases, the music material will be stored near the music
suite or the music director's office. Church literature may be kept
in a cabinet in the main media center or in a room nearby.

Since much library staff work is done out of public view,
space must be provided for these behind-the-scenes activities. This
space will allow for processing and cataloging books and audiovisuals as well as for the repair and maintenance of material and
equipment. Poorly located rooms will seriously limit the service
offered. Some persons have identified the best library location as
being at the corner of "Main and Broadway." In most church buildings, this logical place would be at the intersection of the educational
facility and the auditorium. Overall lighting of at least 30 footcandles should be provided. Study areas should have at least 60-80
footcandles of light. Library floors may be of bare hardwood or

MODEL MEDIA CENTER FLOOR PLAN

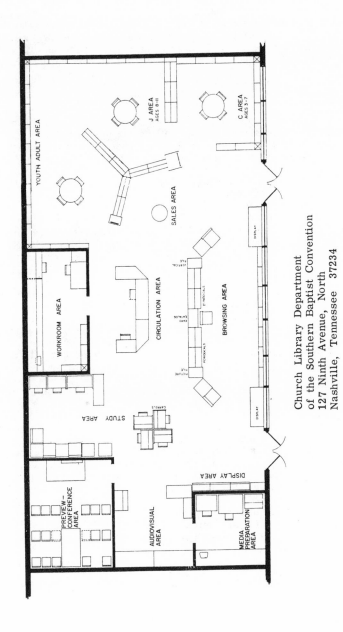

Church Library Department
of the Southern Baptist Convention
127 Ninth Avenue, North
Nashville, Tennessee 37234

covered with carpet, asphalt, or vinyl tile. The walls should be of smooth-finish plaster or sheetrock and painted in a pastel shade in washable, flat, or semigloss paint, with light reflecting value of not less than 50 percent. Ceilings of acoustical material with light reflecting value of not less than 65 percent are recommended.

Services

        Library staff members starting and expanding a library should institute those services which will be the most helpful to their churches. The following services are being offered in many churches and are desirable parts of the church library program:

   a. Guided Study Programs
   b. Hobby Centers
   c. Innovative Educational Technology
   d. Special Services. The library may be used as the main
         ministry to the deaf. It may purchase Bibles in braille
         economically from the American Bible Society. Books
         on the Bible, devotional and religious books may be
         borrowed from the Braille Circulating Library, Inc.,
         2700 Stuart Avenue, Richmond, Virginia 23200. Cur-
         riculum material in braille may be obtained free from
         the Sunday School Board in Nashville, and large print
         books may be secured from book stores. Libraries may
         provide material for parents and teachers of mentally
         retarded children, as well as for the exceptional children
         themselves. "Good News for New Readers" is a program
         sponsored by the American Bible Society which makes
         available carefully graded selections from Scripture pas-
         sages that will help beginning readers through the early
         stages of reading.
   e. Media in Counseling
   f. Public Media Preparation Area
   g. Mediagraphies. Mediagraphies are comprehensive lists of
         library material--usually limited to a specific subject,
         age group, or purpose. When mediagraphies are dis-
         tributed, one copy should be kept at the circulation desk
         and another copy near the card catalog.
   h. Memorial selections
   i. Public Mending Service
   j. Promotion of Church Events
   k. Telephone and Mail Information Service
   l. Sale Items
   m. Story and Film Hours
   n. Cassette Taping Service
   o. Reading Improvement Programs
   p. A Referral Information File

Relationship to the Minister, the Director of Christian
Education, and the Church School

As the church media center, library services should make
available to all leaders all the printed and audiovisual resources
necessary for all teaching, training, learning and ministering functions. The minister's time available for counseling is limited; and
his understanding of the church library is often inadequate. He
must learn that a book can go places where a pastor cannot and it
can stay longer. He should form an alliance with the church library staff which can provide significant privileges: 1) he can pull
from the shelves books related to the immediate need; and 2) he can
send persons to the library with a request for specific titles.

Often the pastor's routine visitation will reveal that a tre-
mendous vacuum exists in lives and that his simple "visits" do not
necessarily mean that an adequate ministry is being performed.
This realization should lead him, as he makes his "house calls, "
to take along library items speaking to personal needs.

The traditional approach to witnessing is worthwhile, but
frequently persons feel that the pastor sees them simply as "join-
ers. " More time is required than he can give to vitally relate to
individuals and to allow for the most effective presentation of the
gospel.   This situation should lead to the method of "cultivation
visitation. " In this approach, on the initial visit, the pastor should
observe family needs and interests. On subsequent visits, he should
relate with a library item, to these needs or interests. Titles
employed can cover popular concerns, such as athletics, hobbies,
occupations, and problems. This fresh communication of concern
on the pastor's part, made possible by committed librarians, will
often cause "prospects" to make the response, "He cares about me
as a person. "

A partnership is essential for an education program of excellence. Suggestions for support of the Director of Christian Education are the following: 1) Give guided study; 2) create home
study centers; 3) demonstrate innovative educational technology; 4)
plan a media preparation area; 5) present mediagraphies; 6) guide
in reading improvement efforts; 7) arrange for story and film hours;
8) offer church literature handling services; 9) check equipment out
on permanent loan; 10) provide media education; 11) furnish media
for preschool and children's departments; 12) allow for preview
sessions; 13) assist small study groups; 14) establish special loan
policies for leaders; 15) keep study course records; 16) sponsor
Vacation Bible School reading clubs; 17) supply vocational guidance
material.

Suggestions for Director of Christian Education support of
the media center are the following:

1. Include the media center in planning meetings
    a.   Church council

        b. Organizational councils
        c. Church staff
        d. Special

    2. Set example in personal opportunities
        a. Mention at appropriate times in writing and speaking
        b. Use media in presentations
        c. Use media in personal study programs
        d. Learn and follow library rules and systems
        e. Recommend specific media for the collection

    3. Support development of the media center staff
        a. Encourage a unified media center staff
        b. Lead nominating committee to fill vacancies and sup-
            port expansions
        c. Enlist media center staff to participate in training
            opportunities
        d. Provide training tools

    4. Support development of media center facilities
        a. Unify facilities
        b. Locate centrally
        c. Enlarge to enable variety of services
        d. Encourage attractive appearance

    5. Encourage adequate financial resources
        a. Lead budget committee to include a library section
        b. Suggest a formula basis for the budget amount
        c. Request media center director to provide itemized
            request
        d. Provide opportunity for director to present budget to
            committee

    6. Include media center in calendar, papers, and reports
        a. Request report in monthly business meeting
        b. Provide regular space in church paper
        c. Include hours in weekly schedule of activities
        d. Encourage an annual media center emphasis week

        As an educator, the effective church school teacher knows
that material must be available to accommodate everyone involved
in the church school's teaching-learning process.   Like other institutions, churches can best handle this assignment through a library.

Relationship to Baptist Publishing Houses and Religious Journals

        The Church Library Department, Broadman Press and Con-
vention Press are members of the Baptist Sunday School Board family.   It is possible, therefore, for the personnel of the three components to work closely together in the entire publishing process.
The Church Library Department suggests to Broadman and Convention Presses certain titles and content for publication, reviews and

evaluates manuscript drafts, assigns technical information, and
projects mediagraphies which include all pertinent information needed
to assist librarians to evaluate, secure, and process the library
additions.

A Typical Southern Baptist Church Library

Beyond the factor of personal dedication, other characteristics
of a typical Southern Baptist Church Library are 1) Operates under
church control; 2) Supported through church budget and memorial
gifts; 3) Has four staff members, none with professional education--
average age 45; 4) Staff receives training through Church Library
Department publications, workshops, clinics, and conferences; 5)
Open on Sunday mornings and evenings and on Wednesday evenings;
6) Has an inventory of 1, 000 book and audiovisual titles; 7) Buys
new material several times a year.

The Church Library Department of the Southern Baptist Convention

The purpose of the Church Library Department which was
adopted by the Baptist Sunday School Board and approved by the
Southern Baptist Convention was the following: to develop service
and material acceptable for use by Southern Baptist churches, associations, and state conventions in establishing, conducting, enlarging, and improving the church library services of providing and
promoting the use of printed and audiovisual media and consulting
with church leaders and members in media use.

In accomplishing its objectives, the Department, consisting
of fourteen employees, provides in-house and on-the-site consultative
services; publishes a quarterly periodical called Media: A Library
Services Journal designed to include inspirational and informational
features plus technical guidance and program-related mediagraphies
and other updating aids; makes available The Church Media Center
Development Plan, a self help system, and other library service
products; operates model church media centers in the national
Glorieta, New Mexico and Ridgecrest, North Carolina Southern
Baptist Conference Centers; conducts national church library conferences at Glorieta and Ridgecrest; provides a package of free library material, valued at $35, to every Southern Baptist Church
which starts library service; and makes available to church libraries
annual planning and achievement guides.

On August 1, 1978, a total of 24, 084 Southern Baptist churches, including some duplication, had registered their libraries with
the Church Library Department in Nashville. To register, a library
need send only its name and address plus the librarian's name to
the Southern Baptist offices in Nashville. Since 1960, the registration process has qualified an average of 1, 000 libraries annually
for receiving the Free Media Offer starter kit and/or guidance material for starting, strengthening, and expanding library service.

Relationship to the National Southern Baptist Convention Leadership

The Southern Baptist Convention is made up of 35, 000 autonomous churches of like mind and faith which have chosen to work together to accomplish cooperatively what one church could not do alone. The chief executive officers of the respective agencies constitute the Inter-Agency Council. Meeting two to four times annually, this Council plans for the agencies' mutual and supportive efforts and considers detailed projects proposed by program representatives. The various program leaders, described as the Coordinating Committee, meet two to four times annually to do extensive and in depth cooperative planning.

The Church Library Services leader is a regular participant in the periodic planning sessions. He focuses attention on the potential plans and proposals for integrating library service and other church programs. An example of implementation of agreed upon approaches for making library service an integral part of Bible Study and Christian Training appears regularly in Media: Library Services Journal. Under the heading, "Media for ...., " the periodical carries a mediagraphy of print and non-print program-related library resources. The titles listed have been selected by denominational Sunday School and Church Training program writers to support the studies suggested for the forthcoming quarter. Subsequently, Church Library Department personnel have assigned cataloging information to each title. The respective programs in turn list the same titles in their appropriate publications. This cooperative planning by national leaders makes possible the most effective work of the learning team (the learner, the leader, and the library) in the local churches.

Among Southern Baptists, the future of church library work is bright. The ever enlarging concept of its potential in comprehensive collections and expanding services makes the library ministry an essential element in the life and work of a growing and ministering church.

LIBRARIES OF THE CHURCH OF JESUS CHRIST
OF LATTER-DAY SAINTS

David M. Mayfield and LaMond F. Beatty

The church of Jesus Christ of Latter-day Saints was organized April 6, 1830, in Fayette, New York, under direction of the Prophet Joseph Smith. Smith's claims of having visions and experiencing other heavenly manifestations incited persecution which forced the "Mormons," as the Latter-day Saints were called, to move from New York and establish headquarters in Kirtland, Ohio, where they built their first temple in 1836. Shortly thereafter, increased persecution drove the members still further west.

From Ohio, the main body of the Church first moved to Missouri, and later to Illinois, where in 1839 the Mormons established the community of Nauvoo. Under Joseph Smith's leadership, beautiful homes and businesses sprang up in an area that was once only swampland. At Nauvoo, for a brief period, the Latter-day Saints lived in peace and enjoyed as rich a social and cultural life as any frontier community of that time. Early in 1844, the Seventies, laymen whose Church assignment is to conduct missionary work, constructed a two-story building in which to improve their teaching and preaching skills. Office space and the "Seventies library" occupied the second floor. Local Seventies requested the townspeople, as well as members of their quorum, to donate books which would contribute to the cultural improvement of the citizens. An early apostle of the Church noted that the Seventies in foreign lands would have ample opportunities to gather "antiquities . . . books, charts, etc., to deposit in the library."[1] Another Church leader suggested that the Seventies were laying the foundation for the "best library in the world."[2] Six hundred and seventy-five books were cataloged for the Seventies library during the first three months of 1845.

The year 1845, however, was a time of increasing difficulties for the Mormons. A few months earlier, Joseph Smith and his brother, Hyrum, had been unmercifully martyred at Carthage, Illinois. Thereafter, mob violence became almost incessant. Crops were burned, homes destroyed, and the very lives of the people were threatened. By midwinter, 1846, the Mormons were being forced to flee across the Mississippi and to begin their modern-day exodus to a "promised land."

Brigham Young succeeded Joseph Smith to the leadership of

the Church and led his people some 1,100 miles across the vast
desert plains to the Rocky Mountains. The first pioneer company
arrived in the valley of the Great Salt Lake in July 1847. Six
months later Church leaders issued a general epistle which contained
instructions to prepare future emigrant companies for the arduous
trek. Interestingly, the epistle closed with an earnest appeal for
all to carry "what books and valuable treatises they have" for use
in their new homes:

> It is very desirable that all the saints should improve
> every opportunity of securing at least a copy of every
> valuable treatise on education, every book, map, chart,
> diagram that may contain interesting, useful, and attractive
> matter, to gain the attention of children, and cause them
> to love to learn to read. [3]

Many families obeyed this admonition. One company of emigrants
that came to Utah in 1850 boasted of having a library in every wag-
on. [4]

        In tracing the evolution of early libraries in The Church of
Jesus Christ of Latter-day Saints after its settlement in the West,
it may be helpful to briefly explain the Church's organizational
structure. The First Presidency, the Council of the Twelve Apostles, and other General Authorities govern the universal body of the
Church. Under their direction are the stake and ward organizations
which are roughly comparable to the diocese and parish, except that
the Mormon units are usually smaller. In mission areas, the stakes
and wards are replaced by districts and branches.

        The stake is presided over by a president with two counselors
and the high council, an advisory group to the stake presidency.
Each stake is divided into four to ten wards, which are the basic
geographical units of Mormon Church life. The ward is presided
over by a bishop, an unpaid part-time official who supervises all
organizations at the ward level with the aid of his two counselors.

        The Church is composed of, and presided over, by laymen.
Every worthy male member, twelve years of age and older, has the
privilege of being ordained to some office in the priesthood. This
priesthood structure is subdivided into quorums which, to a limited
extent, are age graded and which form a progression in the Church.
In addition to the priesthood quorums, the Church sponsors a number of auxiliary organizations: the Sunday School, the women's Relief Society, the Primary Association, and the Young Men and Young
Women's Mutual Improvement Associations. These bodies are organized on ward, stake, and general levels, their structures meshing
with the structure of the Church on all three levels.

        During the latter half of the nineteenth century, libraries,
under the auspices of the Sunday Schools, Young Men or Young
Women's organizations, or Relief Societies, were established in
almost every Utah ward. Their collections, however, were not

always of a strictly religious nature. The old Salt Lake Twelfth
War library, whose books were in use as early as 1855, contained
many of the world's classics. Other ward libraries frequently contained historical material, general reference books, and selected
fiction. Significantly, many of Utah's earliest public libraries trace
their origin to these early Mormon ward collections. For example,
the young people's Mutual Improvement Association of the Lehi, Utah,
Ward operated a "public library" until 1910 when the city levied a
tax for its support. Brigham City's public library began in the
same way when the Mutual Improvement Association library and
reading room were given to the city in 1913. A stake library opened
in downtown Salt Lake City in November 1887. [5] Three-month membership certificates, costing fifty cents, provided access to 500 volumes, including leading periodicals and the daily newspapers. The
Salt Lake Stake library existed until 1897 when the books became
part of the Salt Lake City Public Library.

The establishment of a general Sunday School Union in 1867
provided impetus for the development of the ward Sunday School library program. The founding minutes indicate that the first committee appointed was to decide upon books suitable for Sunday School
libraries. Five years after the organization of the Sunday School
Union, there were 8,645 books in the libraries of the 149 schools
reporting--an average of fifty-eight books per library. [6] In 1876,
the Deseret Sunday School Union general board issued a circular
letter which set forth "Rules for the Guidance of Sunday School,"
stating that a librarian, responsible for preserving and making available the books, was essential in every complete Sunday School organization. Reading in the Sunday Schools was to be confined insofar
as possible to Church works. Following the reading exercises,
books used by each class were to be kept together by strap and
buckle with the number of the class marked on the strap. [7]

At the turn of the century, the Young Ladies Mutual Improvement Association inaugurated a type of interlibrary loan service.
Under the direction of the YLMIA general board, traveling libraries
were instituted in the various stake organizations. The plan was
for each stake to select books to fill one or more boxes, which
could be sent from ward to ward, and from town to town, as they
were read and then passed along. The YLMIA's library committee
noted that "many wards have libraries, but the books, being once
read, are left idle on the shelves. By boxing them up, and sending
them out, they become useful again, while another lot of books from
a neighboring ward finds eager readers in the first association." [8]
By 1908, thirty-seven stakes had well-established traveling libraries
and more than 2,400 books were in circulation. Stake librarians
were instructed to offer variety in their selection of books for distribution. Each box should contain "at least one faith-promoting
book, one on history or poetry, three on fiction, and one of general
information." [9] Ward librarians were accountable for having the
books read, taken care of, and returned promptly.

Although the auxiliary organizations continued to support

separate library programs into the early twentieth century, the concept of a single-ward library, administered by Sunday School personnel, became increasingly prevalent. An example of the interest in this new direction is evidenced in a letter sent to the Deseret Sunday School Union general board in 1912 from Church leaders in Idaho Falls, Idaho. The local leadership specifically sought permission for the libraries in each ward to be consolidated into one general library for all the organizations. [10]

Increasingly, the Sunday School board provided the leadership for strengthening and upgrading Church library services. In 1915, the general board's library committee recommended that the monthly issue of the Juvenile Instructor (the official Sunday School magazine) devote space to the work of Sunday School libraries. The committee further suggested that pictures, illustrating Sunday School lessons, be reproduced in the center of the magazine so that they could be torn out, mounted, and filed in local Sunday School libraries for future reference. Insufficient funds delayed the implementation of these recommendations, but both were eventually adopted. The general board also encouraged the development of library services at Church headquarters to accommodate its own needs. Thus, when the board moved into the new Church administration building in 1917, a small library and reading room occupied part of its office space.

Early in the 1930s the general board's library committee inaugurated a program which influenced library services in the Church for the next thirty-five years. In brief, the committee suggested the following: (1) that a comprehensive educational campaign be launched, using every practical medium available, i.e., the Instructor, the lessons, Sunday School conventions, circulars, the press, and the radio, to develop an incessant demand for the services of qualified librarians, with the goal of providing one in every Sunday School of the Church; 2) that an organizational structure for the library program be established at the general, stake, and ward levels of the Church with representatives at each level from the other departments of the Sunday School serving in an advisory capacity to the library personnel; and (3) that the general board's library committee prepare a list of books and other pertinent material to provide a minimum content for ward libraries. Ward and stake librarians were to make a survey of existing facilities and undertake through proper channels to establish serviceable libraries throughout the Church. Moreover, Church members were asked to donate past issues of Church magazines to ward librarians in order to make this material available for general distribution. [11]

An example of the impact of the library committee's campaign was the program undertaken by the Adams Ward in the Los Angeles Stake. [12] Local members staged a vaudeville, "The Library High Jinks," in the ward amusement hall. The event was well advertised, and exacted, as a price of admission, some contribution to the library, such as books, Church magazines, pictures, library equipment, or cash. Articles which were especially needed were

listed and a copy in letter form was mailed to each family in the
ward.   The event resulted in the receipt of 213 books, 536 magazines, numerous pictures, many pieces of library equipment, and
some cash.   The Sunday School superintendency had been given the
responsibility of organizing the library, but it was established for
the benefit of the officers, teachers, and members of the entire
ward.   It was staffed by six librarians, one representing the Sunday
School and one for each of the auxiliary organizations.   They kept
the library open whenever there were meetings or other activities
in the ward.   The success of the Adams Ward library was widely
publicized and served to stimulate similar efforts elsewhere.

The Adams Ward developed a plan which subsequently was
adopted as a suggested procedure for all ward libraries.   In essence,
the "Adams plan" was as follows: the librarian ascertained in advance what lessons were to be given to each age group on a particular Sunday.   She then drew from her files pictures, references, and
other material which she felt would enrich each class's lesson.   On
the Sunday prior to the scheduled lesson presentations, the librarian
distributed to each teacher appropriate helps from the library.   At
the same time she checked in the material each teacher had used
for the previous lesson. [13]

The Adams plan was part of a larger movement to identify
ward librarians as "teaching aids specialists. "   As early as October
1930, the library committee of the Sunday School general board
recommended the appointment of assistant librarians in each unit to
take care of "all the teaching equipment, such as maps and pictures,
and to make them available as needed. "[14]   This concept had become
fully established by the time the general board published its first
Sunday School Librarian's Guide Book in 1948.   The Guide Book contained detailed instructions for handling books, periodicals, pictures,
maps, charts, and numerous other teaching devices.   Additionally,
it offered helpful suggestions for obtaining library materials encouraging use of the library, and taking advantage of supplementary
sources.

Prior to the mid-1970s, the Guide Book was updated and
supplemented by frequent articles for librarians in the Sunday School's
monthly magazine, the Instructor.   These articles contained technical
instructions on mounting, classifying, and filing pictures.   They
frequently identified the qualities of successful librarians, emphasizing initiative, enthusiasm, experience, intelligence, discernment,
and the ability to work well with people.   The articles described
the steps which had been taken in various parts of the Church to
establish successful libraries.

In addition to the numerous articles for librarians in the
Instructor, occasional visual aid clinics have been held in conjunction
with the Sunday School's general conference meetings.   A model library was constructed for the April conference.   Several ward and
stake librarians had been asked to display simple and inexpensive
visual aids that could be easily duplicated.   The contributed objects

included pictures, grooved boards, a puppet show, an opaque projector, a shoebox theater, replicas of many kinds, a hectograph, dolls, maps, and charts, and samples of pioneer food. Copies of the architect's plan for the library, including material specifications for the cabinets, were made available to interested Sunday School workers. In addition, descriptions, specifications, and drawings of the various visual aids were mimeographed and distributed free of charge. The model library generated so much enthusiasm that it was subsequently put on permanent display at the Sunday School general offices in Salt Lake City. [15]

Church Meetinghouse Library Program

The most significant changes to date in the LDS Church library program commenced in February 1965, when the First Presidency announced the beginning of a correlated program for all libraries and library functions within the Church. In a meeting held in Salt Lake City, Utah, on December 30, 1964, Church leaders agreed that a system of ward libraries, stake libraries, and regional or multiregional libraries should be organized to serve all Church programs. These libraries should be under the administrative supervision of the bishops, stake presidents, and regional officers, rather than being under any auxiliary organization. [16]

The correlated Church library program was implemented so rapidly in the ward and stake meetinghouses that it became necessary to appoint a general Church committee to guide and direct this area of library activity. In March 1971, the Church Meetinghouse Library Committee was appointed. Members of the Committee included representatives from the general priesthood and auxiliary organizations as well as professional librarians, communication specialists, instructional material development specialists, and professionally trained personnel in the fields of educational media and systems development.

The objectives of the Committee, as written in 1971, were: (1) to direct the establishment of a single facility known as the meetinghouse library in each ward or stake meetinghouse, to acquire, organize, and make available instructional material and equipment used in the curriculum and activity programs of the Church; (2) to provide continuing instruction for the proper organization and operation of the meetinghouse library; (3) to maintain a model meetinghouse library where the optimum in library practice is demonstrated; (4) to maintain an up-to-date Instructional Materials Catalog as well as a yearly list of recommended instructional materials for use with specific Church instructional lessons; (5) to maintain an approved list of instructional equipment which can be purchased for meetinghouse libraries with Church headquarters financial participation; (6) to provide input to the Church Building Department in developing plans to accommodate adequate meetinghouse library facilities as well as input on design of classrooms, cultural halls, and chapels to facilitate the use of media; and (7) to correlate with other programs

of the Church in encouraging effective utilization of instructional
material in all programs of the Church. [17]

In 1975, the following additional objective was approved: (8)
to integrate the functions and activities of the branch genealogical
libraries, which the Genealogical Department of the Church had established in selected wards and stake centers, with the correlated
meetinghouse library program.   Thus, rather than functioning independently, the branch genealogical libraries would henceforth serve
as an integral part of the Church meetinghouse library program under the direction of the bishops and/or stake presidents where the
branch libraries were housed. [18]   In addition to the above objective,
approval has subsequently been obtained to provide genealogical library service in all of the stakes of the Church. [19]

The meetinghouse library organization is structured at the
ward, branch, stake, and district levels to provide a maximum of
service to individual Church members and to all Church-sponsored
organizations (Sunday School, women's Relief Society, priesthood
quorums, Boy Scouts of America).   At the stake level, the meetinghouse library organization is headed by a stake director of libraries.
The director reports to the high council adviser, who in turn keeps
the stake president informed concerning the stake's library program.
The stake president designates one meetinghouse library to house
stake instructional materials.   The stake director of meetinghouse
libraries provides the leadership, organizational direction, and assistance necessary to promote and sustain stakewide library services.

When more than one ward or branch occupies a building, a
library board consisting of the bishops of the wards using the building is organized with an agent bishop as chairman of the board.
However, when the meetinghouse library serves the stake, the stake
president is a member of the board and is the chairman, unless he
chooses to delegate this responsibility to one of the bishops.   The
library board establishes the policy for directing local meetinghouse
library functions.

The meetinghouse library staff consists of the meetinghouse
librarians, associate librarians, and assistant librarians (see Figure
1). [20]

The meetinghouse librarian directs all meetinghouse library
activities; trains and supervises library personnel; coordinates the
program with the library board and consults with the chairman regarding library policies and procedures; procures library material
by purchase, donation, or local production; directs the coding and
indexing of library material; evaluates the library's physical facilities
and suggests improvements; and consolidates and coordinates all orders from the individual organizations in the building for instructional
materials and supplies to avoid duplication.

The associate librarians--one for each ward, one for the
stake, one for an institute of religion, and one for genealogical

services (see Figure 1)--all serve under the direction of the meetinghouse librarian. The associate librarian operates the library as
assigned by the meetinghouse librarian; recommends, trains, and
supervises assistant librarians; and coordinates the use of library
material and equipment.

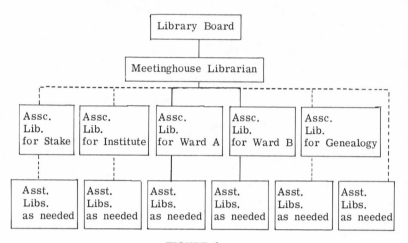

FIGURE 1.

Assistant librarians serve priesthood and auxiliary organizations. One assistant may serve one organization or several, or
several assistants may be required to serve one organization. The
genealogical program in the meetinghouse library may require the
services of many assistant librarians. Assistant librarians serve
under the direction of the meetinghouse librarian or the appropriate
associate librarian. Generally, they work closely with the organizations they are assigned to serve. However, they may be called
to coordinate music material for all organizations; to assist in the
maintenance and storage of motion picture films; to assist as librarians for equipment maintenance, storage, and distribution; and
to serve as librarians in noninstructional service programs (athletics,
Boy Scouts, etc.). Assistant librarians serve individuals as they
require equipment and materials for their personal or family needs.

The meetinghouse library staff functions on a voluntary,
service-oriented basis. No members of the library organization
receive monetary remuneration for their services. Many librarians
donate as much as twenty hours per week for upgrading classroom
instruction and personal development of individual members of the
Church as they seek to utilize library material.

The Church Meetinghouse Library Committee has prepared
numerous instructional materials to assist in the promotion of the
meetinghouse library and to provide training for librarians and

library patrons. Two sound filmstrips, which are widely used throughout the Church, have been remarkably successful: (1) The Meetinghouse Librarian was prepared to give an indepth overview of the role of the meetinghouse library and librarian; (2) Putting It All Together in the Meetinghouse Library was prepared to promote the implementation and utilization of the meethinghouse library. Both sound filmstrips are used in pre-service and in-service training of librarians and in the promotion of the meetinghouse library program.

An individualized, self-paced training manual has been prepared to provide a comprehensive inservice training program for all members of the meetinghouse library staff. The Meetinghouse Library Training Manual consists of four units: (1) "Administering the Church Meethinghouse Library Program, " consisting of ten lessons covering such topics as setting goals; establishing the library program; budgeting; coding and indexing; etc. ; (2) "Production of Instructional Materials, " consisting of fifteen lessons covering such topics as mounting pictures, charts, and maps; reducing and enlarging pictures; making transparencies; principles of lettering; making bulletin boards; flannelboards, etc. ; (3) "Care and Operation of Library Equipment, " consisting of sixteen lessons on how to operate and maintain filmstrip, slide, motion picture, overhead, and opaque projectors; reel-to-reel and cassette records; microform readers, infrared copiers; and the dry-mount press; (4) "Branch Genealogical Training, " consisting of ten lessons covering such topics as organization and administration; assisting patrons; the microfilm card catalog; ordering material and supplies, etc. Each lesson has an introduction, stated behavior objectives, material needed by the user to accomplish the objectives, detailed learning activities, and self-evaluation performance sheets.

A Manual for the Care and Circulation of Motion Picture Films has been prepared to assist in providing in-service training in this important aspect of library service. This manual includes instruction in the following areas: sources of instruction films, circulation policies and procedures, care and storage, cleaning and repairing, and maintenance record keeping.

The Church Meetinghouse Library Committee and the Building Division of the Church Department of Physical Facilities have worked jointly to provide the standard plan for a meetinghouse library in each Church building. The standard plan specifies a 14' x 18' room, containing shelves, counters, slots for library materials, and work space for the staff. [21] One or two adjoining classrooms are made available as workroom(s) or genealogical reading room(s).

The success of the meetinghouse library program is evidenced by the rapid implementation of this standard plan in the wards, stakes, and branches of the Church. No new buildings are approved for construction without the inclusion of the meetinghouse library. Moreover, the remodeling of present buildings to enlarge or include a meetinghouse library has top priority with the Church Building Department.

The costs of constructing meetinghouse libraries in new buildings and of remodeling to provide libraries in older buildings are shared jointly by Church headquarters and the local units. This joint participation is on a 70 percent to 30 percent basis for wards and stakes and an 80 percent to 20 percent basis for branches and districts--i. e. , Church headquarters provides 70 to 80 percent of the necessary funding and the local units provide the remaining 20 to 30 percent. Church headquarters also participates financially toward the purchase of equipment that is approved for the meeting-house library.

Resources

Purchases of library materials, supplies, and film rentals for the meetinghouse library are made entirely from the budget of the local units using the meetinghouse library. These funds come from the donations of the individual Church members. The annual library budget is prepared under the direction of the meetinghouse librarian, working with the associate librarians, assistant librarians, and priesthood and auxiliary leaders, for presentation to the library board. The library board (or bishop in a single ward, branch, or mission) reviews and approves the budget and expenditures. Gene-alogical services are funded by stake assessment or from priesthood quorum dues, as determined by the library board.

The meetinghouse library staff is responsible for procuring the library materials required to meet the needs of ward organiza-tions and Church members. A great many resources have been prepared to assist them in carrying out this responsibility. The basic tool available to the library staff for identifying and ordering, and to patrons for obtaining library material, is the Instructional Materials Catalog. This catalog, which was prepared by the Church Meetinghouse Library Committee, displays a miniature replica and written description of pictures, posters, books, charts, individual frames of filmstrips, overhead transparencies, basic flannelboard characters, maps, etc. , which are available from Church head-quarters for purchase and use in the meetinghouse library. The catalog also provides a description of cassette and reel-to-reel tapes, audio discs and dimensional materials. [22]

The Instructional Materials Catalog contains a subject index to all of the materials listed. By checking the index and then re-ferring to the respective replicas in the catalog, it is easy to identi-fy the material desired by a patron. The IMC provides precatalog-ing and indexing of all materials produced at Church headquarters. This saves thousands of man hours that would otherwise be required to catalog these materials individually in the more than 5, 000 units of the Church throughout the world. Items listed in the Instructional Materials Catalog are available for purchase from distribution cen-ters owned and operated by the Church.

The Church of Jesus Christ of Latter-day Saints publishes a

number of magazines and one newspaper that provide important
articles, reports, bibliographies, biographies, discourses, and practical daily advice for Church members.   The meetinghouse library
maintains a collection of this material for patron use.   An Index to
Periodicals of The Church of Jesus Christ of Latter-day Saints has
been published to assist in locating articles in Church periodicals.
The index is alphabetized by subject much like the Readers' Guide
to Periodical Literature and covers the period of January 1, 1961,
to December 31, 1975, in three volumes.

The Church publishes the Meetinghouse Library Handbook
which outlines the policies governing the meetinghouse library and
explains the organizational structure, financing, physical arrangements, promotion and use, and other operating procedures contributing to a successful library program.   The availability of new material, articles of special interest, instructions needed to clarify,
expand, or update the Meetinghouse Library Handbook, how-to-do-it
articles, and suggestions for improving the meetinghouse library
program are presented to the library staff through the bi-monthly
Meetinghouse Library Bulletin.   This bulletin is sent directly to
every stake president and ward bishop to be read and then delivered
to the meetinghouse librarian.   This routing assures that all members of the meetinghouse library staff and governing board members
are appraised of the latest ideas, innovations, and instructions for
operating the meetinghouse library.   A cumulative index to the Bulletin is available.

Library material must be identified and organized so it can
be located quickly and efficiently.   The Church Meetinghouse Library
Committee has developed a subject indexing system to identify and
locate each item housed in the meetinghouse library.   The system is
very simple and is correlated with the Instructional Materials Catalog.   It uses code letters to identify each category of instructional
material, e.g., IP--posters; MP--motion picture films; OC--charts,
flip charts, graphs; OH--overhead transparencies; OP--pictures,
etc.   Material assigned to a given alpha code is then given a number
in sequence to identify it from other items in that alpha code.   The
combined alpha code and serial number becomes the location and
retrieval number for each item, and thus becomes an integral part
of the printing, distribution, and filing of each item.

All numbers from 000 to 999 are reserved for materials
produced by the Church; numbers from 1000-up are used by the local
meetinghouse library to identify materials that have been locally
produced or secured.   The coding and indexing system on the local
level uses a "Code Serial Record Sheet" (see Figure 2) to record
these locally produced materials. [23]   The maintenance of these record
sheets provides a record of the items produced or procured locally
and a chronological listing of the materials.   This location code
system identifies each item uniquely and the specific location where
the item is filed in the meetinghouse library.

CODE SERIAL RECORD SHEET		
Serial Number	Most Obvious Title	Remarks (Subject Headings, Source, Number of Copies, etc.)

FIGURE 2

A Subject Heading List has been prepared by the Meetinghouse Library Committee to provide library personnel with standard subject headings for instructional materials.   A set of preprinted Subject Index Cards to the material listed in the IMS, designed to form the basis of the card catalog to the meetinghouse library, has also been prepared.

Each meetinghouse library has a variety of library equipment available for patron use, including the following items: filmstrip projectors, slide projectors, 16 mm motion picture projectors, overhead projectors, cassette and reel-to-reel tape recorders, record players, microfilm readers, microfiche readers, opaque projectors, a spirit duplicator, an infrared copier, drymount press(es), large paper cutter(s), and portable screens.   All pieces of equipment are available to support the instructional programs, individual research and study, and general patron use in family activities, socials, etc.

As noted above, numerous meetinghouse libraries offer genealogical reference service.   As such, they provide microform readers, reference books, a reading room, specially trained library personnel, and microform records shipped from the main Genealogical Library in Salt Lake City.

The development of the meetinghouse library program and availability of all kinds of instructional material and equipment has increased immensely since the inception of the meetinghouse library program in the 1960s.   Today, Church members have at their disposal a wealth of material with the support of trained library personnel to assist them in teaching, in doing genealogical research, in preparing talks, or pursuing individual study for personal improvement.

Seminary and Institute Libraries

LDS institutes of religion provide a program of religious instruction for college-age Latter-day Saints.   Regular weekday classes
are offered on a variety of subjects, with emphasis, however, on
the scriptures and doctrines of The Church of Jesus Christ of Latter-
day Saints.   Full- or part-time institutes of religion are established
near colleges and universities throughout the United States and in
other parts of the world.   The full-time program is usually conducted in buildings constructed by the Church, and under the direction of a full-time institute director.   Part-time institute classes
are conducted in rented quarters or in LDS chapels close to college
campuses.   An LDS seminary is a facility where Mormon youth in
grades 9 through 12 are instructed in Church-related subjects.   In
areas where released-time programs are available, students are
officially excused one hour each day from regular classes in their
high schools to go to a building adjacent to the public school for
religious instruction.   They are taught by full-time professional
teachers who are selected by the Church Education System.

There are more than 200 LDS institutes of religion, and approximately an equal number of released-time seminaries, which
provide some library services.   The Department of Seminaries and
Institutes located in the Church Office Building in Salt Lake City
provides centralized library processing for seminary and institute
libraries.   The Library Services Division offers cataloging materials
for more than 3, 500 widely disseminated LDS books.   The cataloging
material includes a spine label, the number labels for the book
pocket, checkout cards, and catalog entries consisting of author,
title, subject, and shelf list cards. [24]   In 1975, library services
handled nearly 8, 000 requests for centralized processing from institutes, and 3, 500 requests from seminaries.   In addition to centralized cataloging, library services publishes a library handbook,
written primarily for the nonprofessional volunteers who assist in
the seminary and institute library program.   Moreover, it distributes
a master list of all books in the institute system that have been
cataloged to date.

The LDS seminary library is unique because it serves high
school students who are predominantly members of The Church of
Jesus Christ of Latter-day Saints; it is intended to house books
primarily pertaining to Mormon history and doctrine; it is staffed
by teachers who know little about library operation procedures; it
does not dispense secular literature; and, the students normally [25]
attend seminary only one period a day on a released-time basis.
A typical seminary library has a limited collection and is primarily
used as a resource for staff members.

Generally, an LDS institute library is headed by the institute
director.   The collection normally consists of a basic set suggested
by the Church Education System and other material frequently obtained by gift.   Institute libraries are financed by general Church
funds, and the annual budget includes a limited amount for acquisitions.

Typically, students use the institute library as a place of study and as a resource center for preparing talks or for completing assignments. More often, the institute library is used by staff members to broaden their own perspective.

Headquarters Library Activities and Services

LDS Church Library Archives

The library-archives of The Church of Jesus Christ of Latter-day Saints enjoys spacious, modern facilities, occupying nearly 67,000 square feet of floor space in the east wing of the Church's recently completed twenty-eight story office building in downtown Salt Lake City. The full-time staff of seventy employees includes fifteen professional librarians and archivists in three administrative areas--acquisitions, public, and technical services.

The Latter-day Saints have long been noted for their vigorous recordkeeping tradition. In the 1830s, Joseph Smith gave the Church instructions, accepted by them as revelation, "to keep a history, and a general Church record of all things that transpire in Zion." [26] Thus charged, literally thousands of faithful Mormon clerks have labored diligently to preserve records and prepare histories. Local units from North and South America, to Europe, Asia, and the South Pacific add yearly to the ever-growing collection of official records as part of the library-archives effort to preserve the history of Church activity worldwide. These records comprise minutes of meetings, including those of the several auxiliary organizations, historical reports, changes of officers and teachers reports, Church ordinance and action records, financial and statistical reports, and numerous other miscellaneous records. In addition to the records of local ecclesiastical units (wards, branches, stakes, districts, and missions), the library-archives accessions the records of the general Church offices, committees, auxiliaries, and departments. Altogether, these collections occupy more than 16,000 linear feet of shelf space and consist of more than 215,000 separate volumes. [27]

The library-archives maintains within its holdings a vast research library on Mormonism. Nearly comprehensive in scope, this collection of more than 120,000 printed items includes books, theses, dissertations, broadsides, serial publications, pamphlets, and magazine articles. Included are works published by the Church and Church agencies as well as works dealing with the Church in any significant way. Interestingly, the library-archives' effort to collect important Mormon-related material has resulted in the most extensive collection of so-called "anti-Mormon" works in existence.

Since its inception, the Church of Jesus Christ of Latter-day Saints has urged its members to keep personal histories or books of remembrance. Because of this practice, the library-archives today contains the diaries, journals, and other personal papers of hundreds of Church members and prominent leaders, as well as those of others

whose lives shed light on the Mormon experience.   A variety of
material is to be found in the manuscript collections, including correspondence, poetry, and other literary pieces.   Another category
of significant source material is that of nontextual media.   This
area of the library-archives includes an estimated 100, 000 photographs, paintings, and pictures; 4, 200 video and audio tapes; 4, 000
disc recordings; and scores of motion pictures and filmstrips, either
produced by the Church, or otherwise significantly relating to Mormonism. [28]

A wide variety of reference and reader services is available
to visitors at the library-archives in four public service areas:
general reference, member services, the model meetinghouse library, and the archives search room.

The general reference collection is arranged in open stacks
and consists of the most widely used LDS books, pamphlets, periodicals, newspapers, maps, and microfilm.   In addition to LDS material, this section holds published works on the history and beliefs
of major religious denominations, secular works on the history of
the West, and complete runs of major Salt Lake City newspapers.
Moreover, this section maintains a number of special reference
aids, including the "Historic Sites File, " a compilation of pictures
and written summaries of LDS historic sites and monuments; the
"Journal History of the Church, " a chronologically arranged compilation of newspaper clippings and other documentary material related
to the Church; and the "Reference Card File, " an incomplete card
index to topics, people, and poems found in various LDS publications.
A unique feature of the LDS Church Library is its use of a modified
Dewey decimal classification system that includes a specially created
M200 section for the large number of Mormon materials.   These
are inserted between the Dewey 200s and 300s.

The general reference staff's foremost responsibility is to
meet the research needs of administrators of general Church programs and departments at Church headquarters.   Each month they
handle an average of thirty-six requests from Church General Authorities and 174 interdepartmental reference requests.   Visitors,
however, are welcome to consult with staff members in developing
search strategies and in using the library's finding aids.   The staff
also answers written queries from Church members, scholars, and
other interested people throughout the world as thoroughly and as
promptly as time permits.   Information for broad research projects
is normally limited to identifying sources in the library-archives
that relate to the writer's inquiry.

Personnel assigned to the member services section search
archival records to assist LDS Church members in obtaining copies
of patriarchal blessings and Church certificates of birth, in tracing
their priesthood lines of authority, and in correcting entries on
original membership records.

The model meetinghouse library was constructed in accordance with the latest plan developed jointly by the Church Building Division and the Church Meetinghouse Library Committee. The model library contains the instructional material that is recommended for use in current courses of study, including pictures, maps, filmstrips, overhead transparencies, current lesson manuals, and instructional equipment such as projectors, tape recorders, and record players, that are approved for meetinghouse libraries with Church participation. Staff members are available to assist visitors in better understanding the meetinghouse library operation, including application of the coding and indexing system, procedures for circulation of library material, and the use of the preprinted subject index cards. The model meetinghouse library also serves as a working collection for use of the departments at Church headquarters.

Due to special requirements governing their use, archival and manuscript material is accessible to the public only in the Archives Search Room. A researcher may be granted archives reading privileges by making application and being interviewed. Staff members are available to consult with patrons about their individual research problems, to help in the use of the finding aids, and to assist in obtaining desired archival material. In addition to the archives card catalog, a detailed listing and description of numerous manuscript collections, Church record groups, audiovisual collections, and photograph collections are available in the rapidly growing number of collection registers. Several of these registers have been published and are available at other institutions which have significant Mormon holdings. Guides that identify sources relating to special topics, such as immigration and women's history, are available.

The Genealogical Department Library

The Genealogical Department of the Church of Jesus Christ of Latter-day Saints is the largest and most active genealogical organization in the world. With headquarters in the new Church Office Building, the Genealogical Department has more than five hundred employees and ninety volunteer aids who compile and organize material for genealogical use and assist patrons. Although the department was founded in 1894 primarily to assist members of the Church in compiling genealogical information, its facilities are available to the general public.

The department is engaged in one of the most comprehensive genealogical record-gathering programs ever known. In locations the world over, more than seventy microfilm photographers are filming records--parish registers, marriage and probate records, census returns, deeds, land grants, cemetery records, and other sources of genealogical value. Each month approximately 4,000 one-hundred-foot rolls of negative microfilm and 12,000 one-hundred-foot rolls of positive microfilm are processed in the Church's modern film developing and printing laboratories. The microfilm negatives are filed in one of the huge storage rooms of the Granite Mountain Records Vault, a unique storage facility built by the Church in a canyon southeast of Salt Lake City to protect this valuable collection.

The Genealogical Department Library in downtown Salt Lake City houses positive prints of most of the collections.

Nearly a half million patrons visit the Genealogical Department Library each year. Area specialists assist patrons with their genealogical research problems in records from throughout the world. More than 130,000 volumes of family genealogies, genealogical periodicals, and published and manuscript histories of towns, counties, states, and countries are displayed on self-service open stacks. Some 240 microfilm reading machines are available to the public in the library's reading room. More than 880,000 one-hundred-foot rolls of microfilm have been accumulated, representing the equivalent of over 3 million printed volumes of 300 pages each. Under the record tabulation program, hundreds of completed parish records are indexed and printed out in alphabetical order with the names arranged chronologically. Thus, they are available for study, and a search for parish records for a given person can be made quickly and with little effort.

Additionally, the library has a collection of over six million genealogical records of individual families, compiled by members of The Church of Jesus Christ of Latter-day Saints. The genealogical information contained in this family group record collection has been recorded on convenient forms filed in the library in looseleaf binders. The forms--family group records--include space to record the full names of all members of the family unit and the corresponding dates and places of birth, marriage, death, and burial. Information such as the source used to compile the record and any necessary explanations are included. The family group record collection is available to the public in open stacks with convenient reading tables and copying facilities provided.

The Genealogical Department services the more than 225 branch libraries in the United States, Australia, Canada, England, Germany, Mexico, and New Zealand. New branches are established each year. Through an interlibrary loan arrangement, patrons in areas served by the branch libraries have access to the main library's vast microfilm collection. As explained in the section on the meetinghouse library program, the branches are staffed and financially supported by local members of the Church. Each branch builds its own collection of reference books, periodicals, and printed genealogies and histories that are not available on film.

Horizons

The library program of The Church of Jesus Christ of Latter-day Saints continues to expand and improve at a phenomenal rate. In 1976 alone, nearly five hundred new LDS meetinghouse libraries were constructed. The Church Meetinghouse Library Committee's commitment to participate in the establishment and assist in the development of fully equipped, expertly staffed libraries in all units of the Church is well within reach.

At the headquarters of the Church in Salt Lake City, the Library-Archives Division is completing a three-year program of mi-
crofilming its 300,000 volumes of official Church records. This
will enable all units of the Church to more readily obtain copies of
their own records which they have annually been forwarding to Salt
Lake City. The headquarters library-archives is preparing to publish on microfiche the Church's retrospective periodical literature
and other selected reference works. This will enable new meetinghouse libraries to acquire a complete set of basic Church material
which otherwise would be out of print. Access to this material will
be facilitated by the improved and expanded indexes which professionally trained librarians at Church headquarters are now producing.

Access to the holdings of the Church's Genealogical Library
will be enhanced as the Genealogical Department completes it multi-
year program of converting its card catalog to machine-readable
form. Moreover, genealogical services in meetinghouse libraries,
which recently were made available for the first time in England,
Germany, Australia, and New Zealand, will continue to be established
in other nations of the world.

The Latter-day Saints' commitment to their library program
is summarized in the words of Howard W. Hunter, a member of
the Church's Council of the Twelve Apostles:

> The well-organized, adequately stocked, and competently
> staffed library will become the nerve center of the ward
> or branch for more excellence in teaching. . . . [The
> meetinghouse library program] has the immediate promise
> to increase the activity of the entire membership of the
> Church through making the messages of the gospel more
> vital in our lives. [29]

BIBLIOGRAPHY

Adams, Charles P. and Larson, Gustave O. "A Study of the LDS
     Church Historian's Office, 1830-1900," Utah Historical Quar-
     terly XLI (Fall 1972), pp. 370-389.

The Church of Jesus Christ of Latter-day Saints. Index to Meeting-
     house Library Bulletins, 1967-1974. Salt Lake City, Utah
     (1976).

_____. Manual for the Care and Circulation of Motion Picture
     Films. Salt Lake City, Utah, 1975.

_____. The Meetinghouse Librarian. Produced by Brigham
     Young University. Salt Lake City, Utah, 1974. Filmstrip
     (88 frames); cassette (16:30 min.); and script booklet.

_____. Meetinghouse Library Training Manual. (Salt Lake City,
     Utah, 1977)

_____. Putting It All Together In the Meetinghouse Library.
Produced by Brigham Young University. Salt Lake City,
Utah, 1974. Filmstrip (56 frames); cassette (9:11 min.);
and script booklet.

_____. Subject Index Cards for Materials Found in the Instruc-
tional Materials Catalog Plus Selected Additional Headings.
Salt Lake City, Utah, 1972.

Evans, Max J., "A History of the Public Library Movement in
Utah," Master's Thesis, Utah State University, 1971.

Esplin, Ronald K. and Evans, Max J. "Preserving Mormon Manuscripts," Manuscripts XXVII (Summer 1975), pp. 166-177.

The Genealogical Society of The Church of Jesus Christ of Latter-
day Saints. Introducing the Genealogical Society. (Salt Lake
City, Utah, 1975)

Olson, Earl E. "When the Books Are Opened," Library Journal
LXXXVI (1 January 1961), pp. 33-36.

Peterson, Virgil. "Behold There Shall Be A Record Kept Among
You," in Church Archives and History (Bulletins of the American Association for State and Local History, vol. 10, no. 1),
Raleigh, North Carolina: The American Association for State
and Local History, 1946.

NOTES

1. Lyman, Amasa, (Seventies Library) Times and Seasons VI (1
   February 1845), p. 797.
2. "Seventies Library," Times and Seasons V (1 January 1845),
   pp. 762-763.
3. "General Epistle from the Council of the Twelve Apostles,"
   Millenial Star X (5 March 1848), p. 85.
4. Young, Levi Edgar, "The First Library in Utah," Young
   Woman's Journal XXI (October 1910), p. 532.
5. "Stake Library," Woman's Exponent XVI (1 December 1887),
   p. 100; "Utah News," Millenial Star XLIX (26 December
   1887), p. 819.
6. Jubilee History of Latter-day Saints Sunday Schools, 1849-
   1899. Salt Lake City, Utah: Deseret Sunday School Union,
   1900, p. 45.
7. Ibid., pp. 24-26.
8. Fernad, J. C., "The Traveling Library," Young Woman's
   Journal XI (January 1900), pp. 36-37.
9. Eddinton, Sarah, "The Traveling Library Committee," Young
   Woman's Journal XX (August 1908), pp. 385-389.
10. Deseret Sunday School Union Board Minutes, 19 March 1912,
    vol. 7, p. 263, Library-Archives, The Church of Jesus
    Christ of Latter-day Saints, Salt Lake City, Utah, herein-
    after cited as the LDS Church Archives.

11. Ibid. , 24 January 1931, vol. XII, pp. 53053.
12. Grant, Jay S. , "A Ward Library, " The Instructor LXVIII (September 1933), pp. 403, 425.
13. "Adams Ward Plan, " in Deseret Sunday School Union Board, Sunday School Librarian's Guide Book Salt Lake City, Utah, 1948, p. 39.
14. Deseret Sunday School Union Board Minutes, 26 October 1930, XII, p. 36.
15. Lewis, Hazel W. , "The Model Sunday School Library, " The Instructor LXXXV (June 1950), pp. 180-182.
16. First Presidency to All General Authorities, Auxiliary Executives, and Heads of Departments, 17 February 1965, Circular Letters, First Presidency Records, LDS Church Archives.
17. Meetinghouse Library Committee Minutes, 10 October 1971, Historical Department Records, LDS Church Archives.
18. Church Library Coordinating Committee Minutes, 8 February 1972, Historical Department Records, LDS Church Archives.
19. Ibid. , 15 April 1975.
20. The Church of Jesus Christ of Latter-day Saints, Meetinghouse Library Handbook Salt Lake City, Utah, 1974, p. 4.
21. Ibid. , p. 10-11.
22. The Church of Jesus Christ of Latter-day Saints, Instructional Materials Catalog Salt Lake City, Utah, 1972, unpaged.
23. Ibid. , Meetinghouse Library Handbook, p. 18.
24. The Church of Jesus Christ of Latter-day Saints, Church Educational System, Library Services, Library Handbook Salt Lake City, Utah, 1973, p. 11.
25. Winters, F. Burton, "A Study of L. D. S. Seminary Libraries, " Master's Thesis, Brigham Young University, 1964, p. 5.
26. Doctrine and Covenants, rev. ed. Salt Lake City, Utah: The Church of Jesus Christ of Latter-day Saints, 1923, Section 85:1.
27. "A Report of the Historical Department of The Church of Jesus Christ of Latter-day Saints for the Five Year Period 1971-1975, " p. 5, Historical Department Records, LDS Church Archives.
28. Ibid.
29. Hunter, Howard W. , (Meetinghouse Libraries) Conference Reports of The Church of Jesus Christ of Latter-day Saints (April 1971), p. 49.

UNITED METHODIST CHURCH LIBRARIES

Maryann J. Dotts

The history of United Methodist Church libraries cannot be viewed apart from the history and events in which the church developed. From the founding by John Wesley, the power of the printed word was recognized. He felt that one of his purposes "was to set before the masses in a form they could understand and in a manner they could afford the best the Christian Church had to offer."[1] This led to reprinting the works of many writers in book format or in Wesley's "Arminian Magazine." In addition, there were, as well as the many original articles, tracts, hymns and whole books of sermons which he wrote.

The early American Methodists followed in this Wesleyan tradition. Most of the printed material was available in inexpensive format. Many were works with earlier British imprints. Historian James Penn Pilkington showed that American Methodists had been printing sporadically for fifteen years prior to 1789, in New York, Philadelphia and Baltimore. Some of the earliest titles printed by Methodist book stewards were Christian's Pattern or Imitation of Christ by Thomas à Kempis, Primitive Physic (originally "Physick") by John Wesley, Saint's Everlasting Rest by Richard Baxter as well as The Pocket Hymn Book and various editions of the Discipline (book of church laws).

In 1789, a preacher from New York, John Dickens, was assigned to pastor St. George's Church, Philadelphia, and to be the book steward. Although there was printing earlier than this time, this man is credited with beginning the printing business for what eventually became the United Methodist Church. John Dickens was designated as Agent and used his own name on the title pages as was the practice of that day. His activities can best be described with the word, publisher. He arranged for the material that would be published, edited, contracted for the printing, purchased the paper, financed the payment of bills as well as the dispersal of the printed material to the preachers who were appointed "book stewards." He struggled to collect the receipts from the sale of the books and paid off the bills. The delivery system left much to be desired and was the cause more than once for notices to be sent to the preachers to pick up their two boxes and quickly send their remittances so that additional paper could be bought to allow for more items to be printed.

149

Bishop Francis Asbury was concerned about the book business and had it on the agenda for the Council meeting of December 3, 1789, at Baltimore. At this point there was not even a formal name for the activity. It was called "the printing business" and later "the book concern" and still later "The Methodist Publishing House. "[2]

With the rise of literacy came the need for reading material for all age levels. This included religious books, political essays, and reprints of many classics. Bible Study helps like concordances and commentaries and other books on background for study became popular. Another avenue of publishing that had wide impact were the periodicals like Methodist Magazine (1818). Youth's Instructer and Guardian (1923), along with the weekly newspaper The Christian Advocate (1826), had wide influence.

Within the Sunday school program, the need for a system of study became apparent by 1853 and developed into the Uniform Lessons. The first cycles ran from 1873-79.[3] A graded curriculum for all ages followed and eventually evolved into a highly sophisticated system of children's curricula in 1964. In addition to student and teacher books this graded curriculum for two year age spans included teaching packets containing vinyl records and filmstrips as well as games, teaching pictures and teaching aids. Preferred books and audio-visuals were identified for each quarter. The youth and adult material began to encompass this new teaching material in the years that followed.

For many churches this was a time of renewed interest in the church library. The library developed first in the earliest Sunday Schools. A basic set of books was made available for sale to Sunday Schools. If the newly formed groups could not afford the price of the set, frequently it was made available as a gift. This is further testimony to the power of the printed word to evangelize the "new fields of work." This principle of pioneer Methodism was expressed in Pilkington's history,

> The propagation of religious knowledge by means of the press is next in importance to the preaching of the gospel. To supply the people therefore with the most pious and useful books, in order that they may fill up their leisure hours in the most profitable ways, is an object worthy of the deepest attention of their pastors.[4]

It is important to note that there were two types of Sunday Schools begun as early as 1786. One was for an hour of religious instruction, and the second was for poor children who needed to learn to read and write. In 1790 the General Conference enjoined the establishing of Sunday Schools.

The classes often met from six o'clock in the morning till ten and from two o'clock in the afternoon till six, with time to attend public worship as a group. These early schools were not considered successful, but they presented the need to provide material that could be used by the students. As the curriculum changed from "acquisition of human learning to primarily teaching of the Bible, the school burgeoned and comprised one of the chief audiences for publications of the Methodist presses. "[5]

The need for material beyond The Horn Book, The Alphabet of Lessons for Youth, The Westminster Catechism, Webster's "Blue Back Speller" and The New England Primer gave rise to a whole new field of writing. Stories were developed for children and youth with a moral twist. Frequently they were first printed in one of the periodicals and then put into book form. All of them were printed as inexpensively as possible for wide distribution.

Each Sunday School developed a library for its students. [6] As early as 1820, some of the schools had respectable collections for their scholars. In a catalog entitled "Sunday School and Youth's Library Catalog, 1842, " we have a listing of more than two hundred titles. They were often published in a series and sold for ten- to twenty-five cents apiece. The paper bound juveniles were sold for about sixty cents a dozen. They appeared in paper covered book cases with leather spines and corners. They ranged in subject matter from Sunday School instruction to juvenile fiction.

The impact on the culture of this early publishing has been evaluated by C. A. Bowen. [7] The Sunday Schools were carrying on about all the adult education of which America could boast at that time. One of the most effective forms of attack upon illiteracy was the establishment of libraries and publication of books for general reading. From the beginning, the publishing and the Sunday School libraries were broad and diversified, which is a common thread that can be found in many of our libraries today with the pluralistic character of the denomination.

From the earliest times, the emphasis of the library was on the upbuilding of the reader, as a part of the Christian moral development. This abides still as the purpose in many church libraries. In a large number of libraries the emphasis is on training material and good reading material. Even though the name has been changed to Church Library from Sunday School Library, the emphasis has stayed with Christian Education material. In communities where no public library is available, often there is a wider scope of secular material, but most church libraries are focused on Christian Education material.

The church library has never received special emphasis from the General Conference (the governing body of the United Methodist Church), the former Board of Education or the present Board of Discipleship. The services that have been provided are channeled through Cokesbury, the retail division of the United Methodist Publishing House.

These services began with a 1948 letter from a local church,

which asked for help in organizing the books in their library. A
committee was formed from several regional divisions, under the
direction of Lloyd Snyder. It was the committee's intention to provide a non-revenue seeking service for church librarians. This remained the organizing principle for almost twenty-five years. Some
of the services provided were: a manual of procedures, a 20 percent discount to libraries, supplies carried in Cokesbury stores and
catalog, training offered in leadership schools, a newsletter, book
lists and some promotional posters and ideas for observances such
as Library and Children's Book Weeks.

        The impetus for service has resided in the merchandising
unit of Cokesbury Book Stores. The book stores service library
needs and often send questions to the appropriate staff persons for
more detailed answers. At different points in time, the personnel
who have had responsibility for providing services have varied from
an interest in libraries with no professional experience to an educated
children's librarian to a marketing specialist. Over the years, additional staff members have been employed to carry the responsibility
for securing teaching material, evaluating, creating book lists, editing newsletters and carrying out correspondence.

        One of the most helpful services to the librarian has been a
manual that provides for simple classification and cataloging in
keeping with good library procedures. These manuals have been
written in such a way that a nonprofessional librarian could follow
the steps in setting up and arranging the library material. The
most recent manual was published in 1975 by the Abingdon Press. [8]
Another service was a newsletter which carried support articles by
librarians, promotional ideas, excellent book lists on timely topics,
all geared to the needs of the church librarian.

        In 1975 an effort was made to restudy the facets of this serv-
ice. A thorough evaluation showed that the denomination has never
formally recognized the contributions of the church library sufficiently to assign this emphasis to one of the program agencies. The
Cokesbury Division of the United Methodist Publishing House is not
a programming agency; rather it is responsible for distribution. As
a result of this re-examination, steps were taken to provide the
services that sell book and non-book material used by church libraries and not to put an emphasis on the programmatic or training
services.

Mission, Scope and Characteristics of Methodist Libraries

        There is no statement of mission for the denomination. Its
purpose has been to undergird church education for all ages. Each
local library is encouraged to develop its own purpose and policy
statement. With little national direction, the local church library
has developed to fit the needs of the individual congregation. An
early manual suggested that the purpose be defined "to provide the
material needed in carrying forward the program of the church." [9]

The largest percentage of the library holdings are related to biblical material. They include dictionaries, concordances, commentaries, various translations of the Bible, study books on the life of Jesus, Paul and biblical characters. Some collections have large holdings in the areas of theology, church history (especially for the United Methodist denomination) and mission studies. Usually there is a large collection of children's books including biblical stories as well as general topics. The Youth collection is often weak. Other subjects included to a smaller degree are the arts, games, psychology, child rearing, fiction and biography.

In most cases the church library does not try to compete with the services of the public library, but acquires those items that are supportive of the teaching ministry of the local church. In situations where there is no public library service, those libraries are likely to have a much larger percentage of recreational reading items. Most libraries have a limited number of periodicals. The majority are related to their denomination or church school subjects.

With the increased availability and use of audio-visual material through the 1960s came a change in policy to include records, tapes, filmstrips, transparencies, kits and other items. The 1975 manual recommended that all of these items and books be listed in one alphabetical catalog for easy access. With the shift in emphasis, there remains the fact that books still provide the largest number of items in any library.

In terms of library procedures, most librarians have little difficulty in getting new material on the shelves for users. The largest problem seems to be having the skill to know which material to weed out of the collection, so many libraries have much material that is out of date or not useful to today's leaders.

Church Library Personnel, Finance and Quarters

The librarian and staff are volunteers who are committed to the importance of providing reading/teaching material for the members of the congregation and its constituency. Most of the library workers have not had professional library education. Some have worked in public libraries or attended workshops on library skills. A number of professionals volunteer their service. "On the job" training is the style used for most of the volunteers. It is recommended that at least two persons be trained to be responsible for each phase of library technical processing.

In 1968 the training of librarians was added to the laboratory enterprises which is the model used to develop leaders of children, youths and adults. The model includes concentrated study for a week to cover all aspects of librarianship. Individuals have the opportunity to enter the laboratory at any level of experience and participate in the group sessions. They work on specific areas where they feel that their competencies need to be improved and relate learning to their "home" situations. [10]

It is the responsibility of each library to work out financing with its sponsoring organization. It is recommended that an amount be allocated for the library budget each year. Additional funds or items are acquired through memorials, gifts and teaching material used for specific units of study and given to the library.

The size of the libraries varies from one unit to another. They may consist of a shelf of books in a classroom to several well appointed rooms. Libraries in United Methodist Churches run the whole gamut. A location convenient to the flow of traffic is always recommended for the best placement of the library.

Services

Within the local library, service, too, varies. Most of the libraries are self service without a librarian on duty. Many try to have a staff person in the library on Sunday morning to help persons secure the library material needed.

The relationship to the church full-time staff members is unique to each congregation. If there is a multiple staff, the responsibility for the library will usually be in the job description of the person responsible for Christian Education. Staff persons are often asked to make suggestions of appropriate new material, including areas of study and congregational needs.

The relationship to the Sunday School is one of providing resources that help teachers and students with resource needs growing out of the curriculum material. Often their material is purchased through curriculum budgets, used in the classroom for the quarter and then permanently accessioned into the library's holdings for wider usage.

There is no direction relationship between the libraries and the secular Abingdon Press which is operated by the United Methodist Publishing House. Many of the items printed are appropriate for United Methodist libraries. Graded Press is the imprint that produces curriculum material for this denomination, and many items with this imprint are found in every library. Of the denomination journals, none relates directly to the library.

A Typical Library

It is easier to identify one library in terms of outstanding service, than to find a typical library. The Anderson Library in Belmont United Methodist Church, Nashville, is outstanding in the way that it serves the 2300 member congregation. This memorial library has book and non-book material. It operates with a library committee composed of three regular librarians, several assistants and other volunteers who work as needed. Each person is related to some group within the congregation. One of the persons is a professional librarian.   The various aspects of the work are divided: one librarian is responsible for the catalog and adult work, one is research librarian, does the ordering and conferring with the staff, and one is responsible for audio-visual material.

There is an excellent relationship between the librarians and the employed church staff which gives a great deal of support.   One example is sending those who need counseling to the library for books that will help them understand their problems and grow through reading.   This support is felt from the assistant minister, the minister, Director of Christian Education, business manager and secretaries.   The library staff is working to upgrade the audio-visuals, equipment, storage and card catalog of audio-visuals.

An example of the kind of use the library gets is seen in the support services to third and fourth grade teachers and students. The elementary classes come to the library to learn how to use a Bible Dictionary, concordance and a harmony of the gospels.   This is scheduled during their unit on "Understanding the Bible. "   The students check out books for home reading that are mentioned in their curriculum unit.   They find Bible story books, easy biographies, including those of Rachel Carson, Cesar Chavez, Jane Addams, and Mary McLeod Bethune.   The teachers follow up on the visit by using the large Bible concordance with the class in finding favorite scripture passages on Thanksgiving for plaques, place cards and prayer cards.

Other activities include: 1) a kindergarten class which comes to the library to look at selected picture books that show how people care for birds, animals, and plants.   Each child shares the pictures she/he found.   2) One class of second graders comes to the library when they have a session on prayer to use books of prayers which they can read aloud and talk about and to listen to a story, "Bless Grandpa, " which tells about a child who puts his prayer into action. 3) Teachers and assistants come with children to help them check out books that supplement their classroom learning.   4) A senior high school class asks to have some interpretation of the Book of Revelations.   Some of their friends have quoted verses from the book to predict that Christ is coming soon and that the end of the world is coming.   The library furnishes many books at the table for background reading and their teacher helps to lead the discussion.

The most common requests are for books in all areas of Bible study, child study and family life problems, devotional books, children's books of all kinds, some fiction for adults, books on crafts and recreation, United Methodist history and other religions. The librarians keep in contact with program plans for the whole church and put on the reserve shelf books for special studies, task force committees, one-parent groups, women's studies, church seasons, recommended books for children and youth curriculum units.   Book lists are often furnished on special subjects.

One of the ways that this library serves the church school is

through providing the book and audio-visual material recommend for
each quarter of the curriculum. Approximately 40 items are ordered
each quarter which makes their $400 material budget go a long way
toward serving this large congregation. Service is their ministry.

Denominational Library Services

The upcoming development of a Cokesbury Church Library
Association membership fee will be the vehicle for service to
church librarians. the purpose is to help librarians secure the best
resources for the budget dollar. This yearly membership package
will include a courtesy card and number, an annual subscription to
the publication Church Library News (sent five times a year), a
discount of 20 percent on books purchased, free information brochures and other promotional help. The Church Library News will
offer ten or more books/material for sale at an individual or a
group price. Other news items may include descriptions of a local
church library, calendar announcements, helpful hints, readers
response along with the order blank.

Another service is the Church Library Guild which is a membership previously known as the Westminster Plan, now assumed by
Cokesbury to offer to church librarians new books four times a year
prior to publication date. A church member of the Church Library
Guild automatically becomes a member of the Church Library Association without paying the membership fee.

At the present time the marketing department of Cokesbury
is not staffed to handle technical questions from church librarians,
plan staff training events or compile extensive bibliographies. It
is equipped to sell religious books and that will be its emphasis at
this time. The present church library registration is over 18,000.
Of this number, 14,000 are United Methodist Church libraries, which
comes closest to identifying a figure for the number of these libraries. Cokesbury is the official supplier for United Presbyterian and
United Church of Christ libraries, also.

National Leadership

Curriculum writers often refer to the church library, an
occasional article appears on the library, but there is no direct
national responsibility for this phase of work in the local congregation. As a librarian, I have some doubts about the vision of a
leadership which does not see the great power still at hand, power
which was seen by the earliest book stewards and by John Wesley
himself.

Believing that "reading Christians will be knowing Christians,"
Wesley bent his energies toward opening books all over England.
And subsequently over America as so many were reprinted here
from the British editions. Reading is still in style, even with media

on every hand, and the ministry of the librarian who can be approached by a person with a need and can place the right book/material in his or her hand is following in the great tradition of developing "knowing Christians."

BIBLIOGRAPHY

Brown, Marianna C. Sunday-School Movements in America. New
    York: Revell Co., 1901. 270 pp.

Bucke, Emory Stevens. The History of American Methodism.
    Nashville: Abingdon Press, 1964. 721 pp. 3 vols.

Chandler, W. A. The History of Sunday Schools: A Brief Historical
    Treatise. Macon, Georgia: J. W. Burke and Company,
    1881. 150 pp.

Vernon, Walter, N. "Good Reading: The Sunday School Library,"
    The Church School IX (January 1977), p. 21.

NOTES

1. Pilkington, James Penn, The Methodist Publishing House.
    Nashville: Abingdon Press, 1968, Vol. I, p. 89.
2. A complete history of the United Methodist Publishing House
    will be achieved when Dr. Walter N. Vernon finishes the
    years following the Pilkington volume.
3. A history of the Methodist Church-School Curriculum through
    1950 is documented in Child and Church by Cawthon A. Bo-
    wen, New York: Abingdon Press, 1960.
4. Pilkington, op. cit., p. 110. This is a quotation from the
    "Journal, 1976," in Journals of the General Conference of
    the Methodist Episcopal Church, I, 1796-1836 (New York:
    Carlton and Phillips, 1855), p. 17.
5. Pilkington, op. cit., p. 93.
6. A chapter on "Sunday School Libraries" is found in Bowen,
    op. cit., pp. 79-87.
7. Bowen, op. cit.
8. Dotts, Maryann J., Church Resource Library. Nashville:
    Abingdon Press, 1975, p. 48.
9. Your Church Library. Nashville: The Methodist Publishing
    House, 1960, p. 17.
10. Information on presently scheduled laboratories or help in set-
    ting up training events may be secured by writing the Director
    of Laboratory Training, Division of Education, Board of
    Discipleship, Box 840, Nashville, Tennessee 37202.

UNITED PRESBYTERIAN CHURCH LIBRARIES

Ruth H. Winters

In 1958, the Presbyterian Church in the United States of America and the United Presbyterian Church of North American merged to become the United Presbyterian Church in the United States of America. The early history recorded here relates to the former Presbyterian Church organized in 1789.

"Elias Boudinot established at the time of his death in 1821 a Trust Fund to provide books for ministers. He bequeathed money to the Trustees of the General Assembly, Presbyterian Church in the United States of America (now known as The United Presbyterian Foundation), the interest from which is to be used to provide "useful books" to churches, "unable to provide for themselves."

"The books are to be selected by the pastor for his use, but as the property of the church would always remain with the church." Boudinot further stipulated "who shall direct the manner in which they shall be kept with regard to their preservation against being improperly lent out..."[1]

Who was Elias Boudinot? He was a member of the Continental Congress and became its president in 1782. He was the first president of the United Presbyterian Foundation. He was a Trustee of the College of New Jersey, now Princeton University, and a founder of Princeton Theological Seminary and the American Bible Society. After 155 years this Fund continues to build up sizably and gifts are still being made to ministers and churches. Just how much is the Boudinot Fund paying out? Gifts to each church have been $50. With discount available, this made the gift worth about $75. Three hundred gifts have been given in the last decade.

In reviewing the early reports of Willard M. Rice, History of Presbyterian Board of Publications and Sabbath School Work, as early as 1839, the church recognized the necessity to establish a publication division in order to produce Sabbath School material. [2] By 1870 about 600 works for use in the Sabbath School library were listed in the catalog. Copies of these lists were made available to the churches. [3] Added to these materials were Bible dictionaries, commentaries, maps, guidebooks, roll books, church hymnals and song books, later good juvenile reading books, plus recommended reading material from other religious publishing houses.

In smaller towns and villages, the Presbyterian Church Library serves the community, especially where there is no public library. Too, certain books in a church library, because of their very nature, are not generally to be found in small public libraries. A recent letter from an active church librarian states how they have an agreement with the local public library to check before purchases are made, thus avoiding duplication.

The growth of public libraries may have taken some of the edge off of the necessity for developing a library within the church building, especially in the larger cities. Public libraries had the funds to secure books in all subject fields, including religion. The early church book collections consisted mainly of Bibles in various translations, books dealing specifically with the Presbyterian Church, its government and history, missionary study books and guides (revised every seven years), and child pedagogy. In the larger cities, public libraries were cooperative in assisting churches to provide additional reading matter for church school teachers.

Often churches have not included in their building blueprints a specific area designated for the library. The minister's study, if one was included, became the depository for the first book collection. Some ministers were willing to share their personal libraries with the members. In the late teens and early twenties, educational programming for youth and church school teachers and leaders took on new dimensions. Leaders who attended summer leadership training schools made available books which they had used there. Back home again in the local church it was a window ledge or a table, perhaps in the ladies' parlor, where these "first book collections" were to be found. There were local teacher training courses and these, too, provided additional study material to be shelved and shared.

Not only was the program in Christian Education taking on new dimensions, but Presbyterian women were making themselves heard. Missionary study books were being written. Later, study manuals on books of the Bible were written by Christian scholars and were added to the collection. It was not by accident that the women named a "literature secretary." Part of her responsibility was looking after the women's material. Seeing the other books gathering on the ledges or tables, in many churches this literature secretary became the unofficial volunteer librarian. And she still is in many of the smaller churches. In such a way, many libraries were born. The writer recalls a number of "literature secretaries" who attended the first Drexel Church Librarians Workshop, 1963.

In 1948 the Presbyterian Faith and Life church school curriculum was introduced. This brought into play reading which encouraged building a home library. The Presbyterian Church in the United States of America had not encouraged library establishment. In the early 40's, as a sales idea, the Westminster Bookstores introduced into their catalog a center spread entitled, "Starter Sets," for church libraries. This became a regular part of the catalog.

The new curriculum listed reference books in its teachers' magazines. There were several "starter sets," varying price. The
first one was priced at $25 and included such basic Bible study
books as The Westminster Dictionary of the Bible, Cruden's Complete Concordance, Westminster Study Edition of the Holy Bible,
plus a book on worship and prayer, and a couple of general Christian education age group teaching and administration titles.

          As denominational publisher sales increased the church col-
lections enlarged and they were forced to take their book collections
more seriously. Westminster was responsible for an early published booklet, a how-to-do-it. This interest in church libraries
led Westminster to develop The Westminster Church Library Plan
in 1944. Members of the Plan received announcements of all the
new books published by the Westminster Press, special catalogs
and a free copy of each edition of the Westminster Bookstore catalog. A 20 percent discount was extended to them on all cash orders for books purchased.

          In the late 1940's the Board of Christian Education took a
hard look at its situation. The largest office book collection was
in the leadership education department, and secretaries and editors
were duplicating titles for use in their own offices. Recognizing
the evident need, a central library was established and a full-time
librarian was employed. This library continued in Philadelphia
until the 1972 restructuring and removal of the offices from Philadelphia to New York.

          In 1956 the maroon binder was introduced as an improved
service to the churches. The Board's full-time librarian, Miss
Merran Henry and the writer, who handled all library inquiries,
revised the "how-to-do-it" booklet. The new and experimental 3-
ring loose leaf binder was mailed to members for the first time.
All new Plan members received a copy of the binder. Membership
was for a church and not for an individual. What did the loose leaf
binder contain? The binder measured 8" x 10" with a hard back
cover and would hold up to 200 pages. The insert pages measured
7" x 9". The binder contained an annotated booklist. The binder
index, by sections, was the following: Basic Reference Books;
Bible; Theology and Doctrine; Worship and Prayer; Church History
and Work; Christian Education; General Education; Church and Society; Fine Arts; General Reading; Other Classifications.

          Some sections contained subtitles: Bible: General Works,
Old Testament, New Testament; Church History and Work: All
Churches Except the United Presbyterian Church in the U.S.A.;
Christian Education: Children, Youth, Adults, Family, Administra-
tion and Leadership, Audio-Visuals, General, Higher Education,
Vocation; General Education: Philosophy, Psychology; Fine Arts:
Art, Drama, Music; General Reading: Children, Youth, Adults;
Other Classifications: Archaeology, Biography, Comparative Re-
ligion, Recreation. The list did not include current missionary ed-
ucation reading books, nor Westminster Press teen-age fiction.

Brief descriptions of these books could be found in special catalogs
available in the bookstores.

The introduction page reads: "Following is a selection of
basic books believed to be essential for a church library, recommended by the Board of Christian Education of the United Presbyterian Church in the U. S. A. A minimum list which can serve as
a starting point for local churches desiring to build a library, it
provides a concise annotation for each book. Supplements will be
sent to members of the Westminster Church Library Plan twice a
year to keep the original list up-to-date, including additions and
deletions. With these carefully annotated compilations the church
will be able to maintain a highly effective, up-to-date library for
its workers. "

The pages for the binder were blocked out for seven listings.
These blocks measured $1\frac{1}{4}$ " x $4\frac{1}{2}$ " plus a blank right hand column for
the librarian to add any notations necessary, such as accession num-
ber, date of purchase, O. P (out of print), etc. Each listing carried
the following format:

> Title. Author. Publisher. Price.
> The Annotation

The twice a year supplements were printed on a special gummed
paper, perforated for separating with specific directions about where
they were to be inserted. If a certain page were to be filled, a
new lined additional page was mailed out with the supplement. The
supplement included an instruction sheet numerically listing all
price changes and a notation if the book was out of print.

The binder was completely revised in 1960. Church librarians were requesting that the Dewey Decimal Classification and a
Sears Subject Heading be added. This service was provided. In
1962, another feature was added ... a notation about whether the
book was basic or secondary reading material for a church library
... and to that an "A, " "B, " or "C" for easy, average, or advanced
reading.

With these additions the listings appeared thus:

> Title. Author. Publisher. Price.
> The annotation
> Dewey Decimal Classification and   Basic or Secondary
> a Sears Subject Heading   "A" "B" "C"
>   "R" (reference)

About 300 book titles were listed in each revision of the
binder. Books were recommended by staff members, carefully annotated by them, and they were given the privilege of indicating a
specific classification. The list was carefully edited. Westminster
Press published the material which was free to all members of the
Westminster Church Library Plan. The binder became popular and

librarians from other denominations sought Plan membership.   By
the close of 1970, close to 4000 churches were enrolled.

      About 1962, the Executive Editor conceived a new sales idea,
a Library Guild.   This involved mailing out five times a year of a
new book which an advisory group selected.   They were not always
Westminster Press publications but did often include first edition
publications before they reached denominational bookstores.   Churches
were to budget $25 a year for the project and in turn the church
could keep the book and be billed, including discount, or return it
within a period of ten days.   Bonus books were given at intervals.
Library Guild selections were new titles and church librarians welcomed the idea.   Budget problems kept some from enrolling, but at
the start, 250 churches joined the Guild.   In time the membership
neared 1000.   Each shipment carried with it a paper listing title,
Dewey Decimal Classification, recommended Sears Heading, and a
lengthy annotation.   The latter was shortened but always appeared
in the next supplement for the binder with a note that it was "A Library Guild Selection. "

      In the early 1970's, the United Presbyterian Church did an-
other restructuring and Westminster Press closed down its bookstores.   There was an arrangement for Cokesbury Bookstores to
take them over.   The Westminster Library Plan, the Guild, and the
binder were turned over to Cokesbury which began to serve Methodist, Presbyterian and other church members.   The United Methodist
Church publishing house took over the library plan, but it has developed a different format.   A final edition of the binder was issued in
1972.   The acting librarian for the Board revised the manual and it
reflected the growth of United Presbyterian Church libraries.

Libraries

      The last known survey of church libraries made was through
reports to the Presbyterian General Assembly Office in the 1960's
At that time, about 85 percent of the churches answering the questionnaire indicated that the librarian was a non-professional volunteer.   Area workshops and conferences have helped to raise this
standard.   Since the Church and Synagogue Library Association was
organized, the percentage of non-professional librarians with workable knowledge of a library has shown an upward trend.

      There are 8, 685 United Presbyterian Churches.   Just over
500 of them have a membership of over 1, 000.   Just over 1, 000 of
them have between 500 and 1, 000 members.   An average congregation has a membership of 300 to 350.   The more affluent suburban
churches may have a professionally trained librarian on the staff.
In the average church, what is termed a "library" is merely a book
collection.   One might find the books grouped by subject.   A volunteer librarian would probably have markers on the shelves and there
would be a card file.   Checking out and returning books is on an
honor system.   The activity is mostly on Sunday.   Many suburban

churches are leasing their quarters for weekday nurseries and kindergartens, and a few share their books.

Non-print material such as films, slides, pictures, cassettes, and tapes are available from the Christian Education Consultant's office in the Synod or Presbytery. The average church does not have the equipment for projection. Cassettes and tapes belong mostly to the minister and are used for recording sermons and music to be shared later with shut-ins. Two problems most churches face with these additional items are "storage" and "servicing."

Where definitely established libraries exist there is a budget provision, plus established "Memorial Funds." In many United Presbyterian Churches the library is mainly for church school workers. The Women's Organization holds the budget strings and also names the librarian. As interest in church libraries has grown, the session or church ruling body has taken over control through its Christian Education Committee. They appoint the librarian, make the budget provision, and the Church treasurer handles the Memorial Fund. The Christian Education Committee approves any expenditures of this special fund. Some churches have a special library advisory committee through which the librarian functions.

It would be hard to estimate the average library size in volumes. We do know the range is anywhere from 100 to 7,000 volumes. Originally churches were built with no designated library space. The women's parlor became the library. If a church had a Director of Christian Education, or an Assistant Pastor with Christian education responsibilities, it was very likely that the library would be adjacent to his office. It is impossible to pick out any one particular library as being typical. Great variation is the rule, in organization, in physical facilities, in cooperation with the local public library.

Book selection is an important step in maintaining any church library. In 1974 Church and Synagogue Libraries carried a copy of "A Policy for Selecting Materials," the statement prepared by two selection committee members of the Lakewood Presbyterian Church, Lakewood, Ohio. It is easily adaptable for smaller libraries. CSLA presented its Certificate for Outstanding Congregational Librarian to Martha Durbin, Lakewood Presbyterian Church, at its 9th Annual meeting, Philadelphia, 1976.

The library in the First Presbyterian Church, Hastings, Nebraska, was organized in 1949, under the guidance of Mrs. Frank Hewitt. She served until 1960, when Mrs. Hal Shiffler became the librarian. Under her professional, competent, enthusiastic direction, the collection has been reclassified in the Dewey Decimal system, with a carefully maintained card catalog, and has been expanded to more than 5,000 well-selected volumes, a stimulating resource center. The 1976 budget was $700 allocated from the overall church budget. In addition, memorial and other gifts provide extra money for books and equipment. The routines of filing, shelving, and book accessions are maintained by three or four volunteers.

The library quarters are most pleasant and attractive and very well located. They were created from two classrooms and an alcove on the south side of the Memorial Room, beside the sanctuary. The south exposure with stained glass windows, the carpeting, special lighting, the shelves filled with books, and a round study table with comfortable chairs make a most inviting library, which is fully visible from the sanctuary when the sliding doors between the two large rooms are opened.

About 1,900 books circulated in 1975, and 264 books were added, with 96 withdrawn. There are 15 periodicals available. A new addition will be two cassette players which can be taken to shut-ins, with sermons and other programs on tape. Recently, three dozen large print books were purchased with a memorial gift of $300. Attractive book and material displays are maintained at the library entrance, and each week a notice of "What's New in the Church Library" is included in the church bulletin, which is mailed to the membership. Special Reading Lists are made available to all members. Men's Reading List includes: Fiction, General, Biography, History, America, Bible, Church and Religion, Travel and Personal. The Women's Reading List, though not broken down uneer headings, has an interesting "foot note": 6 Books for Certificate; 10 books for Certificate plus Honorable Mention.

There are a number of outstanding libraries in the Philadelphia area. Many churches have historical backgrounds since the city was the birthplace of the Presbyterian church in America. Many of the suburban churches have had an advantage. In their congregations were members of the Church's Boards and Agencies formerly located in the Witherspoon Building. Many of these church libraries became community libraries, since their areas lacked public libraries. Within the last few years a number of these libraries have celebrated their 25th anniversaries.

One of the oldest known Presbyterian church libraries is at Neshaminy-Warwick Presbyterian Church in Warminster, Pennsylvania. The library was created to serve both the church and the community. Many of these early rural churches are now suburban and in rebuilding have included facilities for a library. The Neshaminy-Warwick church library has over 2,000 volumes and serves both the church and the community.

The Abington Presbyterian Church, Abington, Pennsylvania has had a professional librarian who served as a volunteer consultant. Over the 23-year history of this library, on a designated day each week, the volunteer librarians met and worked. Violet M. Neger, librarian, reports:

> It was back in May of 1953 that the Christian Education Committee set up its first library as a community service in the Corner Church House. Since then the library has been moved several times and is now in the Parish House. The philosophy of the library has changed... from a

community library to an integral part of the ministry of
the church.   Opportunities exist for all ages to further
their own personal spiritual growth through reading, i. e.,
church curriculum for all age groups; resource material
in church history; mission; Christian beliefs and religious
living, which may not be found in our public library, make
up the large part of our collection.   An attempt has been
made to increase the number of volumes available on international relationships, economics and labor problems,
family life, recreation, the causes of juvenile delinquency,
especially emphasising how Christian faith is relevant to
these areas of daily living.   There are books for pleasure
reading.   The library today is in the mass media category: audio-visuals, tapes and cassettes of the sermons
and the sacred music events; artifacts; maps; including a
selection of framed reprints of world famous Christian
art.

The Minister of Christian Education for the Abington Church
proposed a separate room for a children's library.   This room was
next to the church library.   It had stained glass windows, built-in
bookshelves, a closet, colorful children's chairs, specially designed
reading tables, bright draperies, etc.   It was shared with a Weekday Nursery School and a volunteer children's librarian served the
youngsters and staff one morning weekly throughout the school term.

"The Volunteers of the Libraries present the following report:

Memorial Room Including Reference Room
General Circulation: June 15 to November 15, 1976
                          Books 159
                          AV-Media--tapes and cassettes 18

Children's Library Room
Circulation: June 15 to November 15, 1976 (children of
                church families)
                    Books 197
                    Records 23
                October 13 to November 15, 1976 (Weekday
                Nursery School children)
                    Books 181
                    Records 16"

From Santa Fe, New Mexico, the United Presbyterian librarian wrote "A long time ago I was introduced to the idea of a 'given
congregation' making use of that which was 'unique' about itself,
rather than doing something someone else had done.   So for two
years, the Library Committee and the Arts Committee have been
featuring at each monthly 'coffee hour' an artist and an author of
the month.   They have helped to focus attention on what we have.
Publicity was provided through newspaper and church bulletins; display space was provided, and in some cases when a new book was
available copies were there for persons to purchase and have

autographed. The First Presbyterian Church, Santa Fe, does have
the advantage of having many authors and artists in its congregation. "

In Anchorage, Alaska, the Immanuel Presbyterian Church
has a program entitled: The Seminary of the church--an ecumenical
center for adult education. The library has over 4,000 volumes.
Church membership itself is smaller than the church school enrollment figures. Here is a minister who is concerned that his congregation read and draw its own conclusions about what they believe
and why. Primarily, the books in this library are on theology, the
Bible, the church, etc... [O]ne can find some fiction... "good
books"... but the library is definitely tied into the church program.
In 1976-1977, Immanuel offered a study course "Organizing Materials
for the Small Library. "

Alaskan Presbyterians can even boast of a mobile library on
the boat Anna Jackman that plies the waters from Sitka Sound up
and down the lanes to isolated fishing communities. The books are
shared with one community after another. The students from Sheldon
Jackson College, a Presbyterian-related institution, take the books
ashore, teach the younger ones to read, and leave books for the
older folks. Since statehood, Alaska is providing books for these
communities, but it is still the missionary, his wife, and the college
students aboard the Anna Jackman who are the volunteer librarians,
checking and rechecking in and out reading material for American
Indians and Eskimos. Isolated communities await the book boat.
You see, Presbyterians do read!

Silver Spring United Presbyterian Church, Silver Spring,
Maryland, in late 1975, honored its volunteer librarian by naming
its library "The Patricia Tabler Library. " Mrs. Tabler, a professional librarian, has served for 17 years. She keeps a collection
of 100 new books in a bookcase at the rear of the sanctuary for the
600 church members. The budget has been reduced from $250 to
$50 a year, but many volumes are donated and many are new and
up-to-date books. The library has 1500 volumes. The oldest book
is The Book of Psalms, Paraphrased, published in London in 1700.
The library room is now used by groups, one being "Inter-Met, the
Seminary Without Walls. " These students are delighted to meet in
this room where they have access to the books and make frequent
use of them.

The next church library discussed could be one of the young-
est and most flourishing libraries in the United Presbyterian Church.
It is the William B. Gamble Library, Valley Community United
Presbyterian Church, Portland, Oregon. It was named for the retiring pastor and dedicated in February 1967. The Librarian has
this to say:

> It all began with a small collection of 125 books housed
> in a portable cabinet opened on Sunday only by the Women's
> Guild. When a new building program was begun in 1966,

plans included a large library room, to be fully carpeted, with lovely dark wood shelving and a 12-drawer card catalog. By dedication day, 1100 more books had been catalogued using the Dewey system. Little did that first proud library committee dream that nine years later the library would have an inventory of 3400 books, circulate 500 books a month, and be one of the most used, best loved rooms in the church building.

From the beginning, the library has contained a variety of books. The library philosophy has been to provide the best reading material that would enrich the "whole person." Art, crafts, games, music, fiction, biography, child care, psychology, etc. complement the large collection of religious titles. There is a superior children's collection of 1200 books in hard-cover, each one carefully selected to be the finest available in content and artwork. A subject card file for children's books helps parents and teachers to locate the perfect book on any subject.

Books for the library are acquired in five ways--

Church Budget	- $400 per year, plus
	$100 per year for supplies
Overtime fines	- $100 per year
Memorials	- $ 50 per year
Library Birthday	- $150 per year
Other gifts	- $ 50 per year

Each February (the library's Birthday month) we celebrate all month on Sundays by serving coffee in the library and having available 50-60 new books for friends to purchase as gifts to the library. The books are priced ahead and each book bought has the donor's name put on a bookplate in the front of the book. Promotion and publicity include a page in the monthly newsletter to the congregation. The librarian reviews important new books via "Personal Previews."

There is a cassette tape library of about 100 tapes, as well as 4 cassette tape players.

The librarian is a professional paid for 8 hours per week. There is a crew of 8 volunteers who take care of the typing, filing, shelving, cataloguing, and the myriad details that keep the library in order.

Valley Community Church has a membership of approximately 1500 members, a very lively youth and Church School program as well as an adult education program that involves 500 adults in classes every Wednesday evening for three terms a year. Against this background, the William B. Gamble Library thrives and grows.

This is an example of what can happen when there is careful planning and the building blueprints include library facilities. In addition, it points up the fact that newer congregations recognize the importance of a church library.

The William S. Culbertson Library of the National Presbyterian

Church was established in the nation's capital in 1969. It is located
in the Church Administration Building, second floor, and represents
the amalgamation of two Bible class collections. It is open Sunday
through Friday from 9:00 to 5:00, Saturday from 10:00 to 4:00. A
librarian is on duty on Wednesday and Saturday. The library is a
collection of books, journals, cassettes, audio records, microfilms,
photographs, paintings, etchings, drawings and maps available for
circulation to all congregation members. Material is loaned for
three weeks, and circulation averages 23 items per week. It provides resources for the study of church teachings by making available those items which are not generally found in local public libraries. The collection contains 3,000 volumes of Bibles, reference
books, bibliographies, fiction, and large print editions. This is a
special collection of material gathered to serve the needs of Church
members. It participates in Inter-Library loan service and is a
member of the Church and Synagogue Library Association. New
book lists are provided.

The Library's governing body is a committee whose members
have been approved by the Church Session. The Library Committee
contains sub-committees on book selection and policy, administration
and property. A branch library serves the educational programs of
the Church School and the Day School. A regular budget is provided
by the Church Session. A set of guidelines has been drawn up for
library development. Book selection policy has been developed to
guide the selection of material.

In 1955 Ghost Ranch in Abiquiu, New Mexico, was given to
the United Presbyterian Church, U.S.A. for a National Study Center.
Merran Henry, then Librarian of the Board of Christian Education, UPCUSA in Philadelphia, built this library from scratch to
7,500 books when she retired in 1975. She planned the arrangement,
selected the materials, cataloged them according to the Library of
Congress classification, processed, and shelved all the books as
well as periodicals. She even sewed curtains and cushions and
caned chairs!

The library is geared to the courses and seminars which the
ranch offers and the recreation of its guests, adult and children.
It has a minimal reference section, a fine collection of religious
books, a well-rounded general collection with a fiction room and a
children's room, plus an increasing Southwest collection. All are
housed in Cottonwood Cottage. The Library is unique in that the
latchstring is literally out 24 hours a day, 365 days a year. Anyone on the ranch may visit and study in the library any time during
his/her stay. Books are checked out by the borrower for ranch
use only, and use is heavy.

The book budget has been $700 per year. This sum is to
cover books requested by seminar leaders, about 35 periodical
subscriptions (including the Sunday New York Times) and additions
to the general collection. This is woefully inadequate in inflationary
times. However, thanks to the Westminster Press, the library

receives sample copies of its publications. Frequently, guests make
gifts, but these undergo a rigid selection process. Since the shelves
are jam-packed, if a book cannot be used, it is refused. Especially
welcome are current fiction, material on the Southwest area, ecolo-
gy, pottery, arts, crafts, and up-to-date encyclopedias.

In summary, we see that great variety exists among these
libraries, large and small. It is difficult to identify similarities
among them. However, all of them have several characteristics in
common, also. In each case, some one person or group had the
initiative and energy as well as the ambition to establish a superior
library. Further, the emphasis in most cases has been on use and
circulation, not just on book collection size. Some have worked
closely with the local public library. Some have served a public
library function and some have related very little to that library.
All have reflected a strong support of the concept that reading is
essential to the Presbyterian way of life. Many of these superior
libraries reflect the influence, somewhere in their make up, of a
committed professional librarian. In many cases, it seems obvious
that the extent and usefulness of the services given have inspired
support and cooperation from church leaders.

Elias Boudinot had a vision. He placed before us an open
door. Presbyterians like to read, so they understand more fully
the mission of the church. There is an ecumenical trend in com-
bining curricula by 1980. We can look forward to a sharing between church libraries within a given community. The librarian
has a contribution to make to the mission of the church. Elias
Boudinot in his will wrote: "I do dispose of the same, and all my
estate therein, in the following manner, wishing to do what I think,
on solemn and serious consideration, will not be contrary to His
divine will, but in the end may advance the honor of His great
name. "

ACKNOWLEDGMENTS

To those church librarians who so graciously shared with me
information about their libraries: Gretchen Lainson and Mrs. Dee
Shiffler, First Presbyterian Church, Hastings, Nebraska; Mrs.
Patricia Tabler, Silver Spring United Presbyterian Church, Silver
Spring, Maryland; Vanna L. Bewell, First Presbyterian Church,
Santa Fe, New Mexico; Glori Rodman, William B. Gamble Library,
Valley Community United Presbyterian Church, Portland, Oregon;
Reverend Hal Banks, Immanuel United Presbyterian Church, Anchor-
age, Alaska; Reverend Marvin C. Wilbur, Assistant Director, United
Presbyterian Foundation, New York, New York; Lidie Miller (Mrs.
W. D.) Billings, Montana; Librarian, Ghost Ranch Study Center,
Abiquiu, New Mexico.

NOTES

1. The Last Will and Testament of Elias Boudinot, LL. D.,
   document held by the Presbyterian Historical Society, Philadelphia, Pa. Permission to quote granted by Marvin C.
   Wilbur, Assistant Director, United Presbyterian Foundation,
   New York, New York.
2. Willard M. Rice, The History of the Presbyterian Board of
   Publication and Sabbath School Work. Philadelphia: Philadelphia Presbyterian Board of Publication and Sabbath School
   Work, pp. 28, 111.
3. The Church Library. Philadelphia: The United Presbyterian
   Board of Christian Education, Division of Publications, 1956.
4. The Amazing Heritage, Margaret D. Hummell. Philadelphia:
   Geneva Press, 1972.
5. Presbyterian Historical Society, 425 Lombard Street, Philadelphia, Pennsylvania.

EPISCOPAL CHURCH LIBRARY ACTIVITIES

Claudia Hannaford

"He that gives alms to the poor, he that clothes the naked, or feeds the hungry, will find it upon his account in the day of Judgment. But then as there are different ways of doing good; so to provide spiritual food for the Souls of men, is a charity of as much more exalted a nature, as the spirit is more excellent than the body." From this premise, developed by The Rev. Thomas Bray in his Bibliotheca Parochialis, published in 1697, libraries in Protestant Episcopal Churches of the United States of America had their beginning.

Development and growth through the years to contemporary time has been largely natural and undirected. The incentive to establish libraries has come mainly from individuals and from parishes, little from dioceses, and little or none from the provincial or national church. Yet the Episcopal Church has a heritage unmatched in awareness of the importance of religious education and a continuing appreciation of man's search for truth, "conducted in the broad perspective of Christian knowledge and faith."[1]

History

With the landing of Chaplain Robert Hunt and his fellow colonists at Jamestown, Virginia, in 1607, the Church of England came to the American shores. The Church of England remained here until 1783, when, at the close of the Revolutionary War, it became the Church in the United States of America. Meanwhile, in 1694 Col. Francis Nicholson, a zealous champion of the Church, became Governor of Maryland. He revived an Act initiated by the former Governor, who had died before it received confirmation by the Crown, to create parishes supported by a tithe on the tobacco crop. Nicholson sent a request from the Assembly that a Commissary be appointed for Maryland.

This request came to Henry Compton, who as Bishop of London was responsible for the oversight of the Church in the Colonies of America and the West Indies. Bishop Compton appointed Thomas Bray to be his Commissary. It was expected that Bray would find clergy for the vacant parishes in Maryland and go to take authority in the province and organize the life of the church.

Bray's standards were high, yet he realized that only the poorer clergy would respond to any invitation to travel to the Colonies. "... [T]o do their duty worthily... they must be fortified by knowledge, and therefore with books; yet these, as [Bray] knew only too well, they could not afford to buy. Then libraries must be provided, and a strong statement of the whole matter was drawn up, with a plea for subscriptions to provide them. With this statement, Bray went to Compton; if he and other bishops would back it, Bray would undertake the task of recruiting men, but not otherwise."[2]

Thus in 1695 a plea was printed for libraries for the missionary clergy in Proposals for Encouraging Learning and Religion in the Foreign Plantations. Canvassing was carried out for subscriptions. One of the first visits was made in the company of the Secretary of Maryland to see Princess Anne who gave a donation of forty guineas. Bray decided to present to Annapolis a library which would be the finest in the Colonies and by April 1696 was ready to send it over.

Money collection continued and libraries were sent out in the charge of missionaries or other people bound for the colonies. To avoid loss or embezzlement every book was lettered. The local minister was made responsible for their care and was required to make a triennial account to the Commissary. In 1697 Bray extended his idea to the development of lending libraries for the "gentry" with the publication of An Essay Towards Promoting All Necessary and Useful Knowledge, Both Divine and Human, in All Parts of His Majesty's Dominions, Both at Home and Abroad. The gentry were allowed to carry the books to their homes.

These lending libraries, his new idea, were to be placed in the market towns, where both clergy and gentry might have access. Another publication declared:

> I shall not only extend my endeavors for the supply of all the English Colonies in America, but can most willingly be a missionary unto every one of those Provinces to fix and settle them therein when they are obtained; being so fully persuaded of the great benefit of these kinds of libraries that I should not think them too dear a purchase even at the hazard of my life.[3]

And so plans developed along three lines: 1) the parochial library, those books provided for the personal use of the clergyman; 2) the layman's library, to be under the care of the minister, lent out by him to his parishioners and which included certain tracts for free distribution; and, 3) the lending library, set in a market town and available to all.

S. P. C. K. and S. P. G.

Realizing that the needs of the colonies could not be met by

voluntary efforts, Bray prepared "A General Plan for the Constitution of a Protestant Congregation, or Society for the Propagation of
Christian Knowledge [S. P. C. K.]. " From this plan developed two
societies, the S. P. C. K. and later the S. P. G.   Four friends met on
March 8, 1699, to form themselves into "The Society for Promoting
Christian Knowledge, " which is still in existence today.   In 1699 its
functions were to discover the best means and methods for promoting
religion and learning in any part of His Majesty's plantations, to
find fit persons to serve as chaplains overseas, and to set up parochial libraries throughout the Plantations.

          After returning from a trip to Maryland, the Society for the
Propagation of the Gospel in Foreign Parts (S. P. G.) was formed.
The S. P. C. K. had been an unchartered body, lacking power to receive, invest, and administer funds.   Incorporated in 1701, the
S. P. G. had the powers which the S. P. C. K. lacked, and so to it
was handed over responsibility for the colonies and for the funds
collected for their benefit.

          Bray kept in touch with his missionaries in Maryland and
distributed long letters in 1700 and 1701.   One dwelt on the importance of catechetical instruction and stated that if some of the Negroes could be instructed they also should join in the Sacrament.
The second letter discussed the importance of preaching and of "the
disposing and dispersing of good books among the people, "[4] since
in such extensive parishes it was impossible to visit and teach them
all.   Obviously, Bray felt them both to be important activities.
This letter listed the volumes that should compose such libraries
with the number of copies needed of each title.   "Some, " he said,
"with an Asterism prefixed, " were for "persons of better conditions, "
who would have leisure to read them; "the smaller pieces are to
be serviceable to the edification of all indifferently, and therefore
there was a larger proportion of them provided. "[5]   Complete lists
of library holdings were requested in 1724 in order to know how
they were being maintained.   The answers showed that a few had
been forgotten and neglected, but many libraries were still treasured
and kept in good use.

          In 1730, Bray formed another body to carry on library work
and to administer copyrights.   Early visits for subscriptions had
been made to the Secretary of the King of Holland, Abel Tassin
Sieur D'Allone.   At that time D'Allone became interested in the idea
of converting the Negro slaves in the colonies to Christianity, gave
money and promised more later.   When D'Allone died, his will provided these funds.   Interest from this gift was used to employ cate-
chists to serve among the Negroes, under the direction of missionaries, and to supply books and advice for their work.   Early library
efforts were directed more toward laymen's education than toward
church worker education.

Colonial Libraries

          And so these library projects spread their influence far and

wide, strengthening the pastoral work of the clery, and spreading
the knowledge of Christian doctrine. Episcopal church historians
are emphatic on the importance of the literature provided, not for
the clergy only, but also the settlers, where, with the possible exception of New England, books were very hard to obtain.

In a thesis entitled Colonial Libraries in America, Austin
Baxter Keep, Instructor at Columbia University, wrote that "Bray's
'Provincial Library,' was the first free circulating library in the
United States."[6] Writing for Historical Magazine in 1946, S. C.
McCulloch stated that "Bray's lay libraries comprised the main
body of reading material available to colonial Americans."[7]

A manuscript in the British Museum indicates that about the
year 1708, of the several libraries founded by Bray in America in
five strategic centers, there were in Maryland 1100 books at Annapolis and 1500 books in twenty-nine other places. In Virginia
there were two libraries; in New York (including New England),
four; in Carolina, one; and in Philadelphia, one, numbering 327
volumes. This last library was at the historic Christ Church.

At the time of the two hundred twenty-fifth anniversary of
the founding of Christ Church, its Rector, the Rev. Louis Washburn,
said:

> Perhaps the most vital treasure preserved by us on Second
> Street is a Library, the foundation of which was laid as
> early as 1696, by that singularly gifted man of God, Com-
> missary Bray.[8]

Keep found, while researching his thesis, that there were still some
300 among its books which belonged in the Bray Collection. Sandra
Thornton, Christ Church Bicentennial Coordinator, wrote for an "in
house" publication that this is the oldest library in Pennsylvania, its
volumes having survived fire, salt, and water damage acquired during their long voyage from abroad, and dampness, dust and temperature changes ... in the Church. The collection was transported to
the Library Company, Philadelphia, in the 1950's to ensure its
care.

Later Libraries

In 1839, three years after the death of Bishop William White
of Christ Church, Philadelphia, a Parish Library Association was
organized to honor his memory, by "an earnest churchwoman of the
same city" for the purpose of supplying feeble Parishes and Missionary Stations with Theological Books for the use of the Rectors
or Missionaries in charge.[9] Giving uninterrupted service down to
the present day, the Association (according to Rev. James L. Shan-
non, present Corresponding Secretary) has distributed grants to each
one of the fifty states and to other continents. Its Constitution states
that books and other reading material will be distributed, so far as

its means permit, "either by direct grant to the clergyman of the
parish for the time being or by gift to the vestrymen and wardens
of the parish for the parish library or in such other manner as the
Board of Managers may desire." The history of Episcopal church
libraries is long indeed.

There is little reference to libraries in national papers of
the Episcopal Church, although in 1859, "By Order of the House of
Bishops, William White, D.D., Presiding Bishop," the Journal of
General Convention of that year carries a list of titles for a "Library for a Parish Minister."

The Seventh Annual Report of the Woman's Auxiliary of the
Episcopal Church indicates the interest of women in establishing a
Domestic Missionary Lending Library at their headquarters,

> ... from which books should be sent out to the Mission-
> aries, retained by them for one or two months, as time
> for reading required, and sent back through the mail.
> Should the Missionaries feel unable to meet any expense
> connected with the Library, the whole cost of procuring
> books and of sending through the mail was assumed by the
> members of the Woman's Auxiliary interested in the
> plan. [10]

This library was begun in 1880, after one of the members, who had
heard of the "great destitution of many of our Missionaries regarding
books," urged its establishment and gave a contribution as the beginning of a library fund. Circulars were sent to the Missionaries,
telling them of the idea, asking their advice concerning it, and requesting them to suggest titles for books to be placed in such a library. Under "Woman's Work" in Spirit of Missions, Vol. 45
(1880), the official publication of the Episcopal Church at the time,
is an article about this library which states that it is intended only
as a supplement to the Bishop White Parish Library Association,
and is not meant to supersede gifts of books sent out in Missionary
boxes each year.

At this same time, the Secretary of the New York Committee
on Work for Foreign Missionaries originated the idea of forming
another collection, to be called a Lending Library for Missionary
Workers. It differed from the Domestic Missionary Library

> in that, while the one is intended primarily for the benefit
> of our Missionaries, this is intended to benefit them only
> in a secondary way, as acting upon the hearts and under-
> standings of our workers here at home, and disposing
> them to increase their interest, their prayers, and offer-
> ings for Missions and Missionaries at home and abroad. [11]

Gifts of books and money for this library were solicited through
diocesan and parish officers of the Woman's Auxiliary. The collection encompassed books on foreign or domestic mission work and

also books of travel "bearing on the countries in which our Missions
have already been established."[12] Secretaries of the various parish
organizations connected with the Woman's Auxiliary were encouraged
to draw out volumes for circulation in their respective parishes for
a certain length of time, perhaps six months, with the idea that
such "diffusion of information is the surest way of enlisting sympathy
for Mission work."[13]

Meanwhile, in New York City, women were banding together
to pack and send church periodicals to missionaries in remote
places.   Church women had been sending church magazines to isolated clergymen, some of the material going westward on Wells
Fargo coaches.   In 1888 at the Church of the Holy Communion the
first official meeting of their Church Periodical Club was held.   By
1892 there were 48 dioceses interested and a need for incorporation.
From this beginning grew a national organization which is today an
affiliated agency of the Executive Council of the Episcopal Church.
By 1920 the General Convention recognized the missionary work
being done and put the Church Periodical Club on its budget.

CPC projects range from giving a single book or subscription
to a shut-in, or one hospitalized or imprisoned, to provisioning entire schools and complete libraries from Appalachia to Southern
Asia, sending material to reservations, ghettos, rural missions,
and seminaries.   CPC is unique among Christian denominations in
that recipients are given material of their own choice and in a wide
variety.

Through all the expansion of its activities, a basic principle
of the CPC is still personal sending and the promotion of friendliness by an exchange of letters.   The organization is supported by
contributions and most of its work is done by volunteers.   Needs
that exceed local resources are referred to the National Books Fund,
a committee which meets in the national office to consider requests.
When CPC was faced with a budget deficit in 1976, women again
showed their concern for this "Ministry of the Printed Word" when
a portion of donations from the United Thank Offering of the Church
were made available in a matching fund campaign.   Perhaps it should
be noted that many of these early library efforts were initiated by
women parishioners and were originally designed to aid missionaries.

CPC's Newsletter, the CPC NBF Quarterly (Church Periodical Club/National Books Fund), reported in 1975 that only two
churches among all major Christian denominations had agencies
specifically and solely designed to meet needs for printed material:
The Church Periodical Club of the Episcopal Church, and the Anglican Church's Society for the Propagation of Christian Knowledge.

In the autumn of 1953, in the Midwest, another idea was
born for the Episcopal Church.   This idea was that laymen wanted
to know more about the Church and that a book club would answer
that need.   The Episcopal Book Club was started with a local mailing list from a small parish.   This club has functioned without

diocesan or General Convention appropriations or assistance from
any arm of the national Church.

The Episcopal Book Club operates in much the same manner
as other book clubs, with certain exceptions. It does not publish
books, but acquires them in wholesale quantities, selecting titles to
be issued four times a year on the basis of their literary value as
well as their doctrinal content. Profits from sales are used to
promote and encourage the arts and knowledge which speak of the
Church and to sponsor new projects in those fields. One project
came into being in 1971: Operation Pass Along, the Anglican Book
Depot, which distributes second-hand books about the Church to sem-
inarians, priests, and churches. The books are free, the recipients
reimbursing only the postage. Books have been sent to APO and
FPO locations and to foreign countries.

National Headquarters Library

Paralleling these individual and unrelated efforts to spread
the Christian message through the printed word, a headquarters library was established for the Episcopal Church in the year 1832.
It began as a Missionary Library through the Church's Domestic
and Foreign Missionary Society. Only occasional references to this
library appear in printed Committee proceedings, and these generally
pertain to procuring material. Having been started to supply missionaries with reading matter, a step beyond was to provide information about missions to those who were supporting them.

In 1919 the Board of Missions and the other agencies became
the National Council of the Church. Church members were now
supporting a unified program through the Every Member Canvass
and needed information on all aspects of that program. The Library
that developed in response to this need was broadened to cover all
of the various activities of the Church's National Council.

The Library moved into larger quarters several times. It
carried on a large lending service, much of it by mail. The only
charge was a small rental fee for each book borrowed, plus the return postage. The collection emphasized the three main activities
of the Church's work--domestic and overseas missions, Christian
education, and Christian social relations. Perhaps the most valuable
feature of the library was its collection of books on the history of
the Episcopal Church.

The official house organ of the Episcopal Church in 1957,
Churchways, featured the library in a series on services of the
National Council, and described it as a means by which the Church
is able to reach its people in all parts of the world. Reference inquiries then almost equalled book circulation:

The librarian's day is a busy one. People are constantly
writing, telephoning, or calling in person to ask for

information on such varied subjects as the population of
New Mexico, the Episcopalian's view of the Russian Orthodox Church, and embroidery directions for altar hang-
ings. [14]

Headquarters library service may have reached its peak in
the fifties, while the Rt. Rev. Henry Knox Sherrill was Presiding
Bishop of the Church. In 1963 the National Council Library and
the Christian Education Library were combined in a spacious room
given and furnished in honor of Bishop Sherrill. [15]

In succeeding years, as more local parish and public library
services developed, the National Council Library received fewer
calls. When the Church's national budget was drastically reduced
in 1970, the library budget was cut in half. "Christian Education"
had developed a Program Resource Center and "Service to Dioceses"
had developed a Diocesan Information Center, both of them quite
active. In 1971 the lending function of the Library was discontinued,
many books were disposed of and those which remained were combined with the Program Resource Center and Diocesan Information
Center material. [16]

Parish Libraries
──────────────────

On the parish level, there is no comprehensive information
available regarding libraries for congregational use. A communicant at Christ Episcopal Church, Bronxville, New York, described
how an unexpected gift enabled that church to furnish rooms in the
newly constructed parish house for use as a library. For several
years before, a table at the back of the church held a number of
books on religious subjects, most of them having been purchased by
the Altar Guild to stimulate and enrich the devotional life of parishioners. More than one person, exasperated by the poor service,
had expressed the desire for a properly organized parish library.
But no one had a very clear idea about what a parish library ought
to look like or contain. [17] This is a typical example of how a library starts.

It appeared that while many parishes might have an assortment of books which parishioners could borrow, few had a carefully
selected and cataloged collection that could be graced by the term
"library." From data gathered for a directory of church libraries
published in 1967, this picture of the church library emerged:

> Almost without exception church and synagogue librarians
> were volunteers, although many were retired professional
> librarians or married women with library science degrees.
> In some cases, accurate records of accessions and circu-
> lation were kept, but since the majority operated on a
> self-service basis, many kept no circulation records and
> some did not have exact records of the number of vol-
> umes. [18]

Other examples can be given.   At St. Paul's, Washington, D. C., a parish of 450 communicants, one of the devotional societies sponsored the library, supporting it with yearly grants and personnel toward the time it should be self-supporting.   Proceeds from a booth at the annual bazaar and a book rental fee provided additional funding.[19]   A small mission in Duluth, Minnesota, allocated one percent of its yearly budget for a library.   It had no special room, no staff, no regular hours.[20]

At the Church of the Holy Faith, Santa Fe, New Mexico, amateurs devised a cataloging system and operated a parish library with under fifty books.   This library was not included in the church budget, but with three to eight women meeting weekly to care for its business, and under the devoted direction of Marian Wasson, in thirteen years the collection grew to 2,000 volumes.[21]   There was no coordination or direction for any church library efforts from the national headquarters of the Episcopal Church.

In 1958 a group of dedicated Texas women concluded that their jobs as parish librarians required much more than they had realized.   In an attempt to help each other with suggestions, questions, and helpful hints, they began a Round Robin letter for interested persons.   Library and parish bookstore operators, largely from Texas, but including others from several sections of the nation, contributed to the letter, sending book notes and sharing informational items.   For a few years they held annual interdiocesan bookstore and library conferences at which workshops dealt with the practical aspects of operating parish libraries and bookstores.

Their letters, copies of which are in the Archives of the Episcopal Church Historical Society at Austin, Texas, indicate the service orientation of both libraries and bookstores--a book bank enabled mission congregations to start libraries; surplus profits from some bookstores were distributed for missions, college work, or Christian education projects.

By 1961 their Round Robin publication had grown to such a size that they found themselves unable to continue it.   The Texas group shared its experiences with the national church's Department of Christian Education, and its publisher, the Seabury Press.   Their Round Robin became the forerunner of the Parish Library Newsletter and sparked a new parish library program for the Episcopal Church. The Parish Library Newsletter was published and distributed free nationally by the Seabury Press and the Department of Christian Education.   First issued in June 1961, it acted as a vehicle through which parish librarians could exchange information and experiences. Readers supplied much of the content.

A large staff and comprehensive program in Christian Education marked the sixties for the Episcopal Church.   Its National Council had published a small pamphlet entitled When a Parish Starts a Library, an outline to help vestries or parish planning committees. A more detailed Guide for Parish Libraries followed, with the Texas

"Round Robin" librarians contributing to the manuscript. An extensive list of "Recommended Books for Parish Libraries" was compiled.

The Seabury Press initiated a Parish Library Book Plan and
also a Christian Education Publications Plan, by which subscribers
automatically received material considered suitable for parish libraries and for study courses which were prepared for the national
Department of Christian Education.

In 1965 Christian Education Findings began carrying a "Parish
Library News" page, which replaced the Newsletter. The magazine
regularly included book and audio visual reviews, and periodically
there were reading lists and feature articles of interest to librarians. It was first a monthly (except summer), then a quarterly,
and was last issued in 1971. Presently, the Episcopal Church cooperates with several other denominations in publishing J E D Share,
a quarterly paper for teachers and leaders, with minimal direct
reference to libraries.

In the fall of 1976 the Seabury Book Service began publishing
a monthly magazine of special interest to religious libraries. New
Review of Books and Religion is designed to be "the most comprehensive critical review medium for religious books in the English-
speaking world. "[22] One-source ordering of any book reviewed on
its pages is offered as well as a reduced price for the book featured
editorially each month; there is freedom of selection with no auto-
matic shipments. This publication and its Book Service are available to all interested persons.

Meanwhile, the Parish Library Plan of the Seabury Press
continues to offer its book acquisitions program for churches, with
discount prices on selected books. Today each new member of the
Plan is given a free copy of a handbook on publicizing and promoting
congregational library use, and reaching people through programs
and other library-sponsored events. [23] This helpful book is the work
of a non-Episcopal author and publisher.

In spite of its traditional regard for education, however, and
a stated belief that the more thoroughly and reliably informed
Churchmen are about their faith and its application, the more effective their witness will be in the world, parish libraries in individual
congregations have been allowed no official relationship to national
Episcopal Church leadership or program.

Among the small number of items pertaining to parish libraries in the Archives and Historical Collections of the church,
only one national Church publication could be located. It is a draft
copy of a Christian education pamphlet incorporating a suggested
reading list with suggestions for building a parish lay library. [24]

The Church's national headquarters has no information or
statistics regarding the number, location, or size of parish libraries.

The Episcopal Church Annual is compiled from material supplied by its various dioceses, Executive Council departments, and parochial institutions and organizations. The yearbook's alphabetical index has no listing pertaining to libraries. There is nothing in the table of contents under "Institutions and Organizations, Education, " "Other Institutions and Organizations, " nor their subdivisions, "Miscellaneous" and "General. " Parochial reports, filed annually, provide no space for data about libraries although at least one communicant has officially requested, without success, that this be included.

The Current Picture

For Maryland, however, where Thomas Bray's efforts to establish religious libraries first touched the land which was to become the United States, certain current information is available. Data were gathered in 1973 by Joyce L. White, an Episcopalian, in compiling a Directory of Church and Synagogue Libraries in Maryland. Among those responding to a mail questionnaire, a few Episcopal churches provided statistics regarding their collections, finances, and services. A summary of them follows here:

> Most of the libraries were established in the nineteen sixties.
> All are operated on a self-service basis during hours the building is open, though some are staffed in addition at certain stated times.
> All personnel are unpaid volunteers.
> While the majority are non-professionals, one-fourth reported libraries under the direction of a retired or active librarian.
> About $87\frac{1}{2}$ percent have an annual operating budget under $100, which helps to explain other statistics reported in the Directory. One-half have no non-book material. Two-thirds have a collection of only 500 or fewer books.
> Even so, three-fourths of them attempt to serve the entire congregation. About ten percent are children's libraries. Another ten percent report service to the local community.
> The majority circulate less than ten books per week. [25]

The present Presiding Bishop of the Episcopal Church, The Rt. Rev. John M. Allin, has stated:

> A parish library can be a resource for Christian education and spiritual discipline, or a prison for otherwise useful money that is locked within unused books on neglected bookshelves in parish halls. People in the congregation who care and share books are the difference between a useful spiritual and educational resource and a memorial to waste. Many congregations do better to share and support circulating-lending libraries, rather than investing in volumes that will be seldom used. Every library

to serve a congregation is dependent upon someone or
some group who continually offers available books to others. 26

With no national directives or guidelines, and obviously little
national interest or encouragement, individual libraries differ in
scope and characteristics, as well as in their relationship to the
official parochial structure.   Often they have been established to
provide resources for Christian education or collections for children.
Their physical quarters vary greatly.   Their "staff" may consist of
only one person.   The following are profiles of several Episcopal
Church Libraries which illustrate this diversity.

St. Paul's Parish Library, Greenville, Ohio was begun in
1961 when the Rector suggested that they should "do something"
about the many books scattered around the church building.   St.
Paul's is a congregation of 120 communicants.   The church is located on the edge of the business district in a rural community of
15, 000 persons and is the only Episcopal church in the county.

The congregation contained no librarian, but an interested
parishioner received advice from the city library on organizing a
collection for effective use.   The church library was begun with
books already on hand.   They were placed on a 30-inch wide, two-
shelf metal cart with casters.   This unit was located in an entryway
on weekdays, then rolled into a lounge where Sunday coffee hours
were held after morning services.

In the beginning there were no budgeted funds.   Occasional
donations were received, and for a few years the largest source of
income was the proceeds from weekly Lenten luncheons served by
parish women after services and open to the community.   The annual amount realized from this source grew from $15 to $80 in
four years.   In addition, the church school department and the Episcopal Churchwomen's Association provided funds to develop a basic
collection in the library's early years.

Resource material for the church school, books for children,
encyclopedias and other Biblical reference material, and volumes
on theology, ethics, history, psychology, biography and fiction comprised the collection.   There were no audio visuals.   Reading clubs
for youth and talks to various parish groups were the prime means
of publicity.

The library grew to 600 volumes and some recordings, first
requiring a second cart, and later additional shelving.   For this,
the bell tower area, approximately ten feet square, was utilized.
This was first floor space previously considered unusable, but well-
located, just off the main entrance and nave.   A parishioner mounted
hanging shelves on a wall and around a corner.   There was space
for a chair and a card catalog stand.

Books were listed by author, title, and subject, and the

standard format was used on catalog cards. The classification system was developed by two church women. The call number contained a letter of the alphabet to designate a broad subject category
plus the book's accession number. Since the bell tower afforded no
work area, all book processing was done in the librarian's home,
where supplies and files were kept. A self-service book circulation
system was established, with one of the original metal carts providing the facility for borrowing and returning books.

During the fifth year of operation, expansion in the church
parish hall made a larger area available for library use. A room
18' x 12' located next to the main worship area and adjacent to a
lounge, was fitted with shelving, storage, and display space. A
handsome dining room table and chairs, paintings, and a chandelier
were given to the church to furnish its new library room.

There is now regular financial support, approximately $150
annually, part of the church's Christian education budget. The
church school is the largest library user. One individual is responsible for the library, a lay person recruited by the Senior Warden to serve an indefinite term. This parish volunteer worker relates directly to the Senior Warden and to the Rector.

Occasionally, a new book is highlighted in the parish newsletter, but no special promotion or service is offered. There is
no affiliation with any library association as a source of information
and help. For the last decade the collection has not increased
measurably in size, and numerous personal changes have occurred.
These factors may account for the fact that, although open five days
a week plus Sundays, and available to the general public, the library
is used by very few adults.

Revitalization and major enlargement of the parish library at
the Church of the Mediator, Allentown, Pennsylvania, was undertaken with the coming of a new Rector a few years ago. A small
library had been maintained for several years; then, in 1974, a
Board was organized and the collection and services expanded. A
room twenty feet square, located on the first floor of the main administrative wing of the parish house was redecorated, equipped,
and dedicated as the Harry Green Memorial Library.

Its collection, which includes many of the Rector's own books,
totals 3,000 volumes, 65 magazines and newsletters, and 8 journals.
Categories are restricted to religion, psychology, history, biography,
reference and curriculum resources. Audio visuals include tapes,
records, films, and filmstrips. About $750 is available annually
for operation, largely realized from gifts, memorials and book
fairs. A small amount is provided from the general church budget.

The library hours are from 9 until 4:30 five days a week,
and from 9 to 12:30 on Sunday. The collection is open to the public
for reference use. Area college students use the library for research and paper preparation. Books are loaned on a self-service

basis to church members, and, on application, to other interested
persons.   The Church of the Mediator, with 700 communicants, is
a center of operation for two other Episcopal churches in the immediate area, and the library serves them, too.

The Parish Education Commission appoints Library Board
members for two-year terms.   The Board reports to the Vestry
which is the governing body of the church.   Board members serve
on working committees--Administration, Book Selection, Classifications, Circulation and Publicity, and Equipment.   The chairman is
a lay person.   Professional librarians, members of the Associated
Episcopal Parishes of Allentown, catalog the collection and use the
Dewey Decimal Classification system.   Children's books are color-
coded by subject.   Services include story hours, book reviews, and
church school class visit for instruction in library use.   The library
is rapidly establishing itself as a vital functioning part of the
church's ministry.

Proceeds from church bookshop sales provide funds for operation and for a part-time paid Director for the Parish Library
at St. David's, Austin, Texas.   The interest and work of one individual, supported by the Rector, was largely responsible for the
establishment of the library.   It was started in 1954 with books
placed on a cart in a corner of the parish house.   This was soon
changed to a room where the library and the bookshop were located
together.

Presently, a room 10' x 25' serves as the library.   The
collection consists of 1,200 books, mostly religious and inspirational
literature, including biography and religious fiction, and a section
of reference books.   There are no audio visuals.   Cataloging is
done by a lay person who uses the Dewey Decimal Classification
System.   The library is open to church members and other persons
who are interested.   Regular hours are 9:30 to 5 five days a week,
and from 9 to 10:30 on Sunday mornings.

The Rector chooses an Executive Committee, and its chairman selects volunteers to staff the bookshop and library.   The volunteers operate independently from other church organizations.
There is one paid General Manager who functions both in the bookshop and in the library.   St. David's is the largest congregation
(1500 communicants) among a dozen Episcopal churches in the city.
This church is one of those responsible for arousing the interest of
its national headquarters in parish libraries in the nineteen sixties.

Substantial financial support is evidence of the interest of
Trinity Church, Newtown, Connecticut, in its parish library. $550
is allocated annually from the congregation's operating budget.   Approximately $300 additionally is received from memorial gifts,
profits from a semi-annual poster sale, and other fund-raising activities.

The church was founded in 1732 and the First Rector had a

parochial library provided by the Society for the Propagation of the Gospel in Foreign Parts. No trace of this historic collection remains. A nineteenth-century Sunday School Library existed also, but only a list of titles remains of that. Six years ago Trinity's library was comprised of several hundred old and unused books. The present librarian, an interested lay volunteer, was able to convince the Rector and the Vestry that an investment in renewal would create a used library.

There are 2200 books, including children's books and fiction, and 200 recordings, in the present collection. Recently, cassette tapes have been added to the holdings. Originally purchased for church school use, they now include sermons and recordings of special events of the local church, as well as tapes purchased on a wide variety of subjects. Trinity Church Library is housed in a second-floor general meeting room 15' x 45' in size. The library is open whenever the church itself is open, and the collection is available to the public. A self-service system has been established for circulation of materials.

Books are shelved in alphabetical order by the author's surname within broad subject categories. Close cataloging is not done. Books on personal problems and social welfare, for example, are grouped together. Worship, music and art are combined in another division. Children's books are classified according to age group rather than subject matter--pre-school, primary, junior or intermediate, junior high, and senior high. The simple method of classification is adapted from a plan devised by Erwin E. John, author of The Key to a Successful Church Library. [27]

The staff is selected by the librarian, who is an ex-officio member of the Christian Education committee, which is chaired by a Vestry member. The present librarian, a housewife, became so interested in developing Trinity's parish library that she returned to college and recently received a Master's degree in Library Science.

One of the many services offered by the library committee is direct classroom delivery of appropriate material. Since the church school is structured on five week "mini courses" created at Trinity, and taught by a succession of different teachers during the year, this specialized attention is very important and helpful.

Newtown is a bedroom community for nearby Bridgeport. Population in the township is 18,000. Trinity's membership is approximately 400 communicants. As the church approaches its 250th anniversary, the parish library, after numerous unsuccessful beginnings in the past, is now firmly established.

An Award-winning Library

At the 1970 annual Conference of the American Library

Association, the John Cotton Dana Award was presented to Christ
Church Library, Oil City, Pennsylvania. [28]   Oil City is an industrial
center with 18,000 population, and Christ Church's communicant list
numbers 550.

The following newspaper report outlines that library's services:

> Presentation of the John Cotton Dana Award to Christ
> Episcopal Church Library comes exactly five years after
> the library was established at the church by a committee
> of interested persons.   An Open House marked the dedi-
> cation of the Library in June, 1965.   There were approx-
> imately 300 books in the beginning collection, many of
> which were donated or used copies.   Since that time the
> library's holdings have increased to nearly two thousand
> books and recordings, a picture file, pamphlet file, and
> audio visual material.   The library has been administered
> and operated by a committee of lay volunteers and is open
> daily on a self-service basis.   All books come from do-
> nations and memorial gifts.   Church library resources
> have regularly been made available to those outside the
> Church.
>
> Early in 1969, the library, cooperating with the Oil
> City Ecumenical Commission, initiated a special ecumeni-
> cal book collection to meet the requests of persons in the
> community participating in Living Room Dialogue groups.
>
> Christ Church is one of four Oil City members of the
> national Church and Synagogue Library Association which
> make their books available to public library patrons through
> interlibrary loan.   It sponsored the first tri-city church
> librarians' Round Table, and last fall again hosted this
> group for an all-day training session which was free to
> interested persons.   The library sponsors each year a
> monthly book discussion program for adults open to the
> public and in 1969 began a similar program for community
> teenagers.   Books have been taken to meetings of the
> NAACP for loan and to the Handicapped Persons Associa-
> tion of Venango County.
>
> An active library program within the parish includes
> summer story hours, reading clubs, home book delivery
> service for shut-ins, reference instruction classes for
> church school students, and special events such as recog-
> nition of National Library Week, Children's Book Week,
> etc.   The library committee directs locally the Church
> Periodical Club which is an agency of the national Epis-
> copal Church formed to provide books and magazines for
> missions.   Recently, high school students interested in
> helping with the church library organized formally as Li-
> brary Aides.   They elected officers and meet regularly
> for programs and work sessions.   This group raised its
> own funds to attend a conference of the Church and Syna-
> gogue Library Association. [29]

This library grew out of the need felt for a centralized collection of material pertaining to the Episcopal Church.   Its annual
reports indicate that a group of interested persons met to formulate
plans, then organized and continued regular meetings, becoming the
parish library committee.   Their activities included arranging fund-
raising projects and establishing a Gift Nook, with proceeds for the
support of the library.   Purchase of supplies and other material
was later underwritten by a $100 annual amount in the general church
budget.

The Christ Church library accepted the charge to serve the
entire person for immediately after its organization, programs and
services were designed and extended for the benefit of the local
community. [30] Approximately one-third of its book circulation was
to persons outside the parish.

Gifts of these people and parishioners enabled the library to
add an average of more than 300 books a year in its first five years
of operation.   Its relevant collection reflects this statement of the
Religious Book Publishers Division of the Association of American
Publishers:

> Religious books are also about love, sex, politics, war,
> peace, ecology, theology, philosophy, drugs, race, dis-
> sent, ethics, technology, hippies, morality, revolution,
> rock, God, beauty, psychology, dogma, the underground,
> the establishment, death, and... life. [31]

Today it is accepted that religious libraries are tools for
communicating the Church's wisdom.   Thomas Bray's biographer
wrote of his deep insight in realizing that "an informed mind is not
enough; it must lead to a dedicated heart: that is the aim of religious education. "[32]

The Future

In October 1977 Bray's Societies became the pattern and
English counterparts of a new venture for Episcopalians.   At the
invitation of the Presiding Bishop, nineteen prominent Episcopal
Church personalities gathered in New York City to found "The Seabury Society for the Advancement of Christian Literature and Learning. " The membership brochure states:

> Like Thomas Bray and his colleagues who organized,
> nearly three centuries ago, the Society for the Propagation
> of the Gospel and the Society for Promoting Christian
> Knowledge--to which the American Church owes an enor-
> mous debt--we should sense, with no little urgency, the
> need in our own time to promote Christianity and Godly
> learning. [32]

The stated purposes of the Society are 1) to focus the

attention and to enlist the support of responsive churchpeople in an effort to meet the need, in an increasingly secular age, for the advancement of literature and learning shaped by theological perception and molded by moral imagination; 2) to awaken throughout the Church an awareness of the importance... of literature and learning which is distinctly Christian... 3) to sponsor and promote appropriate research and development programs which will assist... to achieve these purposes.... [33]

This fledgling Society appears so far to be a funding base aspiring to future publications of Christian classics, the church's doctrine, prayer book interpretation and an audio-visual program "to make the teaching and texture of Christianity available in new, enriching ways."

The invitation to membership is extended to all persons and begins:

> Episcopalians are traditionally people of the word and sacrament. We have long believed that the word, in all its subtle shadings of meaning, is both enlivening and enlightening. We have seen that it can instruct and entertain and challenge to action; we know it can console, convert, and galvanize. We therefore cherish the Book and all books written by those wise and eloquent in their instruction. But what we cherish we do not always properly use. [34]

While Bray is lauded in this leaflet, libraries are not mentioned. "What we cherish we do not always properly use," the Society recognizes. It is hoped that the Episcopal Church will one day recognize that it can use religious libraries as tools for communicating The Book and all books of the Church's wisdom.

BIBLIOGRAPHY

Allin, John M., Presiding Bishop, Protestant Episcopal Church. Episcopal Church Center, New York. Form letter, n. d.

Bishop White Parish Library Association. Charter-Constitution and By-laws. 1976.

Bishop White Parish Library Association. 136th Annual Report. Philadelphia: n.p., 1975.

Buzzard, Mary. "Hillspeak's Sensible Dreamer." The Bulletin, Evanston, Ill.: Seabury-Western Theological Seminary, n.d.

CPC NBF Quarterly. New York: Church Periodical Club (1974, 1975, 1976).

Christ Church, Oil City, Pa. Annual Report (Mimeographed) 1965-1970.

Emery, Julia C. , A Century of Endeavor: 1821-1921.   Chicago:
    Hammond Press, 1921.

Episcopal Church.   Archives - Historical Collections.   The Round
    Robin No. 10 (February 1961) (Mimeographed)

Episcopal Church. Dept. of Christian Education.   Building Your
    Parish Lay-Library.   New York: National Council, n. d.
    (Typewritten)

Episcopal Church. Dept. of Christian Education.   A Guide for Par-
    ish Libraries, Greenwich, Conn. , 1961.

Episcopal Church Annual.   Edited by Ronald T. C. Lau.   New York:
    Morehouse-Barlow Co. , 1976.

Fainter, Ruth, General Manager, St. David's Bookshop and Library,
    Austin, Texas, Personal letter, April, 1977.

Foland, H. L. , Episcopal Book Club, Eureka Springs, Arkansas.
    Personal letter, August 1976.

Johnson, Margaret. "Of Making Many Books There Is No End, "
    Spirit of Missions XCIV (1929), pp. 672, 673.

Lewis, Marianna O. , Ed.   The Foundation Directory, 4th Edition.
    New York, Columbia University Press, 1971.

MacMillan, A. Malcolm, Rector, Church of the Mediator, Allentown,
    Pennsylvania, Personal letter, April, 1977.

NOTES

1.   Chitty, Arthur Ben, The Episcopal Church in Education.   Cin-
     cinnati: Forward Movement Publications, n. d. , p. 20.
2.   Thompson, H. P. , Thomas Bray. London: S. P. C. K. , 1954,
     p. 15.
3.   Washburn, Louis C. , Christ Church Philadelphia: A Sympo-
     sium Compiled in Connection with the Two Hundred and
     Twenty-fifth Anniversary.   Philadelphia: Macrae Smith Co. ,
     1925, p. 159.
4.   Thompson, op. cit. , p. 65.
5.   Ibid. , p. 65.
6.   Washburn, op. cit. , pp. 160-61.
7.   Ibid. , p. 105.
8.   Ibid. , p. 280.
9.   Bishop White Parish Library Association, "Its Nature and Ob-
     jects, " Charter (of Incorporation): Constitution, By-laws and
     Explanatory Statement.   Philadelphia: McCalla & Stavely,
     1865, p. i.
10. "Woman's Work: The Domestic Missionary Lending Library"
     Spirit of Missions XLV (1880), p. 177.

11. "Woman's Work: Our Lending Library for Missionary Work-
     ers," Spirit of Missions XLV (1880), p. 327.
12. Ibid., p. 327.
13. Ibid.
14. "National Council Library Serves You," Churchways XI (No-
     vember-December 1957), p. 7.
15. Good Samaritan, Inc., DuPont Building, Wilmington, Delaware,
     Incorporated in 1938. "Broad purposes: charitable giving,
     with emphasis on higher education." Marianna O. Lewis,
     Ed., The Foundation Directory, 4th ed. New York, Columbia
     Univ. Press, 1971, p. 57.
16. Avis Harvey, Librarian, Henry Knox Sherrill Resource Center,
     Executive Council of the Episcopal Church, New York. In-
     terviews and correspondence, May 1976 - February 1977.
17. Scott, Charles Wheeler, "From Book Table to Parish Library,"
     Findings X (May 1962), pp. 14, 15.
18. Rodda, Dorothy and John Harvey, compilers, Directory of
     Church Libraries, Drexel Library School Series No. 22.
     Philadelphia: Drexel Press, 1967.
19. Sargent, Robert, "Problems and Pleasures," Parish Library
     Newsletter II (January 1963), unp.
20. Litras, Harriet F., "What Basic Books to Buy," Parish Li-
     brary Newsletter I (June 1962), unp.
21. Wasson, Mrs. Alexander, "Do-it-Yourself Project Flourishes,"
     Parish Library Newsletter II (June 1963), unp.
22. "A Statement of Purpose," The New Review of Books and Re-
     ligion I (September 1976), p. 2.
23. Smith, Ruth S., Getting the Books Off the Shelves: Making
     the Most of Your Congregation's Library. New York: Haw-
     thorn Books, Inc., 1975.
24. Hearn, Elinor S., Assistant to the Archivist, Archives and
     Historical Collections, Episcopal Church, Austin, Texas.
     Personal letter, June 1976.
25. White, Joyce L., Ed., Directory of Church and Synagogue
     Libraries in Maryland. Bryn Mawr, Pa.: Church and Syna-
     gogue Library Association, 1973.
26. Allin, John M., Presiding Bishop, Protestant Episcopal Church,
     Episcopal Church Center, New York, Personal letter, Feb-
     ruary 1977.
27. John, Erwin E. The Key to a Successful Church Library,
     Minneapolis: Augsburg Publishing House, 1967, pp. 7-11.
28. "John Cotton Dana Award to Oil City Church," Church and
     Synagogue Libraries III (July 1970), p. 3.
29. "Christ Episcopal Church Library Chosen to Receive Special
     Award," Oil City (Pa.) Derrick CXXXIII (6 June 1970), p. 3.
30. Quoted in Findings X (May 1962), op. cit., p. 15.
31. "The Editor's Pad," Church and Synagogue Libraries VI (May-
     June 1973), p. 2.
32. Thompson, op. cit., p. 109.
33. The Seabury Society for the Advancement of Christian Litera-
     ture and Learning. Membership Brochure. New York:
     Seabury Press, n. d.

34. The Seabury Society for the Advancement of Christian Litera-
    ture and Learning. The Past Is Prologue. New York:
    Seabury Press, n. d. , p. 1.

35. Ibid.

CHRISTIAN CHURCH (DISCIPLES OF CHRIST) LIBRARIES

Fay Wiseman Grosse

The Disciples of Christ began on American soil in the early nineteenth century. With the pioneers they began in West Virginia, Pennsylvania, Kentucky and North Carolina and moved westward. They were described by Winfred Ernest Garrison in his book, Whence and Whither the Disciples of Christ, as "a few free and friendly spirits who wanted to find a way by which all sincere followers of Jesus Christ could be united on the original, simple and saving elements of Christianity and could at the same time have complete liberty in all matters of opinion."[1] For them, liberty and union must go together. They considered themselves a religious movement and not a denomination, but a denomination they became.

From the beginning they believed in education, both for their ministers and their membership. They believed in simplicity but not ignorance. In fact, their first leaders, Barton W. Stone, Thomas Campbell, Alexander Campbell and Walter Scott, were all scholars and teachers who believed in a head and heart religion which required the education of the whole person. Early they established colleges (Bacon in 1836 and Bethany in 1840), and, believing in the printed word, they began publishing periodicals in 1823, and by 1845 there were fifteen monthly publications and two weeklies. Claude E. Spenser's Periodicals of the Disciples of Christ, published in 1946, lists 1,000 titles, only a small fraction of these being in existence at any one time.[2]

All publishing companies were privately owned until 1910, when R. A. Long bought all the stock of the Christian Publishing Company, which published the Christian-Evangelist, Sunday school material and books. He made it a non-profit corporation controlled (as most of Disciples' colleges are) by a self-perpetuating board of trustees. Its charter, received in 1911, stipulated that surplus income not needed for improved services or plant expansion shall be used for the support of one or more of the missionary, benevolent, church extension, educational societies or other agencies of the Christian Churches (Disciples of Christ), as the Board of Directors may elect.[3]

The following is the statement of purpose of the Christian Board:

The purpose of this Brotherhood-owned publishing house is to serve the churches of Disciples of Christ by publishing (The Disciple), a journal of information, interpretation and inspiration; by publishing periodicals, books and curriculum materials to propagate and support an effective program of Christian education in the local church; and by providing through (assembly) service and other channels audio-visual materials, Bibles, books and all other supplies which are essential for an ongoing program of Christian evangelism and Christian stewardship in the local church.

In providing this service to the churches of Disciples of Christ, the Christian Board of Publication cooperates with all (regional) and national agencies of Disciples of Christ, with the National Council of the Churches of Christ in the United States of America, and with educational and publishing boards of other communions, and with the World Council of Churches. [4]

By this time the groundwork had been laid for Disciples' libraries--a pattern of belief (mission), the freedom to cooperate with other communions, a publishing house (a central source of material) and a basis for grants-in-aid for future designated commissions or agencies out of the surplus over-and-above plant expansion and improved service. Early Disciples leaned heavily upon their colleges and publications for educating their older young people and for keeping adults informed. However, the earliest parish libraries were the private collections of the pastors which they shared with their parishioners.

The first Sunday schools were organized in 1831 and were met with disapproval by some Disciples because of no mention of Sunday schools in the New Testament church. Disciples have always affirmed: Where the scriptures speak, we speak; where the scriptures are silent, we are silent. In regard to Sunday schools, this was soon forgotten, and Sunday schools flourished, particularly after the International Sunday School Association, an interdenominational agency, produced the Uniform Lessons in 1872. This was the first plan for an orderly program of Bible study.

About this same time (1874), the women organized the Christian Woman's Board of Missions and began almost immediately to publish the monthly Missionary Tidings through which they carried missionary education to every church and into a large proportion of Disciple homes.

Through the years the women were the ones who collected the missionary study books, books of religious fiction and missionary biography and brought them together on the window sills or on some do-it-yourself shelves in a corner of their meeting room, or under the stairs in the basement hallway to be read by their missionary society or other members of the church. Sunday school teachers and leaders did the same, and if the church were large, there was a separate library in every classroom.

Sometimes a church's collection of books served as the library for the entire community. This was particularly true before public libraries developed. With the coming of public libraries, the role was usually reversed. I know of one large church in a city where the selection of books was brought from a lending library for the benefit of the women who attended the Missionary Society. This was in 1923. On the other hand, persons in rural areas had little more than their Bibles and Sunday school lesson material to draw upon.

In 1944 the Disciples' interest in printed material culminated at their International Convention in Columbus, Ohio, in the creation of a Commission on the Promotion of Christian Literature. At this same convention they unanimously adopted a resolution designating the last week in October or the first week in November as Christian Literature Week. This was at the height of World War II and Disciples were concerned about helping prepare citizens and Christians for a new kind of world, a post war world involved in rehabilitation and the pursuit of enduring peace.

The Commission adopted the theme, "You Are What You Read," which recurred for many years, and sent out packets to the churches with material and suggestions for Christian Literature Week. In 1950, a resolution was passed at the International Convention reaffirming the 1944 endorsement of the observance and urging "that all churches set aside this week in the calendar of the churches for the all-important task of encouraging the reading of Christian Literature in order to cultivate a more intelligent Discipleship."[5]

Not until 1954 was a report made to the International Convention of its activities. At that time, it determined its purpose and function, including church libraries:

> It is the purpose and function of the Commission on the Promotion of Christian Literature, not only to promote the observance of Christian Literature Week, but to urge churches of Disciples of Christ and their membership throughout the year to follow a plan of daily Bible reading; to read more and better books and magazines, especially in the field of religion; to encourage the launching of new church libraries; to encourage subscriptions to religious journals, and to urge the exhibition and use of church literature of the highest quality and Christian education value. By such promotion it is hoped to exalt the place of Christian Literature in the life of the church until it shall be considered one of the prime requisites of the church and church school.[6]

The Commission was a representative group of twenty-three persons with a wide range of interests. According to the first report, the following material was included in a packet sent to all churches to assist them in preparing for Christian Literature Observance that year:

1. Large Display Poster;
2. Manual containing suggestions for planning the observance of Christian Literature Week;
3. A reading plan suggesting regular daily Bible readings, twelve outstanding books, and magazines and periodicals published by and for Disciples of Christ;
4. Three minute talks. Three suggested short talks to guide ministers, church school superintendents, presidents of Christian Women's Fellowships, and other church leaders to stimulate the reading of Christian Literature.

The Commission also sponsored a book-of-the-month program, which called for a well-read Disciple to choose and review a book each month. And the for first time, the Commission sponsored a basic library project, the purpose of which was to establish a basic library in every church or church school in the brotherhood.

The report indicated a share in the Disciples' Long Range Plan for the years of 1958 and 1959. The Local Church emphasis for these two years was Christian literature, and the Commission set the following goals:

Daily Devotions

1. Provide every family in the brotherhood with The Secret Place--the Disciples of Christ daily devotional guide.
2. Encourage young people to begin or continue some kind of personal devotions, such as "morning watch" in conference or camp.
3. Encourage family participation (including children) in devotion planning and observance.

Bible Reading

1. Every home to secure and read the new Revised Standard Version of the Holy Bible.
2. Read the "Bible Book of the Month" as suggested by the Commission on the Promotion of Christian Literature.
3. Encourage Bible reading among all ages.

Christian Journals

To increase interest among church members in reading the journals of Disciples of Christ such as The Christian-Evangelist, World Call, The Christian Plea, and the state missionary society papers.

Reading Books To Stimulate Christian Growth

To interest a larger number of church members in reading for personal enrichment books of a religious nature, including those which will provide a better understanding of people of other races, nationalities and cultures.

Church Library

1.   A library representing all phases of the Christian life in every church.
2.   A program to promote the reading of the books of the library.

Christian Education Material

1.   A Christian periodical of personal enrichment and help for every person in the church constituency: a) A Christian family magazine for every family of the church; b) An age group periodical for every person; c) A periodical on methods for every educational leader in the church.
2.   The use by every church of teaching materials that are graded to the abilities of the learner and take into account the full range of his religious needs... that bring the unique resources of the Bible to bear upon all activities of life... that contribute to the understanding and support of the missionary, educational, benevolent, and other enterprises of our brotherhood. [7]

The expenses of these programs were underwritten by the Christian Board of Publication and were included in the Grants-in-Aid of that agency.   This was planned when the Christian Board was first chartered.   Over one thousand churches reported observing Christian Literature Week in 1954 and five hundred were provided with book exhibits amounting to $56,000.   Book purchases amounted to $18,000.

As a result of the previous literature and library emphasis, Disciples of Christ libraries were well underway when in 1955, Bethany Press, the book publishing division of Christian Board of Publication which became a special department of that agency in 1954, published its first library manual to guide the widespread library development, How to Build a Church Library, by Christine Buder.   During that same year, the Christian Board began registering church libraries and offering a 20 percent discount on books purchased.

In 1957, The Church Library Book Nook began publication for church librarians.   In addition to all kinds of "how-to" articles and information, it carried lists of basic books for religious libraries, and Family Bookshelf lists.   In 1959, the Christian Literature Commission adopted the following statement of purpose and function:

> It shall be the purpose and function of this commission to promote the observance of Christian Literature Week; to urge the Christian Churches (Disciples of Christ) and their membership to follow a plan of regular Bible reading throughout the year and to read more and better books and magazines, especially in the field of religion; to encourage the establishment and development of church

libraries; to encourage subscriptions to religious journals; to urge the exhibition and use of church school literature of the highest quality and education value; and to exalt the place of Christian literature in the total life of the church until it becomes a requisite of the church and church school; to stimulate an awareness of the total church on the part of the reader; and to create and develop an appreciation of the Disciple Thought and Disciple Literature.[8]

This Commission met once a year to plan the work to be done by the executive secretary during the ensuing year. It carried out many of the plans and goals set by the former Commission and initiated some new ones. Christian Literature Week continued to be observed. A new theme each year replaced the old "You Are What You Read, " and posters were designed to represent the theme. Consignments continued to be offered.

A ten-year Disciple Reader's plan was launched in 1960 in which 14, 000 individuals participated. A five-year Bible Reading Plan became available for a nominal charge. Two thousand libraries had been registered and were taking advantage of a many faceted program. Book-of-the-Month reviews were sent to and used by state newspapers and agency publications and the Campus Life Center Basic Library Plan initiated in 1961 was continued.

Offered for the first time in 1963 was the Review-by-Mail Plan for registered libraries. With this service, carefully selected books (5 or 6) on various subjects and for different age groups were sent once a quarter. The librarian had the opportunity to examine them, keep all of them at 20 percent discount, or return all or any part of them without charge, except for the return postage. Dewey Decimal classification and Sears subject heading listings accompanied the brief description of each book. This Review-by-Mail Plan and registration of libraries were available not only to Disciples librarians but to all other communions as well.

An annual workshop for church librarians was held at the International Conventions. The Church Library Book Nook, begun as a separate bulletin, was published in the Bethany Preview, a quarterly publication of Christian Board which listed its current, and sometimes seasonal, books.

With the vote by the International Convention in 1968 to restructure and reconstitute the Christian Church (Disciples of Christ), the Christian Literature Commission voted itself out of existence in 1973 in favor of the Church Libraries and Christian Readers Department. The executive secretary of the Commission became director of the new department and editor of Bethany Press. As a department of Christian Board, it continues to be supported by that board.

The Christian Literature Week Observance is being continued, as is the Library Registration Plan, the Review-by-Mail Plan, the Book-of-the-Month review, the five-year Bible Reading Plan, a

workshop at the biennial General Assembly (former International
Convention), book consignments to churches during Christian Literature Week and at other times upon request, and library services,
upon request.   Obviously, reading and library use are busy activities
in Christian churches.

The Christian Literature Week packet, a particularly attractive
package sent to the churches annually, was based on an appropriate
theme for the year and included a poster, a planning manual, a consignment list, a flyer on a particular topic to aid librarians with
development and promotion, a copy of the Christian Reader's Guide
for the year, a bookmark telling where to write for information on
Christian reading plans and church library services and an order
card for requesting quantities of both free and cost material for
the Observance.

The Christian Reader's Guide included in the Christian Literature Week packet was adopted in 1970.   It was an annotated list of
current books for children, youth and adults produced annually for
members of the Christian Church.   Pastors, church school teachers
and librarians in several representative congregations were asked
to make recommendations as well as persons in the national, regional and other offices of the church.   The list of books for youth and
adults was evaluated by church leaders in the Division of Homeland
Ministries, the Department of Church Women, the Department of
Church Men, the Division's Administration office and by editors in
the St. Louis offices of the Christian Board.   A Christian Board of
Publication committee finally made the decision as to which ones
were included.   The children's workers in the local Church Curriculum Division of the Christian Board of Publication carefully chose
the books recommended for children's reading.

Christine Buder's church library manual has been replaced
by The Church Library--Tips and Tools by Gladys E. Scheer, Lex-
ington Theological Seminary, former Christian Literature Commission
member and CSLA vice-president.   At regional and general assemblies of the Christian Church (Disciples of Christ), there is always
a section set aside in the book display area for the sale of library
supplies and manuals and someone on hand to help with library
problems, book lists and information.   Four Disciples bookstores
serve ministers, laymen, churches and librarians.   There are
Bethany Bookstores in St. Louis (1941), Indianapolis (1955) and Los
Angeles (1961).   The fourth is a cooperative project with the United
Church of Christ and the Protestant Episcopal Church in Seattle.

While Bethany Press produces books of particular interest to
Disciples church members, the Christian Board of Publication produces curriculum material and religious publications.   The editor of
Bethany Press is also Director of the Church Libraries and Christian Readers Department so is related to librarians in all services
to them.   The Christian Board supports Bethany Press and the
Church Libraries and Christian Readers Department and makes the
20 percent discount possible to registered libraries.

In addition to The Disciple, the Christian Board produces
printed material informing Disciples of the work of the various units
of the church: Vanguard (the church's program planning journal),
Social Action News Letter, Cutting Edge, DPF News Notes, Glance,
ACCE Notes, Discipliana (Historical Society news), and Family Talk
(publication pertaining to the benevolence homes). In place of the
Bethany Guide (the education journal), church subscription to JED
Share (Joint Educational Development), a denominational/ecumenical
publication, is encouraged. The following three magazines are published: Children at Home (a weekly for ages 4 and 5), Alive (a
monthly for young teens) and Youth (a monthly for those in senior
high school). All should be in the library to be shared with the
teachers and membership (congregation).

General catalogs listing books and church and library supplies
and supplementary special catalogs are available from The Christian
Board of Publication, P. O. Box 179, St. Louis, MO   63166.   In-
formation regarding library services should be requested from
Sherman R. Hanson, Director, Church Libraries and Christian
Readers Department at the same address.

The local church library of the Christian Church (Disciples
of Christ) was essentially a ministerial and service tool. Its mission was the same as that of the church which it served, to provide
the best attainable resources related to worship, the sacraments
and ordinances, preaching, pastoral counseling, parish administration, evangelism, stewardship, social action and teaching. In other
words, it undergirds the total church program, and wherever the
church went to reach people---within its own walls, in the immediate
neighborhood, the community or world---church library resources
were available "on location" to lend support to that part of the
church's work. Furthermore, its mission was to help persons find
meaning for their lives through learning, growing, loving and serv-
ing---the Christian way.

There is no typical Disciples library, since each one is as
unique as the congregation which it serves. Although most of them
occupy a separate room in the most accessible place available and
are staffed by volunteers, some perform effective ministries with
only a book cart or portable cabinet. Others share an ecumenical
religious section of a public library usually staffed by the public
library but supported by the participating churches.

As with most communions, the women have been influential
in creating libraries in the churches. Just as they were the ones
who gathered the books together for the missionary society and the
Sunday School classes, they were the ones who began to gather all
the books about the church into one collection to serve the entire
church. In about 1950, leaders of our Christian Women's Fellowships became interested in setting aside a room or an area where
they could catalog the books according to the Dewey Decimal System, including the newly formed library in their budget and assuming
the responsibility of staffing it. In many of these organizations, the

vice-president was put in charge of acquiring and promoting Fellowship study material and automatically became librarian for a year.
As collections grew and changing volunteer librarians became un-
satisfactory, a volunteer librarian was appointed for a longer period
of time.

The women have had Bible reading and other reading programs
for years.   For the last fifteen or more years, the International
Christian Women's Fellowship has offered a balanced Reading Plan in
addition to Bible reading where the women are encouraged to read
books in three categories (spiritual enrichment, missions and Christian social concerns), The Disciple (Disciples' national publication),
their regional paper, and one of the following: The Church Woman
(ecumenical), The Christian Home (United Methodist), and The Christian Century (ecumenical).   Certificates are awarded at the end of
the year for the Participating Reader (6 books and The Disciple),
the Qualified Reader (12 books, The Disciple, state paper and one
of the other three) and the Superior Reader (24 books and the same
publications required for the Qualified Reader).   The librarian guides
the readers and awards the certificates.

Probably budgets for Disciples libraries range from $25 to
$1,000 per year.   Many libraries are included in the Christian
Women's Fellowship budget, others in the church budget.   Some receive equal amounts from the women's organization, the church
school and the church.   The bills are paid either by the church or
the women.   Many receive additional funds from memorials and
birthday gifts, book fairs and from consignment books sold during
Christian Literature Week.

The majority of Disciples libraries are staffed by nonprofessional volunteers.   However, since there are more church members
with library science degrees than fifteen to twenty years ago, more
of the volunteers are professionals and lend their expertise to the
position.   While one or two churches may have had paid part-time
librarians, there are still many small churches where the first
vice-president of the Christian Women's Fellowship is in charge.
The number on the staff is determined by the size of the collection,
the availability of the library and the number of hours each staff
person can give as a volunteer.

Sherman R. Hanson, Director, Church Libraries and Christian Readers, in the flyer, "Build Up Your Church Library, " in
the 1978 Christian Literature Week packet, described the Disciples
librarian as an associate minister and said that a good church librarian did more than arrange and manage a collection of books.
He or she was a leading member of the church, aware of what the
church was doing and planning to do and what the needs and interests
of the church members were.   As an associate minister he or she
was sensitive to the concerns, joys and frustrations of particular
members of the congregation and could call their attention to helpful
resources.   Not only was technical knowledge necessary, but a
knowledge of the church and a sense of ministry and commitment
were essential.

A large percentage of books in Disciples library collections are religious, but believing in a ministry to the whole person, Disciples include books in all categories if space and budget permit. Librarians of libraries situated near a public library familiarize themselves with the public library's collection and direct their borrowers to the public library when possible, limiting their collections to that material not available in the public library. Library collections range from less than 100 to 7,000 books.

Though most Disciples libraries have book collections only, the trend is toward including non-print or multi-media resources. Larger churches are already developing media resource centers, and in metropolitan areas denominations are developing area communication or media centers shared by all their churches. In some areas, even ecumenical communication or media centers are being considered.

Independence Boulevard Christian Church in Kansas City houses and participates in an ecumenical resource center. Media included are hardware (movie projectors, film and slide projectors, opaque projectors, tape recorders, etc.) and software (tapes, films, film strips, slides, tapes, records, etc.) pictures, art objects, maps, books and periodicals.

No library collection is complete without denominational and ecumenical periodicals. Even secular magazines that fulfill needs can be added if the budget allows or members donate them.

A very important area of Disciples libraries is the reference section. Librarians strive to supplement the minister's library when it is inadequate and to provide basic material for Sunday school teachers and information for information-seeking lay persons. Equally important are the books and other teaching tools which Disciples librarians provide for teacher training and supplementary material for Sunday school lessons. East Dallas Christian Church, Dallas is planning a resource center in which the children's books will be as much a teaching tool as other media. Recreational reading will be important but secondary. A library or media center attains its maximum function when the minister, the director of Christian education, the Sunday school superintendant and the librarian support one another.

The future seems to lie in the shared approach--curriculum, resource centers, and organizations like the Church and Synagogue Library Association (CSLA). Disciples have been interested in CSLA since its inception and will continue to share with, lend support to and benefit from the organization. Believing with Thomas Campbell that the Church is "essentially, intentionally, and constitutionally one," Disciples find it easy to share; and believing in education for their ministers and membership, they will continue to provide the best in education for the whole person.

Like the founding fathers, present-day Disciples are vitally concerned about Christian education for the whole person, believing

it will enrich lives and promote understanding of and appreciation
for the church, the world and all God's people.   They firmly believe a well-organized, well-supported and well-promoted church library is the essential undergirding tool which will help them accomplish their goal in our time.

BIBLIOGRAPHY

Cochran, Louis and Leroy Garrett.   Alexander Campbell: The Man
    and His Mission.   Dallas: Wilkinson Publishing Company,
    1965.

Garrison, Winfred Ernest and Alfred T. DeGroot.   The Disciples of
    Christ: A History.   St. Louis: Christian Board of Publica-
    tion, 1948; revised 1958.

Gross, Fay, "Church Libraries Are Doing Things," World Call
    (June, 1971), p. 12.

McAllister, Lester G. and William E. Tucker.   Journey in Faith:
    A History of the Christian Church (Disciples of Christ).   St.
    Louis: The Bethany Press, 1975.

NOTES

1.   Garrison, Winfred Ernest, Whence and Whither the Disciples of
     Christ.   St. Louis: Christian Board of Publication, 1948,
     p. 1.
2.   Ibid., p. 58.
3.   Ibid., p. 59.
4.   1965 Year Book of the Christian Churches (Disciples of Christ).
     Indianapolis: International Convention of Christian Churches
     (Disciples of Christ), 1965, p. 47.
5.   1954 Year Book of the Christian Churches.   Indianapolis: In-
     ternational Convention of Disciples of Christ, p. 254.
6.   Ibid., p. 254.
7.   Ibid., pp. 255-256.
8.   1965 Year Book of the Christian Churches (Disciples of Christ),
     op. cit., p. 63.

THE BETHESDA UNITED METHODIST CHURCH LIBRARY

Ruth S. Smith

In the autumn of 1955, the minister of Bethesda Methodist Church, Bethesda, Maryland, returned from his vacation full of enthusiasm. He preached a sermon that reached a young housewife, formerly a librarian. His sermon urged each church member to use the talents possessed, no matter how insignificant they were.

This was a suburban church outside Washington, D. C. Membership numbered 2, 000 persons with a healthy church school enrollment. Surrounded by the National Institutes of Health, a National Naval Medical Center and the National Library of Medicine, this was considered to be a high IQ area. So, I was surprised to learn that the church did not have a library. He suggested that I write to Cokesbury in Baltimore for a copy of Your Church Library, the denomination's booklet. I wrote for the booklet and visited other libraries. I talked with librarians and gathered ideas and suggestions, including the names and sources of resources, such as library supply catalogs, audio-visual material, and wholesale book dealers.

At the same time, the Church School Secretary, and another librarian-member of the congregation gathered together the books that were scattered throughout the church. They weeded out undesirables. The 83 books that remained were stored in a glass-enclosed bookcase in the Youth Building, which was on a far corner of the church property and locked most of the time. However, supplies for cataloging the books were ordered and charged to the church school budget.

I approached the minister and suggested that we needed a library committee to represent the major church activities and help in book selection. It could be a channel of communication to and from the congregation and would help to establish basic library policies. He named five people plus himself and me.

The Library Committee held its first meeting in January 1956. By that time the 83 books had been cataloged, but no organized method was available for circulating them. They were still in that locked glass-enclosed bookcase, and some had found their way back to the classrooms. The committee talked about where to house the books, a policy for circulation, training helpers, funding the library, selecting books, and getting a room for the library into the plans for a new Education Wing.

Budget money was sought. We presented a report of activities and plans to the Education Commission and the Women's Society for Christian Service (WSCS). Funds were promised, but for the next year: $50 from the Education Commission for supplies and $200 from the WSCS to buy books. For the present, we asked for gifts of new books for the library.

We posted a list of "desired" books in the main hallway. The Children's Division purchased 16 of them. They were cataloged for the library and displayed at a reception for the new Director of Christian Education. A Book Sale was set up in the Narthex, with a consignment of new books which could be purchased as gifts for the library or for personal use. Notices about the Book Sale were sent to the various church activities and the minister called attention to it in his letter to the congregation and from the pulpit. Needed book titles were listed in the WSCS newsletter, also.

As the library grew that first year, the library committee expanded. Among the new members were the new Director of Christian Education, a "wheel" in the WSCS, and a person who served also as Chairman of the Building Committee. Soon the entire collection was moved from its glass-enclosed bookcase into the main church building to a first floor cloak room off the main Narthex. The WSCS person influenced continued financial support from the women's society when we needed it. The minister managed to find a room for the library in the new building plans--on the first floor along a traffic corridor--and later obtained approval for the purchase of new library furniture.

By the end of the first year, we had 500 cataloged books and, with an honor charging system, an average of six books a week were circulated. Each Sunday a library aid was on duty between the services to help people find material, to accept books returned, etc. Seven library committee members attended a training class for volunteer workers sponsored by the Bethesda Public Library to learn more about standard library procedures. The library staff served the congregation in other ways, too. The librarian read a Christmas story at a WSCS circle meeting as part of the Christmas program. The sixth grade church school learned how to mend books.

The library had to be moved again. While it was in a first floor classroom the books were covered with a sheet, but the collection grew to 806 books and circulation jumped to an average of twelve a week. After alterations were completed, the library found a temporary home in one of the new offices.

Plans were drawn up for furnishing the new library, which

would be shared one hour on Sunday with the senior adult Wesley class.   Through the sale of books and a series of book reviews and story hours, we earned over $270 toward the furnishings.   However, that was not nearly enough.   The minister came to our rescue and a recommendation from him to the Building Committee brought in the rest.   The furniture was selected and ordered.   The library was asked to obtain selected books: 89 were requested for the curriculum, others were purchased to supplement the WSCS study program and the Prayer Group.

A Lenten Reading List was prepared and inserted in the Sunday Bulletin.   A booklist on Jesus Christ was prepared at the request of the minister for a jurisdictional study he was to conduct on St. Mark.   Requests from individuals came in for material on topics such as migrant workers, devotional readings, and church related vocations.   In addition, a crew of library workers sorted and mended all the church hymnals.

The new education wing was completed in the spring of 1958. The library room was 428 square feet on the first floor, along a corridor that ran between the Sanctuary and the parking lot.   The Men's Club painted the walls and helped to install the furniture: bookshelves, card catalog, librarian's desk (with circulation file and typewriter) and a round cornered square reading table with chairs. The Explorer Scouts moved all the books.   The Women's Society ladies, having selected the draperies, helped to hang them.   Everything was in place for the Consecration of the new building in March 1958.

Dedication of the library itself was held later that year, in October 1958.   The Dedication service was preceded by a Tea in Fellowship Hall.   To begin the program in Fellowship Hall, I gave a short talk on how the library started.   The guest speaker was the Chaplain of the U. S. Senate.   These talks were recorded on tape, and pictures were taken for the record.   The Service of Dedication was held in the library.

The library received favorable publicity that year, both nationally and locally, and it was used as a model for other church libraries.   Articles about the library appeared in national magazines and the local press.   People from other churches who were thinking about starting a library or improving one already in existence came to visit.   As a result, Bradley Hills Presbyterian Church (Bethesda, Md.) borrowed 55 books to enhance a book display at their own Library Dedication.   St. Paul's Methodist Church (Kensington, Md.) reviewed the children's collection to select titles for their library. McKendree Methodist Church (Washington, D. C.) borrowed the procedures manual compiled by the librarian to copy it for their own use.

The American Association of University Women used the library as a meeting place to study and discuss good books.   The Bethesda branch of Montgomery County Libraries referred one of their patrons to our library, where they knew he would find a copy of the Interpreter's Bible (12 volumes, Abingdon).   He was an adult class teacher at the First Baptist Church (Bethesda, Md.) and soon became a regular patron.   That was a good year, both in local service and in the satisfaction of broadened horizons.   The collection expanded to over 1,000 books, circulation grew to an average of 23 books per week, and service to the church continued.

By the end of the first five years, the library committee had expanded from four members to nineteen, each with a job and each responsible for a part in the whole.   An Assistant Librarian for the Church School was appointed to look after the needs of that demanding area of library service.   The annual library budget was averaging $500, plus memorial gifts and donations.   The first of a series of workshops for church librarians was held in the church and attracted 31 attendees from 13 local churches of various denominations. The first meetings of what later became the Church Library Council were held, initiated by the church library.

Within the next two years, the collection grew to 2,154 books and 246 media.   Circulation climbed from an average of 50 to 75 per week.   Use of the audio-visuals and the picture and pamphlet files increased, due largely to the promotion given this material by the Director of Christian Education.   The Assistant Librarian for the Church School helped select the material, prepared booklists for the teachers, took groups of books to the classes and arranged for classes to visit the library.   A reading table and chairs were ordered for the children's corner.

Workshop classes were conducted on behalf of the Church Library Council and the Council of Churches of Greater Washington. We produced a set of 39 color slides on "Building Your Church Library" which subsequently were borrowed, or copies purchased, by many libraries and other groups.   Other aids for library volunteers were developed, also.

During this period of expansion, three new Methodist congregations were being established in the rapidly growing suburbs of Bethesda.   Soon they began drawing members from the church, quite often the younger families who lived in those suburbs.   The congregation gradually receded from 2,000 to less than 1,500 members. Even though the library collection grew and outreach continued, these changes in the congregation had their effect.

A decrease in church and church school attendance was evident.   The Story Hour which proved so successful in the first seven years began to have fewer children.   The Book Reviews were abandoned altogether.   Only the Used Book Sale attracted its usual enthusiastic audience.   The circulation of material dropped considerably before the down trend reversed itself again.   The library was being used but not as much.   A college student used references she found there to write a paper.   The Scouts happily ignored the collection of merit badge books, but the Women's Society used the collection of mission material. The Y-Wives, a group that met regularly in the church, asked if they might have a shelf in the library for general reading books, which they would provide. In 1964, at the end of the ninth year, the Library Committee Chairman reported that the church had hired a Business Manager as well as a new Director of Christian Education. These events, in turn, brought other changes.

The library had grown up somewhat autonomously, gaining its support from several sources and reporting informally to the Official Board. Now, the library was designated a committee of the Commission on Education. The library was represented at meetings of the Commission and submitted budget requests and fiscal reports to it. In time, an arrangement was worked out which provided for continuing support from the Women's Society and from donations, as well as the budgeted income from the Church School and the Wesley Nursery School. A report of all expenditures was provided to the Commission on Education.

With enthusiastic support from the new Director of Christian Education, the use of the library and its resources again were promoted as part of the church's education mission. The Wesley Class which shared the library room was moved--along with their piano-- to another meeting place. This made room for additional shelving which was needed for the children's collection. There were changes in the curriculum and changes in class schedules, too. By the end of the tenth year--the end of 1965--the Chairman of the Library Committee was able to make the following observations in a Quarterly Conference report:

"The church library has become a very active place, especially since the institution of a separate church school period between the two services on Sunday morning.... The new curriculum and the expansion of adult study classes have greatly increased the use of the library.... We try to expand our service by taking books and material to people.... [The minister] has promised to assist us in providing brief devotional and sermon tapes which [can be taken to] shut-ins. Recently we purchased a new light-weight tape recorder for this purpose...." The report concluded on this optimistic note: "We hope we can continue to be a vital resource center and, as such, a true ministry to the people of this church, as well as others. Our challenges and opportunities appear to be unlimited."

In its second ten years, the library grew older and so did the congregation. Although there were a number of young people in the congregation, there were fewer children to attend the church school classes. A greater percentage of middle-aged and senior parishioners filled the pews. Memorial gifts were received in abundance, but volunteer helpers became hard to find.

Other changes took place, too. New ministers, associate ministers and education directors came and went. Experimental programs were adopted and later changed or dropped as new ones took their place. The Methodist Church merged with the United

Church of the Brethren to become the United Methodist Church.   The
church commissions were changed into work areas called ministries.
There were adjustments in many ways.   Through it all, the library
reached a kind of seasoned maturity.

The library collection reached its estimated capacity--3,000
volumes--in 1968, its 13th year.   Material was weeded regularly to
dispose of that which was not being used to make room for the new
material.   More careful attention was given to the selection of new
additions.   Storage space became a real concern.   The closet in the
classroom across the hall housed working material for the library,
as well as artifacts and display items.   Church history records
which the library had been collecting, such as the Messenger, were
bound or housed in a file cabinet in one of the church offices.

A complete inventory of books and media showed that after
14 years of operating with the self-charging system, only 136 items
could not be found.   The "loss" was estimated to be less than 4 percent of the total collection, or approximately nine or ten items a
year.   Activities of the library followed the pattern of previous years:
visiting shut-ins, hosting church school class visits, setting up collections of books in classrooms or for special meetings, meeting
with the school department heads and teachers, arranging displays,
etc.   Members of the Committee attended conferences and workshops,
often contributing as leaders.   There was always a need for training
new volunteers.   The library became active in the Chruch Library
Council and the Church and Synagogue Library Association.

By the 15th year, we had lost a number of people from the
library committee.   Then it went down to 17 people, and in another
three years to 13.   We were asked by the minister to help plan the
family Christmas Eve service and made arrangements for stories to
be told.   Two young people regularly set up attractive book displays
in the display case.   A clean-up day was observed.   The librarian
regularly submitted news items to the Messenger, the church paper.

In 1973, the 18th year, the librarian reported that small
groups of books and media were being charged out to the church
school classrooms each quarter.   They were used within the rooms
for extended periods of time.   He also observed: "We have 3,500
books and these, with the furniture and equipment, represent an investment of $16,500."   In a combined annual report for 1974-75, the
librarian reported, "Games have been added to the collection as well
as multi-media kits which may contain games, records or cassettes."

Clearly, a new era was dawning.   The book collection needed
only updating maintenance.   However, the collection of media material was growing.   We requested that a parttime paid librarian
position be established.   This was approved, and this person began
work in January 1977.   The library's unique place in the church was
recognized in 1975--our 19th year--when the library formally was
designated a full-fledged church ministry.   In 1978, the library took
over an adjoining room and began making plans to expand further,

in the direction of becoming a multi-media Information and Learning Center.

Scope and Characteristics

The library is one of the ministries of the church, along with membership and evangelism, education, missions and social concerns. The library committee sets policies, is responsible for overall administration, and reports to the Council on Ministries. The library serves the entire congregation: the ministers and church staff, the lay leaders and workers of the church, the children and adults. It also provides material for the Wesley Nursery School, a church-sponsored nursery school and kindergarten. The library may be used by non-members as well as church members.

Library material is selected to further the work of the church and its programs, to support the teaching, preaching and evangelistic activities, and to encourage individual's spiritual growth and religious education. It is conveniently located on the main floor of the education wing. The room is bright and attractive, with Birch wood standard library furniture.

Library material includes books, filmstrips, records and record albums, tape recordings, slidesets, maps, clippings, pamphlets, periodicals, games, teaching kits, pictures, artifacts, and selected church history records. The material selected must be appropriate for the collection, within the intellectual scope of the congregation, up-to-date, authoritative and attractive. In general, books of popular, short-term interest are purchased in paperback (if available). Examples are the annual mission study books, stories for youth, and controversial topics of social concern.

Books with a longer life expectancy are purchased in hard cover. Examples are reference books, church history, Bible study, and devotions. Although some of this material might also be found in a public library, this special collection provides great depth of material on Methodism, the United Methodist Church, official handbooks and material specifically recommended for use in the church school curriculum.

The library makes this material readily available when and where it is needed. It is open for service at all times that the church is open. Instructions for using the library are posted. Material is charged out on the "honor system." No overdue fines are charged, but voluntary "conscience" contributions are accepted to purchase other new books. Library staff members are in attendance on Sundays between the services to respond to questions and help find material.

The library committee and staff encourages use of the library and its material through a program of involvement and communication. They attend meetings, prepare reports, arrange for class

visits, set up displays, and engage in other activities that promote
the library. Members of the library committee and staff also participate in broader library activities which involve other church and
synagogue libraries. They attend and lead interdenominational conferences and workshops, publish material which helps church library
volunteer workers, and are active members of the Church Library
Council of the Greater Washington, D. C. Area and the National
Church and Synagogue Library Association.

Library Personnel

The library committee is responsible for all library policies
regarding location, financing, book selection, cataloging of materials,
rules for use, librarian and staff, and promotion of the library and
its resources. Members of the library committee generally serve
as the library staff. Members may be appointed by groups in the
church that they represent or may volunteer to serve. We try to
make sure that the major activities of the church are represented:
the ministries, such as education, missions, etc., and groups, such
as the United Methodist Women. Members of the library committee
act as a channel of communication between the library and these activities. They help to select new material and promote its use by
giving short talks at meetings, taking books along to the meetings
to circulate to attendees, and so forth.

The Library Committee Chairman presides at library committee meetings and attends others, such as meetings of the Council
on Ministries. The Chairman sees that a report of library activities
is prepared by the librarian. The Secretary takes the minutes of
regular meetings of the committee and distributes them to members.
The Treasurer receives funds, deposits them in the name of the
committee (in a bank approved by the committee), pays bills, and
keeps records of these transactions. The Treasurer presents a report at regular committee meetings.

The Church Librarian is responsible for operating the library,
with policy guidance from the library committee. The Church Librarian selects material, organizes the collection and makes it available for use; coordinates with the ministerial staff and the various
church departments to make the church library a ministry that serves
the entire church; works along with and helps to train the volunteer
library staff; promotes use, and prepares reports. As delegated by
the Church Librarian, the Church School Librarian acts as the liaison between the library and the church school. As delegated by the
Church Librarian, the Audio-visual Librarian directs the development
and growth of the library's collection of special media material and
works with the Church School Librarian on the selection of material.
This person also helps to process and care for this material. The
Memorials Librarian coordinates the selection, receipt and acknowledgment of all gifts and memorials.

Members of the library staff are assigned specific duties by the Church Librarian.   Some of them are cataloging, circulation, displays, pictures, book processing, and archives.

Library Finance

        The library is financed through the Council on Ministries, but also receives funds from the Church School, the Wesley Nursery School, and the United Methodist Women.   In addition, the library accepts gifts and earns money through special projects.   The total budget was $375 in 1975 and $400 in 1976.   These amounts were used for library materials and supplies.   In 1977 and 1978, the Council on Ministries allocated an additional $1,000 for library personnel; the total budget was $1,450, with a promise from the Church School of $50 at a time beyond the budgeted amount, as needed.   The library committee treasurer may request that these amounts be transferred to the library account.   A record of expenditures is kept and submitted to the Council of Ministries as a part of the annual report. In advance of budget discussions each year, the library committee tries to highlight its activities for each of the supporting groups.

        Gifts are received, either as books, records, tapes, etc., or as money.   The books and other material which are donated generally are from personal collections.   On occasion, an entire collection might be received as a legacy.   Gift books are screened against the library committee's selection policy and those which are not retained are passed along to another library or are placed in the used book sale.

        Money is received from individuals and groups.   This might be a donation to buy needed equipment or to purchase books--some of which are in honor of or in memory of individuals.   These additions are selected by the Church Librarian, working with the Memorials Librarian, and have the donor's approval.   Gifts of money are reported in the financial accounting of library income.   The value of all the material added to the collection is included in the inventory of library holdings for insurance purposes.

Library Collection

        The library has a collection of books for adults and another for children, as well as media material.   A 15-drawer card catalog provides access to the material by author, title, subject and call number.   Subjects in the adult book collection range from fiction to biography, with emphasis on religion.   The percentage of books in the various classes is

Dewey Classification	Percentage
Fiction	1%
000--General Works	1
100--Philosophy	3
200--Religion	80

300--Social Sciences	4%
400--Language	1/4
500--Science	3/4
600--Technology	1
700--Arts	4
800--Literature	1
900--History, Travel, Biography	4
TOTAL	100%

The fiction is inspirational in nature. General works include encyclopedias, atlases, and even books on how to operate a church library. The philosophy and psychology section encompasses books on child study, personality and ethics.

The religion section is the backbone of the library. It includes books on the Bible (versions, concordances, dictionaries, interpretations, study guides, archeology and history); doctrinal theology (life and works of Christ, Christian beliefs, etc.); devotional theology (daily devotions, worship, and Christian living); the Christian church (missions, stewardship, education and other programs); Christian church history; Christian churches and sects; and non-Christian religions.

The social sciences include books on social welfare (inner city problems, etc.), education (teachers manuals and methods), customs and folklore. Language books include the standard English dictionaries. Science includes books on zoology (trees, birds, butterflies, etc.) Technology covers agriculture and home economics (quantity cooking, etc.) The arts include not only decoration and crafts, but also music, outdoor sports and recreation (family camping.) Literature generally contains the collections of inspirational and religious verse. History and travel reflects the mission studies of the church and most of the biography of inspirational reading.

The percentage of the various subjects in the children's book collection is somewhat different:

Dewey Classification	Percentage
Fiction (J and Y)	70%
000--General Works	1/4
100--Philosophy	1/2
200--Religion	15
300--Social Sciences	3
400--Language	1/4
500--Science	5
600--Technology	1
700--Arts	1
800--Literature	2
900--History, Travel, Biography	2
TOTAL	100%

The fiction is divided into Juvenile (J) and Youth (Y). Juvenile is suitable for ages up through eight and includes picture books, easy reading stories and large clear print. The content of these books covers God's great big wonderful world--from warm clothing in the winter to the wonders of rain in the spring, from a baby born in Bethlehem to the family at church today. Youth fiction is suitable for ages nine through twelve. Here one finds stories of adventure and excitement, such as the perilous travels of St. Paul, or stories about young people developing skills and getting along with others. Some of these stories are set in foreign lands where the people and their problems help one to understand how others live.

Children's non-fiction is suitable for all ages. It is used in the teaching program of the church and also is taken out for general reading. The subjects range from "how we were born" to "biography." The religion books are similar to those in the adult collection, but at a child's level of understanding. Here one finds Bible stories, a children's Bible, the childhood of Jesus, etc. The science books describe nature--how things grow--such as the seasons and the varieties of trees, rocks, birds, wild animals, farm animals and household pets.

Approximately 18 current periodical titles are housed on sloping shelves, with the current year's back issues on a flat shelf beneath. These include titles such as the Christian Herald, Campus Life, Daily Word, Guideposts, and Mature Years. The National Geographic is a gift to the library. Back issues are held from January 1949 to the present.

A four-drawer vertical file houses a collection of pamphlets, maps and clippings. These are kept in manila folders by subject. They reflect subjects covered by the book collection. A jumbo vertical file with hanging folders contains the collection of pictures. Many have been clipped from magazines or calendars and mounted. Others have been purchased as curriculum material for the church school. This file is arranged by subject.

The library has a variety of media material and artifacts such as a prayer shawl, scroll and incense burner. They are used primarily in the teaching program. Most of the tape recordings were made at the church--music programs, youth programs, guest speakers, sermons and sermonettes.

Special collections are set up for special purposes. For example, specific shelves have been set aside for the United Methodist Women's mission study program, the Scouting program (manuals, books on skills, etc.), the college program (catalogs of church sponsored colleges and universities and information about church-related vocations) and church school teachers (teaching guides, methods, etc.) Current church history is collected in the form of photographs, slides, clippings, booklets, and the church paper (which is bound by the library for archival retention). Reference books, too, are set aside in a special section.

Library Service

The library operates on the honor system. When a library staff member is not present, the borrower signs his name and date on the card in the back of the book and drops it in a box on the librarian's desk. Regarding rules for use, books and other material may be kept for two weeks, unless special arrangements are made. They may be renewed more than once. Books marked "Reference" do not circulate. Borrowers are asked to pay for books that are damaged or lost. A "return" bin (much like a mail box) near the librarian's desk provides a place where books may be deposited when they are returned to the library.

On Sunday each week, a library committee member is on duty in the library before and after each one of the two regular worship services. Typical inquiries cover topics as follows:

Books for various grades	Susanna Wesley
St. Patrick's Day stories	The prophets
The apostles	Going to church
Summer camp	How to make puppets
Plants in the Bible	Hymn "Jesus Loves Me"
Map of the Middle East	Moses
Worship services for seniors	Meditation for a meeting
Spelling of a Biblical name	Picture story about spring
Who were Jesus' brothers?	Church worship around world
Pledge of allegiance to the Christian flag	

Sunday is the day that the library is used the most. Families of members who must come early to rehearse for choir find the library a good place to wait, to browse and to read. Church school teachers come in for last minute references and material-- maps, pictures, records, etc. Others come to return books or to select books to take out and they often linger to chat awhile before they move on.

School children take advantage of the library being open on Sunday and ask for material that will help them in their school work. We cannot supply material on dinosaurs, voodoo or the Boxer Rebellion, but we can recommend books about people (biography), the Bible and church history, race relations, games and customs of other lands, or church related vocations. Church school classes visit the library as groups on Sunday and occasionally collections of books are taken to them in their classrooms. Teachers sometimes send students to the library to look up the answers to questions that come up in class.

Lists are prepared to recommend reading for special events or seasons, such as Lent. The ministers are encouraged to par-

ticipate in the selection of the titles.   Lists of curriculum resources
available in the library are prepared on request, for each one of the
quarters in the teaching year.   Such a list might be media only or
be complete with reading recommended for parents and children as
well as teachers.

On special occasions, such as the Family Advent Workshop
before Christmas, Vacation Bible School or the Church-Wide Mission
Study, displays of books are set up wherever meetings are held to
encourage interest in related information and to circulate books on
the spot.   Book displays reflecting current programs and seasonal
interests are arranged regularly in the built-in library display case
in the hallway.   Books and other material, such as sermonettes recorded on tape by the ministers, are taken to shut-ins.

Relationship to Minister and Education Work Area

The library serves the preaching and teaching programs of
the church.   In order to do this, and because of the turnover in
personnel, communication with the ministers and the education work
area is nurtured continuously.   The Minister and Associate Minister
are appointed or reappointed by the Bishop for one-year terms.
Similarly, with the church school, the two lead teachers who handle
the elementary and junior grades have one-year renewable contracts.

The members of the library committee talk with the ministers
whenever an opportunity presents itself.   This enables the library to
serve the ministers better and it helps the ministers to understand
the library program and promote it.   We invite the ministers to attend meetings of the library committee where we encourage them to
suggest ways in which we can serve them.   Each year when the library annual report is written, the ministers get a copy for information.   In turn, the librarian checks with the ministers or the
church office to keep abreast of events, new programs and other
news, such as who might require a visit with a basket of books for
shut-ins.

The ministers are asked to tell us in advance when they plan
to quote from or recommend a particular book in a sermon.   This
allows time to have it on hand when people come into the library to
look for it.   They advise us of upcoming programs and special concerns, such as a series of talks on families, a study program on
death and dying, or the role of women in today's society.   In turn,
we prepare booklists on these topics, set up special displays and
purchase new titles to fill in the collection.   The library offers to
purchase or borrow new books that the ministers need.   At the minister's request, we route to him the reviews of new books which
currently are on the market.   We also call to his attention new library resources which might be of use in preparing his sermons,
in recommending reading to people he counsels, or for his own enrichment.

The ministers often suggest new titles which they believe
would be good reading for the congregation. We encourage the ministers to review books in the church paper or from the pulpit. Whenever a booklist of recommended reading is being prepared for a special season, such as Lent, they are asked to select some of the
titles.

The library committee works closely with the teachers of the
church school and the Wesley Nursery School. The library is the
focal point for background material on child study and teacher training, as well as multi-media resources for presenting the curriculum
studies to the various age groups--from pre-school through adult
classes.

Whenever the teachers meet as a group to discuss the forthcoming curriculum program, the Church Librarian, the Church
School Librarian, and sometimes the Audio-visual Librarian, meet
with them to review briefly the resources available in the library
and to obtain suggestions for additions that might be helpful. This
not only lets the teachers know the resources available to them but
it also acquaints them with individuals in the library.

The church school librarian coordinates with the teachers to
plan visits to the classes. Sometimes these plans call for the librarian to read or tell stories to the children. Sometimes a collection of books on the topic of the curriculum is taken along to be
charged out by the children, who can make their own selection. Together they plan what will be presented so the library visit will fit
in with the current teaching topics. Plans sometimes call for teaching the children how to make book marks or how to mend books.

The teachers may schedule a time when they bring the class
to the library during a regular teaching period. The librarian tries
to have material related to their study program on display and is
prepared to introduce the resources on the shelf suitable for the
various age groups. The students are encouraged to ask questions.
Younger children might be told a story. Older children quite often
are given questions to look up in the reference books. Adults might
be introduced to how to use the Interpreter's Bible or other reference
tools. All are shown how to borrow and return books. If time permits, they are encouraged to select and check out a book of their
own choosing.

The church school librarian goes through the curriculum
guides each quarter, checks the recommended resources against the
library's holdings and makes sure that the "preferred" titles not in
the collection are ordered. Since the church school librarian knows
the collection well, this person is in a position to recommend resources when teachers come in for material on a certain topic, such
as a story about Easter suitable for nursery age children, or Biblical archeology for third grade students.

The church school teachers are allowed to borrow a collection of

books for use within the classroom for an extended period of time,
such as one to three months.   If needed, the library borrows collections of books from other sources, such as the public library.
This is done for special programs such as vacation church school
in the summer.   A list of the available resources on specific topics
is compiled from time to time.   Some lists contain recommended
reading for parents and students as well as teachers.

The church librarian, in cooperation with adult workers in
the youth division, provides service opportunities for young people--
helping on the library staff, reviewing books for the church paper,
or serving as projectionist for showing audio-visual resources. These
opportunities also are available to the Scouting program, to help
Scouts earn the God and Country award.

Relationship to Publishing Houses and National Religious Offices

The library has no ties or commitments to the Methodist
Publishing House or to Cokesbury, its retail outlet.   At one time we
did "register" our library with the Cokesbury Church Resource Library Service in order to get the 20 percent discount on books ordered for the library from Cokesbury.

Cokesbury Church Resource Library Service is "designed to
supply resources for Church Resource Libraries, and to provide
them with a system of interpretation, guidance and support.   Any
church or library may take advantage of this service." As a member, one receives 1) The Church Resource Library Newsletter, which
is published four times a year as a free service; 2) The Church Resource Library, a new manual of instruction which costs $2.95 per
copy; 3) a 20 percent discount on most books ordered for library
use; 4) free Cokesbury Book and Supply Catalogs; 5) the services and
assistance of Cokesbury Regional Service Centers and Cokesbury
Bookstores; and 6) an invitation to become a member of the Cokesbury Church Resource Library Guild.

The Cokesbury Church Resource Library Guild operates like
a book club.   A "panel of religious book authorities" reviews catalogs and information about new books coming from a number of publishers.   A selection is made.   If the titles are "inexpensive," two
or more might be selected.   My book, Getting the Books Off the
Shelves; Making the Most of Your Congregation's Library (New York,
Hawthorn Books, 1975), which was based on the church library, was
the Guild selection for October 1975.   Another one of mine, Cataloging Made Easy; How to Organize Your Congregation's Library (New
York, Seabury Press, 1978), also based on the church library, was
a Cokesbury Library Guild selection for October 1978.

The United Methodist Church, Education Department, Board
of Discipleship provides guidance to the church in regard to basic
curriculum resources.   It issues a quarterly Forecast, which lists
recommended resources.   The library receives a copy of it from the
Church School.

Other Activities

        We found a need in the community for information about how
a successful library operates--the kind of information born of experience, of trial and error, of actual operation.   In order to get better
acquainted with other librarians, we invited a group of librarians
from seven church libraries of various denominations to get together
for a coffee hour.   The idea caught on and the group continued to
meet and to grow in size.   By 1963 it had become a thriving interdenominational group called the Church Library Council, with forty
member churches from the District of Columbia and surrounding suburban areas in Maryland and Virginia.   It had chapters in the District, Northern Virginia, and two counties of Maryland.   The Northern
Virginia group eventually spun off into a Church Library Council of
Northern Virginia, but the original group continued as the Church
Library Council (of the Greater Washington, D. C. Area.)   In 1976,
it reported over 100 member churches.

        The Council holds meetings every three months at various
churches.   A quarterly News keeps members informed of meetings,
summarizes activities of the Council and its chapters, and passes
along helpful hints about library operations.   Members of the Council
offer advice to libraries just getting started and try to help each
other improve their own libraries.   If needed, they exchange supplies and trade information about new books and services.   Sometimes they lend each other books, tape recordings, filmstrips and
other material.   They share the overflow of good gift books through
a "give away" table at the regular meetings.   With the Council of
Churches of Greater Washington, they sponsor an annual church library workshop.   These workshops have been held for over fifteen
years and the library has provided leadership for many of them.

        Some of the library helps which have been published by the
Council in connection with the workshops have been written or de-
veloped in our library.   One example, a filmstrip on "Promoting the
Church Library" still is available, for loan, from the Church and
Synagogue Library Association.

        The same spirit that stirred the Church Library Council was
evident in other parts of the country.   Groups were emerging and
workshops being held.   Some of us from the Washington area took
part in and provided leadership for church library workshops in cities
such as Baltimore, Philadelphia and Detroit.   Among these were
three annual church library conferences sponsored by the Graduate
School of Library Science, Drexel University, in Philadelphia.   They
were received so enthusiastically that Dean John F. Harvey was led
to call together a group of interested persons to explore the possibility of forming a national association.   The library was represented
at that exploratory meeting and, when the Church and Synagogue Library Association was formed in 1967, I was honored to serve as
the first president.   In eight of the next nine years, the library was
represented on the Executive Board.

REFERENCES

"The Church Library, " In 50 Years at Bethesda Methodist 1914-64,
    Bethesda, Md. : Bethesda Methodist Church, 1964, pp. 17-18.

"The Church Library, " In It Began on a Front Porch; The Story of
    Bethesda Methodist Church, Bethesda, Md. : Bethesda Metho-
    dist Church (circa 1958), p. 17.

"Church Library Council Assists 40 Members, " Evening Star (Wash-
    ington, D. C.) (April 7, 1962), p. A-6.

"Church Library Council Publishes Guide Booklet, " Washington Post
    (November 10, 1962), p. C-6.

"Dedication of Bethesda Methodist Church Library, " Bethesda-Chevy
    Chase Tribune (October 17, 1958), p. 10.

Hannaford, Claudia and Smith, Ruth S. Promotion Planning. CSLA
    Guide No. 2. Bryn Mawr, Pa. : Church and Synagogue Li-
    brary Association, 1975.

Kaegi, Merrill, "The Church Library Council, Washington, D. C. "
    Drexel Library Quarterly VI (April 1970), pp. 154-157.

Nannes, Caspar, "Church Library Story, " Evening Star (Washington,
    D. C.) (November 10, 1962), p. A-7.

Smith, Ruth S. , "Bethesda (Maryland) Methodist Church Library, "
    Drexel Library Quarterly VI (April 1970), pp. 128-130.

Smith, Ruth S. , Building Your Church Library (script for slide-set).
    Bethesda, Md. , Church Library Council and Bethesda Metho-
    dist Church Library, 1961.

Smith, Ruth S. , "CSLA and SLA in Detroit, " Church and Synagogue
    Libraries III (July 1970), p. 12.

Smith, Ruth S. , "The Challenge of Church Libraries, " Library
    Journal LXXXVIII (September 1, 1963), pp. 3000-3003.

Smith, Ruth S. , "The Church and Synagogue Library Association, "
    Drexel Library Quarterly VI (April 1970), pp. 159-165.

Smith, Ruth S. , "Church and Synagogue Library Association, " In
    Encyclopedia of Library and Information Science, New York:
    Marcel Dekker, 1970, Vol. IV, pp. 674-81.

Smith, Ruth S. , "The Church Library Reaches Out, " International
    Journal of Religious Education XXXIX (April 1963), pp. 16-17.

Smith, Ruth S. , "Confessions of an Author/Librarian, " Church and
    Synagogue Libraries V (January-February 1972), pp. 1-2.

Smith, Ruth S., "Getting People to Read," The Christian Educator
    IX (January-March, 1966), pp. 15, 22.

Smith, Ruth, S., Getting the Books Off the Shelves. New York:
    Hawthorn Books, 1975.

Smith, Ruth S., "Organization and Administration," In Church Li-
    brary Guide, edited by Joyce L. White and Mary Y. Parr.
    Philadelphia: Philadelphia Council of Churches, New Jersey
    Council of Churches, and Graduate School of Library Science,
    Drexel Institute of Technology, 1965, pp. 6-9.

Smith, Ruth S., Outline for Building Vitality in Your Church Library.
    Washington, D. C., Church Library Council, 1961. Rev. ed.
    1967.

Smith, Ruth S., Promoting the Church Library (script for filmstrip).
    Washington, D. C., Church Library Council, 1962.

Smith, Ruth S., Publicity for a Church Library. Washington, D. C.,
    Church Library Council, 1962; Grand Rapids, Mich.: Zon-
    dervan Publishing House, 1966; superseded by Getting the
    Books Off the Shelves.

Smith, Ruth S., "The Story Behind One Library," New Christian
    Advocate II (August 1958), pp. 64-67.

Smith, Ruth S., Workshop Planning. CSLA Guide No. 3. Bryn
    Mawr, Pa.: Church and Synagogue Library Association, 1972.

Smith, Ruth S. and Swarthout, Arthur W., "Youth Ministry and the
    Church Library," Workers With Youth XXI (December 1967),
    pp. 6-8.

Smith, Mrs. T. Guilford, "Building Your Church Library," In Pro-
    ceedings of the Second Annual Church Library Conference,
    edited by Joyce L. White and E. J. Humeston, Jr. Phila-
    delphia: Philadelphia Council of Churches and Graduate
    School of Library Science, Drexel Institute of Technology,
    1964, pp. 39-41.

Smith, Mrs. T. Guilford, "Case Study: Bethesda Methodist Church
    Library, Bethesda, Maryland," In Proceedings of the Second
    Annual Church Library Conference, edited by Joyce L. White
    and E. J. Humeston, Jr. Philadelphia: Philadelphia Council
    of Churches and Graduate School of Library Science, Drexel
    Institute of Technology, 1964, pp. 35-38.

Smith, Mrs. T. Guilford, "Library: Bethesda Methodist Church,
    8300 Old Georgetown Road, Bethesda, Maryland," In Planning
    and Furnishing the Church Library, by Marion S. Johnson.
    Minneapolis, Mn.: Augsburg Publishing House, 1966, pp. 42-
    43.

"Some Tell-Tale Evidence of Youngsters' Enthrallment," Washington Post (February 2, 1961), p. A-8.

Tucker, John and Smith, Mrs. T. Guilford, "Basic Cataloging," In Proceedings of the Second Annual Church Library Conference, edited by Joyce L. White and E. J. Humeston, Jr. Phila- delphia: Philadelphia Council of Churches and Graduate School of Library Science, Drexel Institute of Technology, 1964, pp. 51-53.

White, Joyce L., "Church Libraries," In Encyclopedia of Library and Information Science, New York: Marcel Dekker, 1970, Vol. IV, pp. 662-673.

PART V:

RELIGIOUS LIBRARY
ASSOCIATIONS

THE CATHOLIC LIBRARY ASSOCIATION PARISH
AND COMMUNITY LIBRARIES

Bernadette Young

For over fifty years, the Catholic Library Association has declared, "The object of the organization is the promotion of Catholic principles by the improvement of library resources and services through cooperation, publication, education and information."[1] Organized to provide library service for specific interests, the Association first included among its sections, Elementary, High School, College and Seminary. While these objectives were directed toward library service for some of the Catholic population, there was no provision for the great numbers of Catholics outside the direct educational system. Individual parish organizations, feeling the need for Catholic library service, sponsored individual parish libraries. In an effort to unify and provide professional assistance to these parishes, concerned Catholic librarians, clergy and lay people organized a section devoted to those not included in other sections. A Round Table interest group met for the first time in 1954. They formed what is now known as the Parish and Community Libraries Section of the Catholic Library Association.

Representing clergy and lay people, the 47 section charter members were united in purpose. Basing their objectives on those of the Catholic Library Association, their first Constitution and By-laws, adopted on April 5, 1961 stated: "The object of the Parish Libraries Section is to further the objectives of the Catholic Library Association, particularly as they relate to parish libraries and to promote the establishment and maintenance of parish libraries, inter-parochial libraries, Catholic Lending Libraries, information centers and similar Catholic libraries as a means of carrying on the apostolate of literature."

Through this call to action, these dedicated members hoped to provide library service to all Catholic adults and the Catholic children not in the parochial school system. The extent of interest generated at that time can be demonstrated by the fact that in 1960 the Washington-Maryland Unit of the Catholic Library Association printed a directory of parish libraries and Catholic information centers in the Archdiocese of Washington.[2] Twenty-one active libraries were listed at that time, guided and inspired by Rev. James Kortendick, well-known librarian at the Catholic University of America. The libraries ranged in size and service from the mobile book cart to large, well-organized library facilities containing several thousand

volumes. One such library had an extensive children's collection,
book review program, winter forums and vacation time field trips
for youth.

These first Section members organized creative library facilities. Edith Tighe, Section chairperson, 1962-1963 and her committee, formed an interparish library which was the resource center
of its time, serving four parishes. Called St. Thomas Aquinas Library, it acted as library and cultural center with lecture series,
musical programs, adult classes, even the multi-media of the day.
Founded before the Parish and Community Libraries Section was
formed, it was a model for members. Canada boasted a parish-
community library facility. Founded by Edith Peterkin, M.D., this
library-cultural center offered programs in religion, art, music and
literature. [3]

Within the Parish and Community Libraries Section, membership increased dramatically through the 1960's with several states--
Illinois, Minnesota and Michigan--displaying strong membership. As
the 1970's began, problems arose which caused the decline of what
appeared to be a new horizon in library service. Lack of funds,
inadequate housing, women leaving volunteer service to enter fulltime
employment and the decline of the parochial school system had a
drastic effect upon the membership. While membership has decreased
and many of the past model libraries no longer exist, for the current
year new memberships balance lapsed memberships. Throughout
Section history, membership has represented approximately 10 percent of the C.L.A. total.

Parish and Community Libraries Section members lead flourishing libraries: Mrs. Mary Page Irwin, [4] Paulist Library, San
Francisco; Ruth T. Orr, [5] St. Alice's Parish Library, near Philadelphia, which was founded by Rev. Vincent P. Schneider; Mrs. Isabel Bradley, [6] Catholic Lending Library, Ware, Mass.; Mrs. Helen
I. Dempsey, [7] St. Lucian Library, Birmingham, Mich.; Mrs. Agnes
Oberwise, [8] Milwaukee; Mrs. Stephen Kleszewski, Hazardville Catholic Library, Enfield, Conn.; Rev. William R. Walsh, S. J., St.
Ignatius Parish Library, New York, to mention a few.

Section Organization

The Parish and Community Libraries Section receives $2.00
per year out of the total C.L.A. dues for each Section member
registered. It operates independently from headquarters and handles
its own treasury, business, newsletter, printing, mailing, etc. As
in most organizations, annual reports are requested of the chairman,
secretary, treasurer and standing committee chairman. The Section
constitution and by-laws closely follow that of the Catholic Library
Association.

When the Section was formed in 1957, the name Parish Library Section was appropriate. [9] Within a short span of years it was

evident that the name did not reflect the full scope of the Section's objectives.   The present Parish and Community Libraries Section title is one of the steps in the evolution.

National organizations face obstacles in communication.   While the Catholic Library Association has a headquarters which redirects Section mail, the sections themselves have no permanent addresses and so follow the addresses of the current section officers. [10] Most officers and committee members live great distances apart making smooth operations difficult.   Meetings of officers and committees are rare except at the annual conference.

The Section's chairman is responsible for planning and pre- siding at the annual conference Section program.   In an effort to assist the chairman, an Advisory Board was established in 1971. In addition to the Executive Board, consisting of the officers and immediate past chairman, the chairman appoints four to six other members to act as advisors.   They assist in bridging the gap that distance creates.

The Catholic Library Association depends for its strength on its state and regional units.   All of them operate with similar con- stitutions.   State and regional units are able to provide close contact with their members.   Dues structures and distance for meeting at- tendance attract greater numbers to the local organization.

The contrast in membership at the national and local levels is interesting.   In the former, professionalism is a key factor.   A national association must provide specific incentives to attract mem- bers.   In the same manner, to be useful, the local unit must remain active and viable.   The skilled librarian realizes the value of national and local membership in a professional association.   The parish or resource center librarian who lacks a library education background presents a challenge that has yet to be solved.

Local units are able to attract fine attendance for workshops, "How to" activities, panel discussions, book fairs and luncheons, but encouraging the attendees to become continuing members is dif- ficult.   However, the Michigan Unit of C.L.A. began what has be- come a tradition at a Catholic Book Week luncheon of recognizing library volunteers, library aides, student assistants and librarians who have performed a special service.   Begun as a project of the Parish and Community Libraries Section of that unit, this annual award luncheon stimulates membership and provides a necessary gesture of gratitude to many parish librarians.

Parish and Community Libraries Section members receive the Catholic Library World, the CLA official journal, published ten times a year.   Catholic Library World regularly contains a column published as Viewpoint.   Articles are submitted by individual sections and include material of a wide range of interest, thereby enabling the membership to remain in close contact with other sections.

Membership includes the quarterly Parish and Community Libraries Newsletter, also. This publication contains current news, member activities, items of Section importance and offers suggestions of useful print and non-print material. In 1972 and 1973, the Section compiled book lists containing reviews of the most recent religious, social, and biographical non-fiction and fiction. Review copies were mailed to selected members in an effort to create a greater sense of unity and cooperation. The booklist was a helpful tool for prospective library purchases. For the first time, in 1974, the Section sent a Resource Kit to all new members. It included the Parish Manual, recommended books lists, the Standards for Parish and Community Libraries, and other material helpful for beginning resource centers.

The Catholic Library Association has a proud tradition of annual conferences. Since 1921 the yearly meetings have gathered at most large cities throughout the country. The Executive Director is charged with planning the general program. Speakers of national and international renown provide the necessary magnets. An exhibit program is maintained, also.

Annual Section meetings include an Executive Board meeting, a general business meeting and a Section program that will provide inspiration and practical assistance and increase library professionalism and skills.[11] To this end, workshops, lectures, panels and tours are planned to encourage attendance.

While each city brings a one time conference attendance, there is a large and loyal representation from the Parish and Community Libraries Section, including Rev. Angelo U. Garbin from Chicago who not only attended the original Round Tables but also every convention since that time.[12] His guidance and keen judgment have provided inspiration through the years. Rev. Vincent P. Schneider and Rev. Charles Dollen have also given unfailing support.

Two editions of a manual for organizing and operating a parish library have been published.[13] At this writing, a third edition has been completed. Entitled Guide for the Organization and Operation of Religious Resource Centers, this manual has been the combined effort of the Parish and Community Libraries Section and the Religious Education Committee.[14] Guide for the Organization and Operation of Religious Resource Centers is intended to offer help for the present and goals for the future.

A committee composed of Alphonse Trezza, Joanne Klene and Rev. Angelo U. Garbin compiled The Standards for Parish Libraries which were adopted by the Section in 1971.[15] Striving to assist librarians deluged with contributions of older fiction, 1940-1964, the Parish and Community Libraries Section of the Michigan Unit compiled two volumes of Check It! (1961 and 1964) containing more than 10,000 fiction titles. This list was prepared from reviews in recognized critical journals. Wisconsin and New Jersey were among the units with active parish library groups. Excellent organization manuals were prepared by these units to aid their beginning library centers.   The Catholic Periodical and Literature Index indexes 127 Catholic periodicals and national Catholic newspapers.   It is published bi-monthly with a permanent two year cumulation and is most useful in larger library situations.

Relationship with the Roman Catholic Church

The Catholic Library Association and the Parish and Community Libraries Section have maintained a relationship with the Roman Catholic Church on an individual basis.   There has been no official policy regarding either promotion or discouragement of parish libraries.   Prelates such as Monsignor Francis X. Canfield, past president of the Catholic Library Association, have provided inspiration to all library-minded people.   Priests such as Rev. Vincent P. Schneider, Exton, Pa.; Rev. Angelo U. Garbin,[16] Chicago; Rev. James Kortendick,[17] Catholic University of America, Washington, D. C.; Rev. Jerome Fraser,[18] Detroit; Rev. Charles Dollen,[19] Poway, Ca.; Rev. William Walsh, S. J., New York; Rev. Anthony J. Lachner,[20] Minnesota and many other clergy have given encouragement and assistance.   With no specific church policy regarding establishment of library centers, prospective librarians have depended upon their individual pastors for support.[21]

Problems and Opportunities

A lack of funds, lack of general access to the library and changing times have produced discouragement, a decline in Section membership and library closings.   These are some of the major problems facing the parish library movement today.

A lack of funds has been a chronic problem for the clergy responsible for financing and maintaining parochial schools.   It is not difficult to understand that even the most enthusiastic pastor had few funds with which to extend library services to his adults and to the parish children in public schools.   Those pastors willing to provide this service did so with all-volunteer staffs.   In most cases the volunteers were left strictly on their own to use their ingenuity to generate their operating funds.   Librarians forced to support their libraries through creative fund-raising attempts have found membership in professional organizations increasingly difficult.   Personal membership at the national level of the Catholic Library Association begins at $15 per year which includes the Section membership and subscription to the Catholic Library World.   At this writing, many Parish and Community Libraries Section members, all volunteers, maintain their membership and pay their own transportation and expenses to the annual conference.

But money is not the only problem.   Libraries housed in out of the way places discouraged patronage.   Because library regulations stipulated that the school library was for student use only, other housing had to be found.   Libraries were put in hallways, basements and rectories.   Poor accessibility meant poor circulation and discouragement for the librarian.   The changing times have also produced several problems.   As women chose employment over volunteer service, library staffs dwindled.   It is unrealistic to expect a few volunteers to contribute unlimited years of service.   Consequently, administrative and operative functions become slow-moving and burdensome.

Changing times also demand frequent re-evaluation of material. Even some libraries well funded and staffed found their collections out of date.   They had failed to recognize the various interests of their clients.   Lack of patronage forced them to close.   But there is also hope in the changing times.   Changing times are producing an evolving concept of parish libraries as resource centers.   In states where many parochial schools have closed, some flourishing parish libraries were peremptorily closed, then reorganized as religious education centers. [22]   Former school libraries have been expanded to provide service to the parish.   Where parish libraries that formerly served adults exist, they are being expanded to include service for entire religious education programs much as Protestant and Jewish libraries serve their congregations.

With the evolving concept of resource centers, finances and staff must be reviewed.   Thought must be given to providing recompense for professional service.   Some media centers are now funded under religious education budgets in parishes in New Jersey, Washington, Michigan and other states. [23]   This realistic approach to library services recognizes that the proliferation of materials requires time and skill to process.   As the centers become more professional, so must the librarian.   Improved librarianship means increased library education.   Some of that growth can come with membership in professional organizations, through workshops, classes, meetings and conferences, expenses of which must be included in the library budget.   With increased professional skills, the librarian should receive remuneration for services.

These are the challenges facing the Parish and Community Libraries Section.   There is new hope that the Parish and Community Libraries Section can unite the religious education field with fine parish libraries to form a section devoted to Christian formation, a major contribution to Catholic library service.

NOTES

1.   Catholic Library Association, "Constitution and By-laws. " Catholic Library World XLVII (January 1976), p. 251.
2.   Catholic University of America.   A Directory of Parish Libraries and Information Centers in the Archdiocese of Washington. Washington-Maryland Unit, Catholic Library Association, 1960.
3.   Eymard, Sr. Mary, I. B. V. M.   "The Belleville Catholic Lending

Library." Catholic Library World XXXIX (December 1967),
p. 289.

4. Irwin, Mary Page, "Public Relations: The Key," Catholic Library World XLIV (March 1973), p. 502.

5. Orr, Ruth T., "One Parish Library--A Chronicle," Catholic Library World XLIII (May-June 1972), p. 528.

6. Bradley, Isabel. "Parish Library and Religious Education," Catholic Library World XLVIII (March 1977).

7. Dempsey, Helen I., "Special Libraries, a Viewpoint," Michigan Librarian XXXVII (Autumn issue, 1971), p. 15.

8. Oberwise, Agnes, "The Catholic Parish Library Association, Milwaukee Archdiocese," Catholic Library World XXXVIII (April 1967), p. 551.

9. Young, Bernadette, "Needs Assessment," Catholic Library World XLVIII (September 1976), p. 87.

10. Catholic Library Association, 461 W. Lancaster Avenue, Haverford, Pennsylvania, 19401. Handbook-Membership Directory. Vol. 47, Jan. 1976.

11. Lamsey, Marilyn, "Why Walter Wrote That Book," Catholic Library World XLIV (December 1972), p. 291.

12. Garbin, Rev. Angelo U., "The Parish Libraries Movement in the Catholic Church," Catholic Library World XI (April 1969), p. 515.

13. Schneider, Rev. Vincent P., editor. The Parish and Catholic Lending Library Manual. Haverford, Pennsylvania. The Catholic Library Association, 1965, 64p.

14. Corrigan, John T., C.F.X., editor. Guide for Resource Centers. Haverford, Pennsylvania, The Catholic Library Association, 1977.

15. Klene, Joanne, "Standards for Parish and Lending Libraries," Catholic Library World XLII (May-June 1971), p. 574.

16. Garbin, Rev. Angelo U., "Parish Libraries: Fonts of Renewal," The Catholic Standard and Times. (Thursday, April 1, 1971).

17. Catholic University of America, op. cit.

18. Fraser, Rev. Jerome, "Parish Library Service in Changing Neighborhoods," Catholic Library World XLIII (December 1971), p. 222.

19. Dollen, Rev. Charles, "Volunteers: The Heart of the Parish Library," Catholic Library World XLVIII (October 1976), p. 131.

20. Lachner, Rev. Anthony J., "Audio-visuals in Religion," Catholic Library World XLIII (March 1972), p. 417.

21. Favars, Rev. Joseph F., "The Parish Library, a Pastor's Point of View," Catholic Library World XXXIX (February 1968), p. 432.

22. Young, Bernadette, "Where Have All the Parish Libraries Gone?" Catholic Library World XLIV (February 1973), p. 438.

23. Young, Bernadette, "Libraries and Librarians," Catholic Library World XLVIII (November 1976), p. 184.

THE ASSOCIATION OF JEWISH LIBRARIES

Mae Weine

The beginning of the Association of Jewish Libraries dates back over thirty years, when the Jewish Librarians' Association was formed in 1946. This group was composed primarily of librarians in large scholarly libraries, mostly situated in New York, and included representatives of such distinguished institutions as the Jewish Theological Seminary Library, the Hebrew Union College Library, and the Jewish Division of the New York Public Library. However, the organization had no formal program of activities, and was an organization of librarians rather than of libraries. Aside from sponsoring occasional learned lectures, and holding one or two dinner meetings, nothing was done.

In the meantime, several local Jewish library associations had been formed. The Cleveland synagogue librarians formed one group, Librarians of Jewish Institutions of Cleveland, and had for many years worked out a booklet for Jewish Book Month and helped prepare displays for local pedagogic conferences. Librarians in non-Jewish libraries were invited to become acquainted with what was available in the field of Jewish books. In 1956, the Jewish Library Association of Greater Philadelphia was established, which included not only Philadelphia but the nearby communities in Southern New Jersey (Camden, Haddon Heights, and others).

The real credit for founding the national organization as it is today must go to Miriam Leikind, the Librarian of The Temple, in Cleveland. Miss Leikind had been for a number of years a member of the Jewish Librarians' Association and had urged that group to enlarge its scope and assist the small synagogue libraries scattered throughout the country. Many of them were in urgent need of guidance and had nowhere to turn. She had received letters from Jewish librarians frequently in which they asked for aid in setting up libraries. Often she had traveled to their communities in order to render personal assistance and advice. However, the Association, no doubt concerned with its own problems and unfamiliar with laymen's needs, did not respond to her plea.

At one time, indeed, the Jewish Book Council attempted to call a meeting of interested librarians during an educator's conference in Atlantic City, but only three or four people came, including Rabbi Philip Goodman, then the Executive Director of the Book Council, Miss Leikind herself, and the author of this paper. Apparently the time was not yet ripe.

In the summer of 1961, the American Library Association held its annual conference in Cleveland. The local Cleveland group, the Librarians of Jewish Institutions, invited guests attending the conference to discuss the feasibility of a national organization of Jewish librarians. The meeting was held at Miss Leikind's home on July 11, 1961.

Representatives of the Cleveland and Philadelphia groups described their activities. In view of what the local organizations were doing, it was felt that the New York-based Jewish Librarians' Association did not help the small Jewish library, so the group discussed what a national organization could do to help such institutions. However, before proceeding further, Miss Leikind, who was chosen president pro-tem of the tentative "Jewish Library Association," was asked to speak to Dr. Abraham Berger, the president of the Jewish Librarians' Association, to see if he would invite the proposed group to join the original group. This was done later, but Dr. Berger suggested that it would be wiser to organize separately.

Jewish Library Association Formed

Early in the following year, under Miss Leikind's direction, publicity was sent to a number of libraries and Jewish institutions throughout the country which proposed a meeting to form a Jewish Library Association. From May 30 through June 1, 1962, the first conference was held in Atlantic City, New Jersey. The response exceeded all expectations. Some 30 enthusiastic, dedicated librarians came to the conference, from places as far away as Oklahoma and Florida, as well as Toronto and Montreal. The charms of the Atlantic City boardwalk went unheeded while delegates held workshops, listened to speakers, discussed Jewish library problems and laid plans for the future.

Miriam Leikind was unanimously elected president of the new organization, a constitutional committee was organized, and the new organization was underway. A newsletter, originally called The Drop Box, was organized, with Mrs. Elaine Williams of Detroit as its first editor.

From the beginning, the aim of the new association was service to its members. Animated discussions on the need for a satisfactory classification scheme for an all-Jewish library collection eventually resulted in the distribution of two suggested classification schemes for members to consider. One was the expansion of Dewey Decimal numbers worked out by Miss Leikind for her own library in Cleveland (this expansion preceded the later expansions made in the Dewey system by its editors). The other classification by the author of this paper was a modification of Dewey which had originally been designed for the Philadelphia group and had been worked out with the cooperation of its members.

Additional material was added and the whole was combined

in a "membership kit," which was sent without charge to each Association member. Included were such items as the Jewish Book
Council's Manual for Jewish Community Center, School, and Congregation Libraries, by Sophia N. Cedarbaum, and the original children's
book list by the late Fanny Goldstein, also a Book Council publication.

Today, the membership kit has swelled to include not only the
two classification schemes (both schemes have since been revised
and the expanded Weine scheme is now in its sixth edition), but also
two subject heading lists, one Miss Leikind's, the other, based on
the Weine classification, prepared by the Philadelphia group under
the chairmanship of Mrs. Mildred Kurland (now in its third revised
edition); a relative index to the Weine scheme, by Mrs. Anita Loeb;
a basic periodicals list; a considerably expanded children's book list,
published by the Jewish Book Council; a selected reference book list
for a small Jewish library, by Herbert C. Zafren; Standards for a
Jewish Library; an order blank listing the publications available from
the Jewish Book Council; and any new publications which might be
issued from time to time by the Association. The kit is not only
an indispensable aid to the untrained Jewish librarian, it is a powerful magnet which attracts new members.

The very existence of the new organization had important side
effects--some direct, others indirect. Miss Leikind, who had long
been indexing Jewish periodicals for use in her own library, was encouraged to expand the index and to make it available on a wider
scale. As a result, the Index to Jewish Periodicals is now published
independently on a regular basis and is an important reference tool
in libraries throughout the country, both Jewish and non-Jewish, university libraries included. Another publication of the organization,
the Standards for Jewish Libraries, has been added to the publications list of the Jewish Book Council and is available along with their
other publications.

Another long range benefit has been the establishment of
many local library associations where none existed before, including
members who may not be affiliated with the national organization
but yet benefit from a face-to-face contact with their local colleagues.
Often these local groups carry on extensive programs which are in
turn reflected back on the national scene.

An excellent example of the latter is a project of the Southern
California association, by far the largest of the local groups. That
association has prepared an index to Jewish holiday short stories in
collections, with age groups indicated, an invaluable aid to librarians
who serve a school population. Most synagogues maintain religious
schools, usually either the three-day-a-week after-school type or a
one-day-a-week Sunday school.

Since the establishment of the national association, local library groups have formed in Boston, Miami, Southern California and

Detroit, to mention only a few of the larger groups.   Canadian members cooperate actively with one another.   In addition to Canada, the Association of Jewish Libraries now boasts members in Mexico, Spain, Greece, and Switzerland.   A librarian in Mexico City, Mrs. Linda Sametz, has translated the Weine classification scheme into Spanish for use by her library.

The young organization early established an annual award for the best Jewish juvenile book published, as a way of encouraging authors to enter a more limited field for their endeavors than general publishing, as well as making them conscious of the expanding numbers of Jewish libraries for marketing their work.

One of the first projects undertaken by the infant organization was a survey of its member libraries to gather accurate information about their nature, size, personnel, etc.   No information had been compiled before, with the exception of a limited 1947 survey by the Jewish Book Council.   The Council survey covered only 49 libraries, more than half of them in Jewish Community Centers rather than in synagogues.   The results of the JLA survey, covering 92 libraries, were tabulated and reported to all the members.   A second questionnaire was distributed in 1971 to seek more information than the first, and with greater response, 122 libraries.

Comparison of the two surveys showed mixed results.   On the plus side, the intervening years showed improvement in the fields of professional qualifications, the Jewish education of the librarians involved, expansion of library service, greater emphasis on the Jewish nature of the book collections, and greater use of formal classification systems (as opposed to "home-made" schemes).   On the minus side, there was little improvement in the limited number of library hours, the "status" of the librarian in comparison with that of other Jewish professionals, and the correspondingly low salaries. These difficulties, unfortunately, will probably be with us for some time to come, especially in a field where so much of the work is done on a volunteer basis.

All of this activity inevitably attracted the attention of the older group, the Jewish Librarians' Association.   They were disturbed by the similarity in names, and feared that confusion would result in the minds of the public.   Around 1965, when the Jewish Library Association had been in existence for three years, Dr. Herbert Zafren was nominated for the presidency of the Jewish Librarians' group.   Dr. Zafren, librarian of Hebrew Union College-Jewish Institute of Religion (the seminary for the training of Reform rabbis) had always been most sympathetic toward the problems of the small Jewish library, and he accepted the presidency with the explicit understanding that he would explore affiliation with the Jewish Library Association.   Accordingly, a meeting was called in New York in 1966, with representatives of both groups present.   The discussion was animated and prolonged, but a merger agreement was eventually hammered out.

Association of Jewish Libraries, Synagogue,
School and Center Division Formed

Because the needs, size, and make-up of the two groups varied so widely, it was agreed that the overall Association would consist of two autonomous divisions, each one with its own group of officers, with a national slate for the division as a whole. Each group
maintains its own treasury, with a certain percentage going into the
treasury of the Association. Thus, each group has funds available
for the publication of material which may not interest the other group.

In order to eliminate any possible confusion, the name of the
new combined organization was changed to Association of Jewish Libraries (AJL), with the respective divisions being known as the Synagogue, School, and Center Division (SSC), and the Research and Special Libraries Division (R&S). New members may join either or
both divisions, depending on their interests and the needs of their
libraries.

Although not specifically stated, in practice, the custom has
been for the national president to be chosen alternately from each
group. For a time, the presidents of the divisions served as vice-
presidents ex-officio of the overall organization. This situation has
recently been changed, so now there is only one vice-president who
is the president-elect.

The name of the newsletter was changed from The Drop Box
to the Bulletin, and eventually it was expanded from a mimeographed
publication of a few sheets to its present printed and illustrated form
averaging 25 to 30 pages. Where it had formerly been restricted to
organizational news, it now covers, somewhat like Library Journal,
any items likely to be interesting to Jewish librarians. A typical
issue included, for example, items about the launching of a new
Jewish book club; the news that a new typewriter has been developed
which types both Hebrew and English, and can be shifted from left
to right and from right to left; a brief listing of additional headings
in standard Jewish reference books under which material on the Holocaust can be found; a description of a Bicentennial Haggadah; ads for
"Situations Wanted"; a brief annotated list of new books, and sundry
other items.

From the beginning, the new organization held annual conferences filled with workshops, lectures, and visits to local Jewish libraries. With the merger, the custom was instituted of having workshops both separately for each group to discuss its own problems,
and combined for items of interest to both groups. Thus, the small
libraries had their horizons and interests enlarged, while the larger
research libraries were made aware of the needs of the Jewish layman.

Again, as with the founding of the Jewish Library Association
a few years earlier, the gains were not only direct but also indirect.
For years, conference delegates had bemoaned the fact that there was

no specific training school for Jewish librarianship. No library
school in the country offered courses to meet those needs--indeed,
as far as the writer is aware--none does yet. In 1975-76, the Jewish Theological Seminary of America (the seminary for the training
of Conservative rabbis), with the aid of a grant from the National
Endowment for the Humanities, was able for the first time to offer
courses for librarians of Judaica. Courses were offered in Judaica
bibliography and reference, cataloging and classification of Judaica,
and in Hebrew paleography, all on an advanced level with a knowledge
of Hebrew essential. Arrangements were made with New York area
library schools to accept credit for these courses toward students'
library degrees. The response was overwhelming with many more
students enrolling than had been anticipated.

Unfortunately, the grant was not repeated the following year,
and the Seminary was unable to continue. Yet the need continues,
and one hopes that some future library school may eventually institute such courses on a regular basis. Even before the Seminary offered these courses, however, the SSC division had done its bit by
offering a small annual scholarship to library school students who
planned to enter the Jewish library field. This is still being done.

As with the JLA previously, the merger provided the scholarly
libraries of the R & S Division with an opportunity to meet and discuss mutual problems. Thus, Dr. Zafren, chairman of an American
National Standards Institute Committee on the Romanization of Hebrew,
presented a preliminary report to his colleagues at the 1972 AJL conference in Toronto. Judging from their reactions, he felt that the
so-called Keypunch-Compatible Style, which is a consonantal scheme
and ignores vowels (like the Hebrew language) was the one that made
the most impact. This style has since been published as ANSI
"American National Standard Romanization of Hebrew."

Jewish Book Council of America

A word would be added here about the important role played
in the library field by the Jewish Book Council of America. Its beginning goes back to the work of a devoted children's librarian, the
late Fanny Goldstein of Boston. Working in a Boston public library
branch located in a Jewish neighborhood, she started the first "Jewish Book Week" in 1925. The movement grew until 1943 when the
national Jewish Book Council was established. A year later, the
Council came under the sponsorship of the National Jewish Welfare
Board, a Jewish service organization, with which it is still affiliated,
thus making possible a considerable expansion of its program. The
"Jewish Book Week" has grown to Jewish Book Month and is annually
celebrated in the fall in libraries and Jewish Community Centers
from coast to coast. The 1976 observance in the Jewish Community
Center of Detroit, for instance, extended for over a week, with talks
by 20 well-known authors and a display and sale of thousands of
Jewish books.

The Jewish Book Council supplies free posters and bookmarks to all institutions, including libraries, observing Jewish Book Month. The bookmarks list the books which have won the awards which the Book Council gives each spring to the best Jewish books in various categories. At the time of the book awards, the Book Council gives citations to Jewish libraries which meet their minimum standards (size, number of acquisitions, hours open, etc.) Needless to say, this has been a great encouragement to the establishment and improvement of new Jewish libraries.

Even more important than the citations, however, are the publications of the Book Council, which pioneered in the field long before the establishment of the Jewish Library Association. Of particular importance to the untrained (usually a volunteer) synagogue librarian is the previously mentioned library manual by Sophia N. Cedarbaum. This manual includes not only the usual information on how to go about organizing and running a small library (policies, administration, and technical processes) but also special appendices listing such things as names of Jewish publishers (often very small and not listed in the usual library sources), sources for library information and supplies, and information on library courses. All illustrative material concerns items and/or problems of Jewish interest.

Equally important to the beginning and untrained librarian are the selected basic book lists which the Book Council distributes for very nominal fees. Thus, the basic book list for the Jewish adult, or the book list for the Jewish child, as well as lists on special Jewish subject areas (the Holocaust, for example, or Israel, or Jewish reference books), offers invaluable aid to the beginning librarian, overwhelmed by the mass of material available. Realizing the importance of such aids, AJL's membership kit includes three of these lists, the ones for the Jewish adult and child, and for reference books.

All Jewish librarians, whether or not professionally educated, look forward each year to the Council's Jewish Book Annual. This volume contains articles of interest to all persons involved in the Jewish book world--Jewish literary activities all over the world, descriptions of important Jewish libraries, articles on important Jewish writers, and perhaps most important, annotated bibliographies of books of Jewish interest published during the preceding year, including books in Hebrew and Yiddish as well as in English.

Because these aids existed before the establishment of the library association, AJL's policy has always been to supplement, rather than to compete with, the work of the Book Council. Happily, relations between the two organizations have always been cordial and helpful. Thus, when the library association drew up its Standards for Jewish Libraries, Rabbi Goodman asked for and received permission to distribute it as one of the Council's publications. The classification schemes developed for the library association are listed along with others which the Book Council sends in answer to inquiries

on the subject.   Conversely, the order blank for Book Council publications is always included in the AJL membership kit, so members
will know what publications are available elsewhere.

Challenges

The Association of Jewish Libraries is now firmly established.
If any danger exists, it may come if the association should be content to settle into routine.   It must continue to be of service to its
members.   It must revise its publications to keep them up to date.
The Bulletin, excellent as it is, suffers from the lack of a fixed publication date.   Despite the best efforts of its editors, the flow of
material, being dependent on voluntary contributions by members,
is necessarily erratic.

The R&S division has been comparatively inactive; it should
do more both for its own members and for the association as a
whole.   The SSC, so far at least, has not succeeded in raising the
status of the Jewish librarian in the eyes of the Jewish community.
It must redouble its efforts to reach Jewish educators and those who
administer the affairs of the Jewish community.   Above all, it must
make the Jewish public aware of the existence of Jewish libraries.

BIBLIOGRAPHY

The American Jewish Yearbook.   New York: The American Jewish
        Committee; Philadelphia: The Jewish Publication Society of
        America, annual.

Association of Jewish Libraries, Synagogue, School, and Center Division.
        A Basic Periodical List for the Small Jewish Library.   Pre-
        pared by Bertha Cravets and Mae Weine, n.d.

Cedarbaum, Sophia N.   A Manual for Jewish Community Center,
        School, and Congregation Libraries.   New York: Jewish
        Book Council of America, 1962.

Elazar, David H. and Daniel J., A Classification System for Li-
        braries of Judaica.   Detroit: Wayne State University Librar-
        ies, 1968.   192 pp.

Golub, Jacob S., J.E.C. Classification System.   Revised and edited
        by Ruth C. Kanner.   1968.   Apply to United Parent Teachers
        Association, Board of Jewish Education, 426 West 58th Street,
        New York, N.Y. 10019.

Index to Jewish Periodicals.   Cleveland Heights, Ohio: The Temple
        (editor varies).

Jewish Book Annual.   New York: Jewish Book Council of America.

Jewish Book Council of America.   A Book List for the Jewish Child,
    1972.

_____.   Standards for Jewish Libraries in Synagogues, Schools,
    and Centers.   Rev. ed.   New York: Prepared by the Asso-
    ciation of Jewish Libraries, Synagogue, School, and Center
    Division, n. d.

Survey of Jewish Community Center Libraries.   New York: National
    Jewish Welfare Board, 1967.

Jewish Library Association of Greater Philadelphia.   Subject Headings
    for a Judaica Library.   3rd ed. rev., 1972.   Apply to the
    Association of Jewish Libraries, 2 Thornton Road, Waltham,
    Massachusetts. 02154.

_____.   Supplement to the Subject Headings List.   1975.

Leikind, Miriam.   Library Classification System.   Cleveland: The
    Temple Library, n. d.

_____.   Subject Headings.   Cleveland: The Temple Library, 1963.

Loeb, Anita.   Relative Index to the Weine Classification Scheme for
    Judaica Libraries, 1972.

Rubin, Leah, and Wildman, Ruth.   Holiday Bibliographies.   Beverly
    Hills, California: Temple Emanuel Library, 1975.

Weine, Mae.   "Libraries for the Jewish Laymen, " Jewish Book An-
    nual XXIV (5727/1966-67), pp. 50-54.

_____.   "Report on the Library Questionnaire of the Synagogue,
    School and Center Division, Association of Jewish Libraries, "
    1972.

_____.   Weine Classification Scheme for Judaica Libraries.   6th
    ed.   Distributed by the Synagogue, School and Center Division,
    Association of Jewish Libraries, 1975.

Zafren, Herbert C.   Jewish Reference Books, A Select List.   Re-
    printed from the Jewish Book Annual, XXVIII (5731/1970-71),
    New York.

THE CHURCH AND SYNAGOGUE LIBRARY ASSOCIATION

Dorothy J. Rodda

With the acceleration of church and synagogue library development during the decade of the nineteen sixties came the need for a
unifying core for this branch of librarianship. The Church and Synagogue Library Association was founded in Philadelphia in 1967 as the
culmination of the developing interest in church and synagogue libraries of John F. Harvey, then Dean of the Graduate School of Library
Science, Drexel University.

Shortly after Harvey assumed that position in 1958, he came
to realize that certain areas of librarianship had been neglected by
the library school. An outstanding example of this neglect was the
field of church and synagogue librarianship in which no course was
offered despite a relatively large number of such libraries in the
Philadelphia area. While certain library associations provided some
assistance to this field, none of them offered programming and publications aimed directly at this new and growing group. Visits to a
number of these libraries convinced him of the need for education
in the field. Library quality varied greatly, in size, organization
and staffing. Some consisted of a shelf of castoff books which circulated rarely. At the same time, he found some well-chosen and well-
organized collections supervised by professionals who volunteered
their skills to their churches or synagogues. All shades in between
seemed to indicate to Harvey that the library school should be providing service for this group. Furthermore, he felt that it was a
fruitful field for the interest of book publishers and library suppliers.

Harvey discovered that a group of Philadelphia synagogue librarians was meeting to provide mutual assistance in basic library
practice and book selection. Following a number of meetings with
this group, he spearheaded the establishment of the first Seminar in
Synagogue Librarianship, held in 1961 at the Drexel University Graduate School of Library Science under the directorship of Sidney Galfand, Librarian, Temple Har Zion and Chief of Technical Processes,
Pedagogical Library, in the Philadelphia public school system. The
first seminar provided instruction for synagogue librarians over a
period of several weeks, for which they received academic credit.
It was repeated annually for a number of years.

One year after the first synagogue seminar, in 1962, the
First Church Library Conference was held, under the co-sponsorship
of Drexel and the Philadelphia Council of Churches. Unlike the syna-

gogue seminars of several weeks duration, it was held for just one
day, with several plenary sessions being interspersed with groups of
workshops covering the major phases of librarianship, i.e., administration, book selection, cataloging and classification, promotion
and audio-visual material.   No academic credit was involved.   These
one-day conferences became annual affairs and often attracted more
than 200 persons from a number of surrounding counties and states
and many different denominations.

The early sixties saw the rise of a number of other church
and synagogue library groups.   Several denominations had been providing help for their church libraries for many years before that,
usually in conjunction with their denominational presses.   But this
was the period that saw the rise of interdenominational conferences,
assisted by representatives from the library profession.   Regional
groups were formed in the Washington, D.C. and Baltimore areas
and in the Pacific Northwest.

John Harvey's search for Drexel conference leaders brought
to light a number of individuals who were vitally interested in this
branch of librarianship.   He discovered students in the library school
who were interested in working on literature in the field.   One result of this interest was the compilation of the Second Annual Church
Library Workshop proceedings in 1963.[1] Published by the Drexel
Press, it became possibly the first ecumenical congregational library manual.   A second such book, based on papers from the Third
Annual Church Library Conference and entitled Church Library Guide,
was published the following year (1965).[2]

Another student project was the compilation of an interfaith
church and synagogue library directory, again perhaps the first of
its kind.[3]   Though it contained only about 10 percent of the estimated number of congregational libraries in the country, it suggested
the potential field of interest in the subject and became the basis for
Association membership recruitment.

The interest of these students plus that of many established
librarians convinced Harvey that a core of leaders was available to
form a nationwide ecumenical church and synagogue library association.   To test this thesis he invited forty persons to a meeting in
the Americana Hotel in New York during the summer 1966 American
Library Association conference.   Twenty-eight of this group of forty
persons either attended the meeting or expressed interest in the
project.   Represented in the group were persons of all three major
faiths, representatives of denominational and regional congregational
library groups and publishers of religious literature.   All of them
expressed willingness to follow Harvey's leadership in establishing
an association such as he described.

Although an ecumenical association was intended from the
start, the persons who expressed interest represented Protestants
to an overwhelming proportion.   Perhaps this was where the greatest
need lay, since there were already long-established Catholic and

Jewish library associations. Neither of them, however, existed
solely to serve the local church or synagogue library. It was seen
that a new association could provide supplementary services for individual parish and synagogue librarians who shared needs common
to all three faiths.

Thus encouraged, he set out to write a constitution and by-
laws for the group, based on the documents of other national library
associations. This document was subsequently ratified by a mail
vote which Harvey conducted among the "Americana Group. " The
same group voted in a further mail vote conducted by Harvey on the
slate of officers which he developed and which was stipulated in the
new by-laws. These officers, together with the fourteen appointed
committee chairpersons, comprised the first Executive Board. These
were the winners of the first election:

> President--Ruth S. Smith, Chief, Open Library, Institute for
> Defense Analysis, Arlington, Virginia; Librarian, Bethesda
> United Methodist Church, Bethesda, Maryland;
> First Vice-President and President-elect--Rev. Donald L. Leon-
> ard, Executive Editor, Board of Christian Education, United
> Presbyterian Church, U.S.A., Philadelphia;
> Second Vice-President--Miriam Leikind, Librarian, The Temple
> Library, Cleveland;
> Secretary--Rev. Vincent P. Schneider, Librarian, Cardinal
> Dougherty High School, Philadelphia, Founder and Director,
> St. Alice's Parish Library, Upper Darby, Pennsylvania;
> Treasurer--Dorothy J. Rodda, Assistant Librarian, Harcum
> Junior College, Bryn Mawr, Pennsylvania; Librarian, Ard-
> more Presbyterian Church, Ardmore, Pennsylvania.

Eleven members of this group, together with John Harvey,
met for the first time on July 11, 1967 in the Bellevue-Stratford
Hotel in Philadelphia. Harvey opened the meeting with an introduc-
tory statement concerning the background and foundation of the Association and his hopes for its future. Then, before turning over
the brand-new gavel to the President, he told the group that he would
be leaving the country to spend a year as a Fulbright professor in
Iran. This year lengthened into four as he founded the Iranian Docu-
mentation Centre and the Tehran Book Processing Centre and stayed
to develop them. The rest of the meeting time was spent in discussing the functions which the various officers and committee chairpersons would perform.

At the first meeting, the officers recognized the need for an
executive secretary, and the Secretary, Reverend Vincent Schneider,
was asked to perform this function. It soon became apparent, however, that the receipt and recording of memberships was an essential
part of the executive secretary's task. Since membership rolls were
the responsibility of the Treasurer, according to the by-laws, it was
voted at the second Board meeting held on November 30, 1967, to
appoint the Treasurer, Dorothy J. Rodda, Executive Secretary for
a term expiring August 31, 1968, at a salary of $1 per year. At

the same time, she was authorized to rent a post box in the name
of the Association. Since that time, the Bryn Mawr post office has
been the official address of the Association.

Dorothy J. Rodda's appointment was renewed for two subsequent years. From September, 1970, to October, 1973, Joyce L.
White served in that position. Then, Dorothy J. Rodda was reappointed to the position, extending to August 31, 1979.

The first CSLA office was established in 1970 in a room of
Joyce L. White's home in West Philadelphia. A room in Dorothy
Rodda's home in Havertown is now devoted to that purpose. A clerical assistant now works 40 hours per month; the executive secretary
averages 130 hours per month. The salary has been increased each
year to its present level of $4800 per year.

The original Association by-laws stated that "its objective is
to investigate, discuss, and promote every phase of church and synagogue librarianship." With the first revision of the by-laws in 1969,
the purpose was stated in greater detail as follows:

This Association is formed for the following purposes:

a.   To provide an international ecumenical association for those in-
     terested in the work of church and synagogue libraries.
b.   To investigate, discuss, and promote every phase of church and
     synagogue librarianship.
c.   To issue regular and occasional publications relating to the in-
     terests of church and synagogue librarians.
d.   To provide through its membership such counseling and guidance
     services as are incident to its program.
e.   To conduct such conferences, seminars, workshops, or meet-
     ings as will serve the needs of its members.
f.   To foster adherence to educational and religious standards and
     criteria in the development of church and synagogue libraries.
g.   To pursue these objectives without contemplation of pecuniary
     gain or profit, incidental or otherwise.

Subsequent revisions of the by-laws, in 1971 and 1974, returned to a simpler statement that "The purpose of the Association
shall be to provide educational guidance in the establishment and
maintenance of library services in churches and synagogues." Certainly it was evident from the start that the over-riding need was
the provision of informal, though not unstructured, continuing education for volunteer church and synagogue librarians. Many members
were professionals in other branches of librarianship, some were
trained librarians, others were non-career homemakers who had been
educated in librarianship, still others loved books but had no library
education, and yet others were recruited just because the need was
there. All wanted help in relating to congregational libraries.[4]

This help had to be funded with the dues of members. For
the first membership year ending August 31, 1968, 186 members

were enrolled in all categories. Membership has always been open
to any interested person or group without distinction as to race,
color, creed or nationality. For the first nine years of the Association's existence, dues were $5 per year for individual members
(entitling them to one subscription to the official bulletin); $10 for
church or synagogue members (3 subscriptions); $25 for affiliate
members--church or synagogue library--related groups (5 subscriptions); $50 for institutional members--publishers and other interested
groups (5 subscriptions); and $100 for contributing members (5 sub-
scriptions).

Inflationary pressures, especially in the areas of postage,
printing and paper, forced the reluctant decision of the Executive
Board to raise dues in the first two categories for the 1976-77 membership year. Currently, they are $7.50 for individual members
and $15 for church or synagogue members.

The Official Bulletin

The first project undertaken by the original Board was publication of a newsletter, originally entitled News Bulletin. The Publications Chairperson edited the first two issues which were distributed in the spring and fall of 1968. Containing four and six pages
respectively, they included photographs, news of the fledgling Association and articles about successful church libraries. The bulletin
goes to every member; circulation was 1480 in April, 1978.

The Publications Chairperson appointed for the second Association year was given the responsibility for editing the official bulletin. It was renamed Church and Synagogue Libraries, and became
a bi-monthly publication of 12 mimeographed pages. The emphasis
was on practical help for volunteer librarians and news of CSLA conferences. Five issues were published during the remainder of the
second membership year; since then, six issues have come out each
year.

The editorship of the official bulletin was soon recognized to
be a demanding and time-consuming job in its own right. When consideration was given to publications other than the bulletin, the Board
decided to separate the positions of publications chairperson and editor. At that time, Claudia Hannaford, of Erie, Pennsylvania, took
over the post of editor. At the beginning of Mrs. Hannaford's editorship, the official bulletin became a printed instead of a mimeographed publication. It now contains 16 pages in each issue. Selecting material for an issue which will be helpful to large denominational groups and to beginner as well as professional librarians
presents a challenge for every editor. It is indexed in Christian
Periodicals Index. The present editor is William H. Gentz, Senior
Editor, Seabury Press, New York.

The bulletin strives to bring significant news of the congregational library world to its readers, in addition to material of prac-

tical help and inspiration.   A feature of particular interest has been
the development of a book review section.   The first book review
appeared in the July 1969 issue.   Subsequently, a review or two appeared occasionally.   In January 1971, a specific section of the bulletin was set aside for book reviews.   Current bulletin issues contain 15 to 20 book and media reviews.   Special bibliographies also
appear occasionally on such subjects as holidays, bereavement, books
for men, books for young people and reference books for an ecumenical library.

Regular columns of news items of general interest to congregational librarians have appeared with different titles under different
editors.   Specific suggestions for congregational library practice have
appeared for several years.   At present, a column "The Latchstring
Is Out" fills this function.   Occasionally, an entire issue is devoted
to one topic such as religious art in the library or Association chapters.

Most issues have contained photographs, line drawings, and
some advertising, usually by publishers.   Horn Book, Inc., the first
institutional member, was also the first advertiser.   Its first ad appeared in the March 1970 issue, and it has remained a regular advertiser to the present.   However, the possibilities for advertising
income have not been fully exploited.   This is one of several bulletin
problems with which the Executive Board has wrestled.   Finding copy
which has the most usefulness to the members is another.   The current trend toward using material which originates in conferences and
workshops shows promise of being a workable long-term solution.
A third major problem area is getting the issues out promptly.   This
problem, of course, is common to all volunteer publication program.

Annual Conferences

The first year of the Association saw the establishment of
the First Annual Conference.   It was held in Philadelphia at the
Bellevue-Stratford Hotel, May 27-29, 1968, with the theme, "The
Challenge of Books in Today's World."   One hundred fifty-four delegates representing 14 denominations and faiths, from 15 states, attended this conference.   It established the format of a series of
workshops or classes interspersed with plenary sessions addressed
by speakers on topics of an inspirational or informational nature.
Topics covered in the workshops included cataloging, reference work,
book selection, administration, circulation, publicity, and audio-visual
material, in other words, the basic elements of library practice.
A tour of outstanding area congregational libraries was held and 16
exhibits were open to the participants.

This pattern has been followed in the national conferences
held since that time.   Although workshops on the basic elements of
library practice are included each time, many related and enriching
subjects have been covered as well--service to children, young people, men, senior citizens, handicapped persons; relations with the

congregation, clergy, religious leaders, other congregational librarians, public libraries, the community; the handling of non-book material such as periodicals, pamphlets, art prints, recordings and
other audio-visuals; preparing bibliographies, writing book reviews,
giving book talks, storytelling, making banners or posters, handling
repairs; new books, books on special subjects, archives, problems
of censorship, recruiting volunteers, furnishing and financing a library.   And of course the basic elements are often discussed on
more than one level of experience.   Workshop leaders and speakers
are recruited from CSLA and other congregational library leaders
and from the local area.

Beginning with the second (1969) annual conference held in
Washington, D. C. , fees have been charged to commercial exhibitors.
Other library associations, libraries and local civic groups have been
given free exhibit space.   At the 1973 conference in Portland, Oregon, the exhibits chairperson initiated the practice of inviting publishers to send individual titles for a group exhibit as an alternative
to a staffed exhibit at one or more tables.   A total of forty-four
exhibitors in all categories participated in the 1976 conference in
Philadelphia.   An innovation at this conference was the allocation
of a block of time exclusively for visiting exhibits, an idea much
appreciated by the exhibitors and the delegates.

The first conference featured the first Awards Banquet, also.
Mrs. Josephine Kyles, then director of the Division of Services,
Metropolitan Detroit Council of Churches, was honored with a life
membership.   The Awards Banquet became a regular conference
feature.   Early in CSLA history, a solid foundation was laid for the
awards program.   Each year one or two awards were given to persons who had made outstanding contributions to congregational librarianship.   Other award recipients have received official CSLA certificates of appreciation.

In 1976, the Awards Committee recommended the establishment of three categories.   The Executive Board voted to accept this
recommendation and an award was made in each one of these categories at the 1976 conference in Philadelphia, as follows:

Outstanding Congregational Librarian--This award is given to a
    church or synagogue librarian in recognition of distinguished
    service to the congregation and/or community through devo-
    tion to the congregational library.
Outstanding Congregational Library--This award is given to a
    church or synagogue library which has responded in creative
    and innovative ways to the library's mission of reaching and
    serving members to the congregation and/or the wider com-
    munity.
Outstanding Contribution to Librarianship--This award is given
    to a person or institution who has provided inspiration, guid-
    ance, leadership, or resources to enrich the field of church
    or synagogue librarianship.

The official Association seal was adopted by the Association on October 6, 1968. The emblem consists of the Star of David (Judaism) and the Cross (Christianity) superimposed on an open book, all within a circle inscribing the name of the Association and the date of its founding. This seal or emblem has appeared on all of CSLA's publications and promotional literature and was incorporated into a design for pins and tie-tacs which have been sold to Association members.

Following the adoption, at the July 15, 1969, Executive Board meeting, of blue and gold as CSLA colors, an official banner was procured for display at conferences and workshops. The CSLA emblem is embroidered in blue on a gold background. At the same Board meeting, authorization was given to print membership certificates suitable for display by church and synagogue members who receive them automatically when they join the Association. Individual personal members may purchase them.

Organizational Structure

Not surprisingly, need for by-laws changes was discovered by the first Executive Board. Perhaps the most controversial item in the original by-laws was a provision for denominational sections. This was dropped in the first by-laws revision in 1969, as a result of objections by several denominational groups which feared that it represented an attempt to absorb them. Another significant change in the first by-laws revision was the division of active memberships into individual and church or synagogue memberships. The category of Affiliate membership was added for library associations or groups.

A provision was made for three vice-presidents, required to represent each one of the three major faiths: Catholic, Jewish and Protestant. The three were to be members of the Membership Committee. A further revision of the constitution and by-laws was necessary in 1971 to include provisions concerning the use and disposal of Association property, required by the Internal Revenue Service prior to granting federal tax exempt status. Thus, the Association became eligible to receive tax deductible gifts.

Further by-law changes were made in the revision adopted September 7, 1974. The Sites and Exhibits Committee was divided into two committees. It was made clear that the First Vice-President was general chairperson of the annual conference and that all committees relating to the conference were to be under his/her direction. Finance and Chapter Committees were added as standing committees and each church or synagogue member was authorized to designate a representative who would have the same rights and privileges as an individual member. Although three vice-presidents were retained, the requirement that each represent one of the three major faiths was dropped, in view of the disproportionate denominational numbers in the membership.

At the 1978 annual meeting, however, the membership voted to eliminate the office of Third Vice-President. Furthermore, in order to give the First Vice-President and President-Elect more time to become involved in all phases of the Association's activities, the responsibilities of the general chairperson of the annual conference were transferred from the First to the Second Vice-President. The office of Secretary was eliminated and the duty of recording minutes was assigned to the Executive Secretary. At the same meeting, the fiscal year of the Association was changed to the calendar year and the membership year was changed to July 1 to June 30. This was to make it coincide approximately with the new terms for officers who are now to take office at the end of the annual conference.

Publications

The Association publication program got under way in 1969, with the first in a series of guides for congregational librarians. Entitled A Bibliography of Church and Synagogue Library Resources (CSLA Guide #1), it was a 10-page mimeographed booklet. It aroused interest, not only among church and synagogue librarians, but also in the public and college library world where there was an increasing need for information of this kind. Most of the publications have been short bibliographies on topics of interest and usefulness to the individual church and synagogue librarian. They have been advertised in the news columns of the leading general and large circulation library periodicals. They have been sold for barely enough to cover their publication cost until recent years when all expenses plus a contribution toward a revolving publication fund has been built into the charge.

Since 1969, seven additional guides on the basic phases of librarianship have been published. Book selection, cataloging and processing, classification, subject headings, library promotion and congregational library standards have all been treated in CSLA guides. The intent has been to make them accurate and clear and sufficiently detailed for a small to medium-sized congregational library. Two small promotional pamphlets, "The Family Uses the Library" and "The Teacher and the Library--Partners in Religious Education" are suitable for distribution in quantity to patrons and potential users of the library.

CSLA's only venture into non-print media has been a slide set photographed from the Christ Church (Oil City, Pa.) Publicity Scrapbook, which won the John Cotton Dana Public Relations Award. The 100-slide set is accompanied by a cassette narration and may be purchased or rented from the Association.

In 1975, Hawthorn Books (New York), published Ruth Smith's Getting the Books Off the Shelves: Making the Most of Your Congregation's Library, a manual of promotion and publicity. Because of

her long-time association with CSLA, the Association is mentioned
several times in the text. The author made copies of the book available for purchase from CSLA, through an arrangement worked out
with the publisher. This cooperative publishing venture has resulted
in many new members and friends for CSLA. Brisk book store
sales of the book have brought CSLA to the attention of many congregational librarians who had not previously heard of it. A second
co-operative publishing venture was completed in the fall of 1978
with the publication by Seabury Press of Cataloging Made Easy, also
by Ruth Smith.

In 1977, the Executive Board voted to add a part-time publications director to the paid staff. He/she is to be responsible for
carrying out the publications program under the guidance of the Publications Committee. The retiring president, William Gentz, was
named to this new post. After the responsibilities of a new job
made it necessary for the bulletin editor to resign, Mr. Gentz assumed this position as well.

Library Services

In addition to the CSLA publication program, other material
helpful to congregational librarians has been assembled and distributed by the Library Services Committee, established in 1973 and
chaired ever since by Rachel Kohl, a church library laboratory
leader certified by the United Methodist Church.

It is the function of this committee to search out brief pamphlets and other articles on establishing and developing church and
synagogue libraries and to make them available to CSLA members
and other interested people. Much of the material originates in
Church and Synagogue Libraries or at CSLA workshops and conferences. Some is acquired from other sources willing to share.
Checklists of the material are compiled and distributed periodically.
Requests are filled without cost to CSLA members. Non-members
are charged nominal postage and handling fees. This committee replies personally to individual questions and requests for help. On
occasion it has made consulting visits to congregational libraries.

Chapters and Affiliates

In addition to sponsoring its annual conference, the Association has co-sponsored or assisted with the production of a number of
one-day workshops. For the past five or six years, they have averaged about 25 per year. In some cases, it has provided supplies
of material; in others, it has provided suggestions and leaders as
well. Some of these workshops have been initiated by one or more
individual CSLA members, others by denominational groups, still
others by public librarians.

A problem, probably insoluble, is that of meeting the needs

of all the members, who vary so widely in training and experience.
It is faced in planned workshops and conferences and is easier to
care for in a 3-day conference when the series of workshops can be
gauged to appeal to various groups.   Nevertheless, the problem remains of bringing together in a common time and place, those persons with particular needs and the best people to meet those needs.

A number of these workshops have resulted in the formation
of CSLA chapters.   Chapters are intended to provide on-going face-
to-face sharing of opportunities which the national Association can
provide only occasionally in any given area.   The requirement for
forming a chapter is a statement of intention signed by ten CSLA
members.   A constitution and by-laws, including the intended geographic area, must be approved by the CSLA Executive Board as
being consistent with the national by-laws.

A chapter governing body arranges area meetings, frequently
in the form of annual one-day workshops patterned along the lines
of the Drexel workshops of the sixties.   Many chapters also have
briefer seminars or single-subject workshops at more frequent intervals.   Some chapters issue brief newsletters to their members.   The
first regional chapter was formed in 1970 in the birthplace of the
national Association, the Philadelphia area.   Called the Delaware
Valley Chapter, it serves the area within a 100-mile radius of Philadelphia.   The Lake Erie Chapter was formed in 1973 in the counties
surrounding Erie, Pennsylvania.   The same year saw the formation
of the New Mexico Chapter in the Albuquerque area.   It embraces
the whole state plus the El Paso corner of Texas.

Chapter formation speeded up rapidly in 1975 and 1976 with
three additional chapters formed in each one of these years.   In
1975, admission was granted to the Mid-South Chapter, which serves
the 100-mile radius of Memphis, the Maumee Valley Chapter, which
draws its membership from the Toledo-Maumee Valley area and
nearby Michigan counties; and the Northeastern Ohio Chapter, which
covers the northeastern quarter of the state.   Joining in 1976 were
the San Fernando Valley Chapter, serving counties in the Los Angeles area; the North Texas Chapter, in the Dallas area and the
Greater Richmond (Virginia) Area Chapter.   Connecticut and Southwest Pennsylvania chapters were added in 1977; Florida and South-
western Michigan in 1978.

Because there were already a number of active regional congregational library groups at the time of CSLA establishment, provision was made for an affiliate membership in CSLA for groups
which preferred to retain their own identity to becoming a CSLA
chapter.   Any group related to congregational libraries can become
an affiliate member.   Each affiliate member receives five subscriptions to CSLA's official bulletin.   Although not a requirement, it has
worked out in practice that affiliates include CSLA on their own mailing lists; so news is mutually reported in publications.   Frequently,
CSLA people participate in activities sponsored by the affiliates and
vice versa.

The requirement that individual chapter members be national
CSLA members presents a special problem for already established
groups which invariably have members who do not wish this dual
membership. This requirement has been a controversial issue which
has been discussed on a number of occasions. An ad hoc committee
was established in 1972 to study the matter thoroughly. The conclusion was that a close working relationship between CSLA and its
chapters could be maintained only if the requirement were kept. It
was felt that the affiliate membership provided a workable alternative. A significant by-product of this ad hoc committee was the establishment of a Chapter Coordinator as a member of the Executive
Board.

Two regional groups have maintained affiliate memberships
in CSLA. They are the Church Library Council (since 1970) which
serves the metropolitan Washington, D. C. area; and the Church and
Synagogue Librarians' Fellowship of the Baltimore area (since 1972).
The New England Jewish Library Association of the Boston area held
an affiliate membership in 1974.

Other groups keep in contact with CSLA by way of one or
more individual or church memberships held by their members.
Examples are the Pacific Northwest Association of Church Libraries,
the Congregational Libraries Association of British Columbia, the
Church Library Association (Toronto area), the Lutheran Church Library Association, and the Catholic Library Association. Each one
has continued to retain its autonomy.

Contacts with still other groups are maintained through mutual
agreements to exchange subscriptions to official bulletins or journals.
The Evangelical Church Library Association, the Christian Librarians'
Fellowship, the Special Libraries Association and OPTIONS, the Jewish Resources Newsletter, all relate to CSLA in this way.

Contacts with general groups which are related to church and
synagogue librarians are made by the Library World Liaison, the
Religious World Liaison, and the Publishers' Liaison Committees.
It is the function of each one of the individual committee chairpersons, all of whom, like all other committee chairpersons, sit on
the CSLA Executive Board, to create an awareness of CSLA among
those groups and to keep CSLA leaders informed of activities that
are helpful to church and synagogue librarians or that provide opportunities to publicize CSLA.

One of the specific purposes noted at the time of CSLA founding was "to study and guide the development of church and synagogue
librarianship toward recognition as a formal branch of the library
profession." A significant step in CSLA's program to upgrade the
field it represents was taken in 1970 when it was admitted to membership in the Council of National Library Associations, a group
composed of many national library associations. Two CSLA members are appointed for staggered 3-year terms to represent the Association at semi-annual CNLA meetings, and others are appointed

annually to serve on committees such as the Joint Committee on Library Education and the Joint Committee on Prison Libraries. Currently, a CSLA member serves on the CNLA Board. In 1976, representatives from CSLA were appointed to the ALA Anglo-American Rules Revision Committee and the Z39 Committee of the American National Standards Institute.

Continuing Education

Continuing education is one of today's favorite catch phrases. Certainly it has been featured in recent library literature and general library conferences. Long before its current emphasis, CSLA was centering its purpose and program on the concept. Conferences and workshops, the official bulletin, other publications and the work of the Library Services Committee are all geared to provide continuing educational opportunities for church and synagogue libraries. Nevertheless, after the early start at Drexel, efforts to work with library schools in providing course work in congregational librarianship did not get well underway until 1976.

In that year, CSLA President John Harvey initiated correspondence courses in congregational librarianship. The outgrowth of this effort was the establishment of CSLA's Continuing Education Committee whose function is to encourage such developments and serve as liaison between CSLA and the cooperating schools. At this writing, there are encouraging signs that at least three library schools will be adding correspondence or extension courses in congregational librarianship to their course offerings. Professional librarians among CSLA's membership will be writing the syllabi and serving as instructors for these courses. The first one of these courses, prepared and taught by G. Martin Ruoss, is offered by the University of Utah.

Facing Problems and Challenges

It has been estimated that there are between 25,000 and 40,000 congregational libraries in the United States. Although CSLA has had steady growth, with no net declines in its decade of existence, it still has only 1002 members, as of March 27, 1978. Why has it attracted only a small portion of its potential universe?

Gaining the attention of the fragmented religious world has not been easy. For one thing, church leaders are not invariably convinced of the value of libraries. For another, there are no one or two sources, such as Library Journal or Wilson Library Bulletin, which reach the majority of church and synagogue leaders. Many more contacts are needed to spread the word to them about CSLA. And money has not been readily available even for extensive advertising, let alone the expense of making personal contacts.

Membership is undoubtedly affected by the opportunities in

other church library associations such as the Lutheran Church Library Association and the Evangelical Church Library Association. The Church Library Board of the Southern Baptist Convention fills the continuing education need in its own denomination through an excellent periodical and workshop program. Other denominations provide services for their church librarians, also.

Originally, the CSLA structure was patterned after existing professional library associations. Since many of its aims were similar--mutual contact with peers, improvement of library service, recognition by others in the profession--this seemed the logical thing to do. Many of the founders and many of the leaders over the years have been professional librarians. But few, if any, leaders or members at large have been professional church or synagogue librarians. Therefore, the dues structure cannot be based on salaries.

Some members have their CSLA dues paid from the funds allotted by the congregation to the library. Several instances have come to our attention of adequately or even well-endowed congregational libraries. The majority, however, like most of their counterparts in the public and college library realms, must compete with other groups for limited funds. Many congregational librarians pay not only their own dues, but sometimes church or synagogue membership dues, also. And some pay their own expenses to the national three-day conferences.

A sizeable portion of the dues income has been required to publish the bimonthly bulletin, with little left over for promotional activities. Annual conferences have just about paid for themselves and monographic publications have not quite managed to do so. Nevertheless, the monographic publications have been a good source of publicity for the Association and have been an important part of its education program. Most have been favorably reviewed in library literature which has called the Association to the attention of many public and school librarians. Some of these librarians are working in congregational libraries themselves or have patrons who are looking for help with their congregational libraries. Each publication has enabled the Association to educate additional librarians. Intensively promoting publication sale has been carried out as a means of upgrading church and synogogue librarianship. Many librarians have learned how to carry out their jobs by reading CSLA publications.

The problem of finance has only recently begun to be approached from the standpoint of seeking contributions and grants from outside sources. Although the Association was awarded tax-exempt status by the Federal government in 1971, it was not until 1976 that a Fund-raising Committee was established at the insistent urging of the treasurer, who saw clearly that reliance on dues for income was inadequate for CSLA's growth and stability. Contributions on a small scale have been received from friends over the years, and, as is true with all organizations staffed essentially by volunteers, much valuable time has been contributed by leaders. But a concerted ef-

fort to tap sources of funding in significant amounts is yet to be
made.

Membership committees have attempted to contact potential
areas of interest.   Shortly after the formation of the first Executive
Board, a membership mailing went to all those listed in the Drexel
Directory of Church and Synagogue Libraries, which included libraries in all of the states.   Copies of the first newsletter were sent to
library journals, religious periodicals and religious associations.
The Presbyterian-related Westminister Church Library Plan included
the original one-page announcement and membership application in
its regular mailing to church libraries all over the country.   This
is probably the explanation for the preponderance of Presbyterian
members which continues to this day.   The Lutheran Church Library Association has generously included CSLA promotional literature in its mailings on more than one occasion.   It has given CSLA
free exhibit space at its conferences, as has the Catholic Library
Association.   Both of these associations and many other congregational library groups regularly report CSLA news in their periodicals.

Since most congregational librarians are volunteers, the turnover among them is inevitably much greater than among employed
persons and this affects the renewal rate among CSLA members.
This rate has gradually improved, however, and reached 80 percent
in 1978.

In 1972 a questionnaire was mailed to those who had not yet
renewed from the previous year to ask them for the reason.   Of 140
questionnaires mailed, 94 were returned.   About one half of those
returned stated that they still intended to renew, and about half of
that number did.   Another third stated that they were no longer associated with a congregational library.   The rest of the replies indicated that they would not renew for various reasons--some budget-
ary, some because they did not feel they received enough practical
help from CSLA and still others because they thought the bulletin
was not scholarly enough. [5]

CSLA could be justifiably accused of relating more closely to
the needs of Protestant church libraries than to those of Catholic and
Jewish libraries, not through prejudicial intent, but in response to
the needs of its constituency.   To continue to meet their needs, while
attempting to attract more parish and synagogue librarians, is not
easy.   Merely finding an appropriate meeting day is difficult.   Normally, Saturday is the day when most Protestant and Catholic church
librarians have free time for meetings.   This, however, is a holy
day for Jewish members.   A meeting on Sunday afternoon is usually
workable for all three groups, but this does not give enough time
for all-day workshops, just as a weekday evening does not.   This
problem has resulted in establishing the custom of holding annual
three-day conferences from Sunday afternoon through Tuesday afternoon.

The advantages of ecumenism, nevertheless, outweigh these

problems. It has certainly been an advantage in relating to the library world, particularly in working with public libraries to promote workshops and seminars for church and synagogue librarians. Since library service has much in common for the three faiths, sharing in one Association eliminates much duplication of time and effort of leadership. The very concept of libraries is a sharing concept. Persons who have been involved with CSLA for several years can testify to the broadening of understanding, far beyond library principles, which is to be gained from participating in an ecumenical relationship.

Surely, CSLA participation has led many members to have greater understanding and appreciation of their own religious beliefs and those of their church or synagogues. Their understanding of other religious groups and beliefs must have been deepened by their CSLA experience, also. Their volunteer activity has enabled well informed members to support their own churches or synagogues in very tangible and useful fashion. To strengthen and deepen members' understanding of good church and synagogue librarianship is a way of improving the effectiveness of these people and their churches and synagogues.

In the short history of the Association, certain persons have been asked repeatedly to undertake challenging assignments. This could be an indication of dangerous inbreeding. However, it could be an indication of uncommon commitment to CSLA's goals. There are no material rewards to be gained from involvement in CSLA's leadership. It is safe to say that all Board members have been out of pocket, at the very least, for attendance at Board meetings. For a few, this has meant plane flights of up to 3000 miles plus meals and overnight expenses. With a few exceptions, workshop leaders and conference speakers have paid their own expenses.

Nor can participation in CSLA be expected to lead to advancement in one's career. The incentives are intangible: the dubious satisfaction of seeing one's name in print; the possibility of hearing, "Nice job, " from one's colleagues; the likelihood of hearing "That was so helpful" from workshop participants; or maybe only an eventual, "Well done, good and faithful servant. "

Appendix I

CHURCH AND SYNAGOGUE LIBRARY ASSOCIATION

Exploratory Meeting
July 10, 1966
Americana Hotel
New York, N.Y.

John F. Harvey, Convener Dean, Graduate School of Library Science Drexel University, Philadelphia

Alice Booker, Director, Church Librarians Exchange, Graduate
    School of Library Science, Drexel University, Philadelphia

Annette Buurstra, Reference Librarian, Calvin College & Seminary
    Grand Rapids

Lucy Carpenter, Editor, Church Librarian, Faith Temple Church of
    God in Christ, Chicago

Daphne Carter, Baltimore

M. Elizabeth Denning, Washington Bible College, Washington, D. C.

Mildred Eagan, Division of Education, United Methodist Church,
    Nashville

Agnes Ford, The Sunday School Board of the Southern Baptist Con-
    vention, Nashville

Alice C. Gustafson, Cleveland

Stanley Heath, Religious Publishers Group, Philadelphia

Jane Hindman, Catholic Library Association, Haverford, Pennsylvania

Joseph Jacobskind, Association of Jewish Libraries

Ruth Jacobskind, Association of Jewish Libraries

Wilma Jensen, Executive Secretary, Lutheran Church Library As-
    sociation, Minneapolis

M. R. Kindly

Donald L. Leonard, Executive Editor, Board of Christian Education
    United Presbyterian Church, U. S. A., Philadelphia

Juanita Ziegler Oas, Librarian, Public Library, Sturgis, Michigan

Dorothy J. Rodda, Research Assistant, Drexel University, Philadel-
    phia

Ralph Shaw, New Jersey Council of Churches

Ruth S. Smith, Chief, Open Library Institute for Defense Analysis,
    Arlington, Virginia

James G. Stewart, Christian Herald Magazine, New York

Miriam Waggoner, Office of Public Relations, Christian Librarians'
    Fellowship, Johnson City, New York

Margaret Warrington, Administrative Assistant, Graduate School of
    Library Science, Drexel University, Philadelphia

Joyce L. White, Adjunct Instructor, Drexel Librarian, Penniman
Library, University of Pennsylvania, Philadelphia

Ruth H. Winters, Westminister Church Library Plan, United Presbyterian Church, U.S.A., Philadelphia

Marian E. Wolf, Librarian, Parish of Trinity Church, New York

Joseph Yenish, Librarian, Gratz College, Philadelphia

Herbert Zafren, President, Association of Jewish Libraries, Cincinnati

Appendix II

CHURCH AND SYNAGOGUE LIBRARY ASSOCIATION

PRESIDENTS

1967-68	Ruth S. Smith Chief, Open Library Institute for Defense Analysis Arlington, Virginia Chairman, Library Committee, Bethesda United Methodist Church
1968-69	Rev. Donald L. Leonard, Executive Editor Board of Christian Education United Presbyterian Church U.S.A. Philadelphia
1969-70	Joyce L. White, Librarian Maria Hosmer Penniman Library University of Pennsylvania Philadelphia
1970-71	Rev. Arthur W. Swarthout, Assistant Librarian West Virginia Wesleyan College Buckhannon, West Virginia
1971-72	Wilma W. Jensen, Executive Secretary Lutheran Church Library Association Minneapolis
1972-73	Betty Lou Hammergren, Catalog Li- brarian Public Library Minneapolis Parish and Community Libraries Section, Catholic Library Association

1973-74   Claudia Hannaford, Librarian
                     The Diocesan Library
                     Erie, Pennsylvania

1973-74   Maurice Tuchman, Librarian
                     Hebrew College
                     Brookline, Massachusetts

1975-76   John F. Harvey, Dean of Library Ser-
                        vices
                     Hofstra University
                     Hempstead, New York

1976-77   William H. Gentz, Editor of Religious
                        Books
                     Hawthorn Books
                     New York

1977-78   Fay W. Grosse, Librarian
                     East Dallas Christian Church
                     Dallas

1978-79   Maryann J. Dotts, Director of Religious
                        Education
                     Belle Meade United Methodist Church
                     Nashville

Appendix III

CHURCH AND SYNAGOGUE LIBRARY ASSOCIATION

ANNUAL CONFERENCES

May 27-29, 1968   Bellevue-Stratford Hotel
                     Philadelphia
                     "The Challenge of Books in Today's
                        World"

July 13-15, 1969   Shoreham Hotel
                     Washington, D.C.
                     "Libraries in an Ecumenical Era"

May 3-5, 1970   Webster-Hall Motor Hotel
                     Pittsburgh
                     "The Library Serves the Family"

June 12-14, 1971   College of St. Thomas
                     St. Paul
                     "The Library--A Media Center of Ser-
                        vice"

June 17-19, 1972   University of Maryland, Baltimore
County Campus
Baltimore
"Get in Touch With the World Through
Libraries"

July 22-24, 1973   Lewis and Clark College
Portland, Oregon
"Blaze a Trail"

June 23-25, 1974   Simmons College
Boston
"The Freedom Trail Through Books"

June 14-17, 1975   Oberlin College
Oberlin, Ohio
"Church and Synagogue Libraries in
Today's America"

June 20-22, 1976   International House
Philadelphia
"Proclaim Literacy Throughout the
Land"

June 26-28, 1977   Southern Methodist University
Dallas
"Communication is the Key"

June 25-27, 1978   Calvin College
Grand Rapids
"The Library as Ministry"

Appendix IV

CHURCH AND SYNAGOGUE LIBRARY ASSOCIATION

AWARDS

1968   Josephine H. Kyles, Detroit
Director, Division of Services
Metropolitan Detroit Council of Churches
Christian Educator instrumental in
training church librarians in two
large metropolitan areas

1969   Ruth S. Smith, Bethesda, Maryland
Founder, Bethesda United Methodist
Church Library
Founder and First President, Church
Library Council, Washington, D.C.
First President, Church and Synagogue
Library Association

1970   Lorraine Pike, Milwaukee
                       Librarian, Ascension Lutheran Church
                       Instrumental in assisting in the estab-
                            lishment of 79 other church libraries

                       Helen Dempsey, Birmingham, Michigan
                       Librarian, Our Lady Queen of Martyrs
                            Church
                       Instrumental in counselling other par-
                            ish libraries through the Parish and
                            Community Libraries Section of the
                            Catholic Library Association

1971   Erwin John, Minneapolis
                       Editor, Lutheran Libraries
                       Librarian, Mt. Olivet Lutheran Church,
                            Minneapolis for 15 years during which
                            he developed an outstanding art lend-
                            ing section
                       Founder, Lutheran Church Library As-
                            sociation
                       Author, The Key to a Successful Church
                            Library

1972   John F. Harvey
                       Sponsor of Drexel's church and syna-
                            gogue library workshops
                       Founder of CSLA

1973   Helen Carr Baker, Springfield, Virginia
                       Librarian, Springfield United Methodist
                            Church
                       Founder and First President, Northern
                            Virginia Church Library Council

                       Elizabeth Groff, Richland, Washington
                       Special award in recognition of founding
                            the Pacific Northwest Association of
                            Chruch Libraries

1974   No Award

1975   Leonard M. Sandhaus Memorial Library
                       Temple Israel
                       Sharon, Massachusetts
                       Helen Greif, Librarian
                       Award for significant service in its
                            synagogue and community

1976   CSLA Award for Outstanding Congrega-
                            tional Libraries
                       Reveille Memorial Library
                       Reveille United Methodist Church
                       Richmond, Virginia

Alma Lowance, Chairman, Library
Committee
Mrs. Gordon W. Binns, Librarian

CSLA Award for Outstanding Congre-
gational Librarian
Martha Durbin, Lakewood, Ohio
Librarian, Lakewood Presbyterian
Church

CSLA Award for Outstanding Contribution to Church or Synagogue Librarianship
Ruth Roth, Benson, Illinois
Consultant for Church Libraries, Illinois Mennonite Conference
Author of books and columns on church
librarianship

Appendix V

CHURCH AND SYNAGOGUE LIBRARY ASSOCIATION

PUBLICATIONS

Guide No. 1
        Swarthout, Arthur W., ed. Bibliography of Church and Syna-
gogue Library Resources. 1969. 10 p. $0.50.
        Kohl, Rachel and Dorothy Rodda, compilers. Church and
Synagogue Library Resources. Second edition. 1975. 16 p. $2.00.

Guide No. 2
        Hannaford, Claudia, comp. Promotion Planning Calendar for
1970. 1969. 26 p. $1.25.
        Hannaford, Claudia and Ruth S. Smith. Promotion Planning.
Second edition. 1975. 52 p. $2.95.

Guide No. 3
        Smith, Ruth S. Workshop Planning. 1972. 3v. $6.00.
        Part I.   Committee and Chairman's Guide. 34 p.
        Part II. Group Leader's Guide. 13 p.
        Part III. Sample Materials. 43 p.

Guide No. 4
        Swarthout, Arthur W. Selecting Library Materials. 1974.
7 p. $1.25

Other Publications
        Ott, Helen Keating. Helping Children Through Books: A
Selected Booklist for the Seventies. 1974. 16 p. $2.00
        White, Joyce L. Directory of Church and Synagogue Li-
braries in Maryland. 1973. 12 p. $1.25.

Sturtevant, Anne F. and Joyce L. White. <u>Know Your Neigh-</u>
<u>bor's Faith</u>. An Ecumenical Reading List. 1972. Pamphlet.
Single copy, stamped self-addressed envelope; $3.00 for 100.

<u>The Family Uses the Library</u>. 1970. Pamphlet. Single
copy, stamped self-addressed envelope; $1.25 for 100.

<u>Promotion and Publicity for a Church Library: Slides from</u>
<u>the Award-winning Christ Church Publicity Scrapbook</u>. 100 35mm
color slides; reading script; cassette. Cassette narration by the
Rev. Canon James D. Smith and Claudia Hannaford. 1974. $50.
Rental fee $7.50.

NOTES

1. White, Joyce L. and E. J. Humeston, Jr. (eds.) <u>Proceedings</u>
   <u>of the Second Annual Church Library Conference</u>. Philadelphia: Drexel University Press, 1964.
2. White, Joyce L. and Mary Y. Parr, <u>Church Library Guide</u>.
   Philadelphia: Drexel University Press, 1965.
3. Rodda, Dorothy J. and John F. Harvey, <u>Directory of Church</u>
   <u>Libraries</u>. Philadelphia: Drexel Press, 1967.
4. Probably the term "congregational library" originated in CSLA
   in an attempt to find a word that covered both "church" and
   "synagogue."
5. Minutes of Executive Board meeting April 29, 1972, Harrisburg,
   Pa.

REFERENCES

Archives of the Church and Synagogue Library Association and committee reports
   Minutes of the Executive Board and Executive Committee, July
   11, 1967 to September 18, 1976, inclusive

Constitution and By-laws, 1967
Constitution and By-laws, Revised 1969
Constitution and By-laws, Revised September, 1971
Constitution and By-laws, Revised 1974

<u>Church and Synagogue Libraries</u>, Volumes I through IX

Letter from John F. Harvey to Joyce L. White, dated July 27,
   1970, describing his recollections of the background of the
   founding of the Church and Synagogue Library Association

"The Church and Synagogue Library Association." Talk delivered
   by John F. Harvey, July 22, 1973 at Sixth Annual Conference,
   Lewis and Clark College, Portland, Oregon

Articles

Hannaford, Claudia. "An Ecumenical Concern for Quality Service in Religious Libraries," Special Libraries LXI (January, 1970), pp. 9-14.

Smith, Ruth S. "Church and Synagogue Library Association," Encyclopedia of Library and Information Science, Volume IV (1971), pp. 674-676.

Smith, Ruth S. "The Church and Synagogue Library Association," Drexel Library Quarterly VI (April 1970), pp. 159-165.

(White, Joyce L.) "Church and Synagogue Library Association," Journal of Ecumenical Studies VII (Fall 1970), pp. 910-912.

Unpublished Material

Hindman, Jane. "History of the Church and Synagogue Library Association," 1973.

Schnapf, Susan. "The Church and Synagogue Library Association." Term paper for course in Special Libraries, C. W. Post College, Greenvale, Long Island, New York, Spring, 1976.

NOTES ON CONTRIBUTORS

JACQULYN ANDERSON received a B.A. degree from Tift College, Forsyth, Georgia, and a M.L.S. from George Peabody College for Teachers, Nashville. She is a regular contributor to Media: Library Services Journal. She has written How to Catalog Church Music Materials, the Church Library Record and Plan Books (annual) and has coauthored several other books. Miss Anderson is Consultant, Church Library Department, Southern Baptist Sunday School Board, Nashville, and is on the library staff, First Baptist Church, Nashville.

LAMOND F. BEATTY has a B.A. from Utah State University, 1951, an M.S. and Ph.D. from the University of Utah. He has been an elementary and secondary school teacher, an educational media center director and is now Assistant Professor, College of Education, University of Utah. Beatty is a member, Meetinghouse Library Executive Committee, The Church of Jesus Church of Latter-day Saints, Salt Lake City.

MARYANN J. DOTTS has three degrees: B.A. in Religious Education, National College for Christian Workers; M.A. in Christian Education, Scarritt College; and M.L.S., George Peabody College for Teachers. She has worked as a director of Christian education and an elementary school teacher. She has been a freelance writer for the United Methodist Church and has published children's books and a manual for church libraries.

HELEN B. GREIF has a B.A., Brooklyn College, 1942, and an M.A., Columbia University. She has served as a research librarian and elementary and junior high school teacher and administrator, in addition to working in several synagogue libraries. Librarian, Temple Israel, Sharon, Massachusetts.

FAY WISEMAN GROSSE has a B.A., University of Texas, Austin and has been a teacher, secretary, ecumenical worker, and contributor to denominational publications. She has coordinated library workshops for the Christian Church (Disciples of Christ). For six years, she served on the Christian Literature Commission, the Christian Church's (Disciples of Christ) national library department and is currently liaison librarian between the Church Libraries & Christian Readers Department and CSLA. Librarian, East Dallas Christian Church.

CLAUDIA HANNAFORD received a B.S. in Education from Wilmington College in 1951. She has worked as a media library assistant in two public libraries. She has won an American Library Association John Cotton Dana Public Relations Award and served on the Board of Directors of the Council of National Library Associations. Mrs. Hannaford is an instructor in The Schuylkill Business Institute, Pottsville, Pa.

JOHN F. HARVEY, A.B., Dartmouth College, 1943; B.S.L.S., University of Illinois, and Ph.D., University of Chicago. Harvey has had a career in academic library management and library education. Former Dean, Graduate School of Library Science and Director of Libraries, Drexel University, Philadelphia; later, Dean of Library Services, University of New Mexico, Albuquerque.

JANE HINDMAN, B.S. in Education, Temple University; Certificate, Drexel University School of Library Science, 1924. Former Philadelphia public school librarian and former Assistant Librarian, Holy Family College, Philadelphia. Assistant to the Executive Director, Catholic Library Association and Editor, Catholic Library World, 1963-75. Now retired.

WILMA W. JENSEN, B.A., Gustavus Adolphus College, 1938; B.S. in L.S., University of Minnesota. University of Minnesota Library experience. Employed by the National Lutheran Council for several years. Executive Director, Lutheran Church Library Association, Minneapolis, 1963 to date.

MIRIAM LEIKIND is a graduate of the Cleveland College and its library school and she graduated from and later taught at the College of Jewish Studies in Cleveland. She was one of the founders of the Jewish Library Association. She is a past Vice-President and Chairperson of the Northeastern Ohio Chapter of the Church and Synagogue Library Association. She is a founder and co-editor of the Index to Jewish Periodicals and Archivist, Librarian and Curator at The Temple, University Circle at Silver Park, Cleveland.

DAVID M. MAYFIELD has a B.A., University of Utah, 1967, M.A. and M.L.S., University of California, Los Angeles, 1971, and a Certificate of Completion, 31st Institute, Introduction to Modern Archives Administration, American University. He has been a Teaching Assistant in German, University of Utah, Instructor in Library Science, Brigham Young University, Supervisor, LDS Church Library, and is now Assistant Church Librarian-Archivist, Historical Department, The Church of Jesus Christ of Latter-day Saints, Salt Lake City.

ADELE-ETHEL REIDY has a Bachelor of Music, Chicago Musical College and has done graduate work at New York University, University of Alaska and Towson State College. She has worked in the Chicago Musical College Library, the Chicago Public Library, and various school libraries. Librarian, The Cathedral of Mary Our Queen Parish Library, Baltimore.

DOROTHY J. RODDA graduated from the University of Pennsylvania,

A. B. in 1943, Phi Beta Kappa. In addition, she has an M. S. in
L. S. from Drexel University. She has had a career as a securities
analyst, college and school librarian. Ms. Rodda has been Executive Secretary, Church and Synagogue Library Association, 1967-
1970, and 1973 to date. She has published the Directory of Church
and Synagogue Libraries plus articles and bibliographies. She is
Librarian, Ardmore Presbyterian Church, Ardmore, Pennsylvania.

G. MARTIN RUOSS, A. B. , Muhlenberg College, 1933; D. D. and
S. T. M. , Lutheran Theological Seminary, Philadelphia. M. A. in
L. S. , University of Denver. Lutheran Church pastor, 1936-65.
Department Head, General Library, University of New Mexico, 1968-
76. Has published in both religion and library science. Compiled
and published a directory of world theological libraries, 1968. Now
retired.

RUTH S. SMITH, A. B. , Wayne University, 1939; A. B. L. S. , University of Michigan. Experience in the Detroit Public Library, Lt.
WAVES, U. S. Navy. Technical library experience in Philadelphia,
Government Publications Section Chairperson, Special Libraries Association. Librarian, Institute of Defense Analysis, Arlington, Virginia, 1968 to date. Former Librarian, Bethesda Methodist Church,
Bethesda, Maryland.

REVEREND WAYNE E. TODD has a B. A. , Mississippi College,
Clinton, and Th. B. , Southern Baptist Theological Seminary, Louis-
ville. He did additional graduate work at the University of Tennessee, Belmont College and New Orleans Theological Seminary. After
a career as a church pastor, Todd became Secretary, Church Library Department, Sunday School Board, Southern Baptist Convention,
Nashville. He is editor of Media: Library Services Journal and
has published three books in the field. He is a trustee of a Baptist
school and four Baptist hospitals.

MAURICE S. TUCHMAN has a B. A. , Brooklyn College, 1958, M. L. S.
Columbia University School of Library Service, B. H. L. , Jewish Theological Seminary of America, and is a doctoral student at Simmons
College. He has been Librarian, Hebrew College, Brookline, Mass. ,
for the past decade. He has advised various synagogues on library
problems and reviews Judaica books in several periodicals. Tuchman
organized and directed the First Institute for Hebraica and Judaica
Librarians, 1976.

MAE WEINE, B. Litt. , Columbia University, 1932, Drexel University
Graduate School of Library Science, M. S. in L. S. Circulation Assistant, Rutgers College of South Jersey, 1958-70. President, Jewish Library Association, 1965-66. Librarian, Beth Israel Synagogue,
Camden, New Jersey, 1953-70. Author, Weine Classification System
for Judaica Libraries.

JOYCE L. WHITE, B. A. , University of Pennsylvania, 1949; M. S.
in L. S. , Drexel University Graduate School of Library Science. Librarian, University of Pennsylvania Penniman Education Library,
1949-76. Episcopal History Library, Austin, Texas, 1976 to date.

THEODORE WIENER has a Bachelor's degree in history from the University of Cincinnati, 1940, and Bachelor's and Master's degrees in Hebrew Literature from the Hebrew Union College, Cincinnati. After a career as a rabbi in several Midwestern temples, he joined the library staff of the Hebrew Union College where he served for fourteen years. Since 1964 he has worked in both the Descriptive and the Subject Cataloging Divisions at the Library of Congress, Washington, D.C. He has been a leader in the Association of Jewish Libraries and the American Library Association.

RUTH H. WINTERS has an A.B., Hanover College and studied at the Presbyterian College of Christian Education, Chicago. She was a director of Christian education at several churches and Staff Assistant in Parish Education, United Presbyterian Church in the USA, Philadelphia. For 15 years she was contract administrator for the Westminister Church Library Plan. Published church library books and articles. Now retired.

BERNADETTE YOUNG received a Life Certificate from Detroit Teachers College and has carried out further studies at Marygrove College, Wayne State University. She was a supervising teacher in the Detroit Public Schools until retirement in 1973. For several years she was a contributing editor of the Catholic Library World. Librarian, St. Daniel Parish Library, Clarkston, Michigan.

INDEX